Rethinking Language and Gender Research

Real Language Series

General Editors:

Jennifer Coates, Roehampton Institute, London
Jenny Cheshire, Queen Mary and Westfield College, University of London, and
Euan Reid, Institute of Education, University of London

Titles published in the series:

David Lee Competing Discourses: Perspective and Ideology in Language
Norman Fairclough (Editor) Critical Language Awareness
James Milroy and Lesley Milroy (Editors) Real English: The Grammar of English Dialects in the British Isles
Mark Sebba London Jamaican: Language Systems in Interaction
Janet Holmes Women, Men and Politeness
Ben Rampton Crossing: Language and Ethnicity Among Adolescents
Brian V. Street Social Literacies: Critical Approaches to Literacy in Development, Ethnography and Education
Srikant Sarangi and Stefaan Slembrouck Language, Bureaucracy and Social Control
Ruth Wodak Disorders of Discourse
Victoria L. Bergvall, Janet M. Bing and Alice F. Freed (Editors) Rethinking Language and Gender Research: Theory and Practice

Rethinking Language and Gender Research: Theory and Practice

edited by

Victoria L. Bergvall
Janet M. Bing
Alice F. Freed

LONGMAN
London and New York

Addison Wesley Longman Limited
Edinburgh Gate
Harlow, Essex CM20 2JE
United Kingdom
and Associated Companies throughout the world

Published in the United States of America
by Addison Wesley Longman, New York

First published 1996

ISBN 0 582 265746 Csd
ISBN 0 582 265738 Ppr

British Library Cataloguing-in-Publication Data
A catalogue record for this book is
available from the British Library

Library of Congress Cataloging-in-Publication Data
Rethinking language and gender research: theory and practice / edited
  by Victoria L. Bergvall, Janet M. Bing, Alice F. Freed.
      p.   cm.—(Real language series)
  Selected rev. papers, with one additional paper, of a conference
held during the 1993 Linguistic Institute in Columbus, Ohio, July
16–19, 1993; the conference was sponsored by the Committee on the
Status of Women in Linguistics of the Linguistic Society of America.
  Includes bibliographical references and index.
  ISBN 0–582–26574–6 (cased).—ISBN 0–582–26573–8 (paper)
  1. Language and languages—Sex differences—Congresses.
I. Bergvall, Victoria L. (Victoria Lee), 1956–   . II. Bing, Janet
Mueller, 1937–   . III. Freed, Alice F., 1946–   . IV. Series.
P120.S48R48   1996
306.4′4—dc20   96–20024
                                                             CIP

Set by 8 in 10/12 pt Sabon

Produced by Longman Singapore Publishers (Pte) Ltd.
Printed in Singapore

Contents

Contributors

Victoria L. Bergvall is Associate Professor of Linguistics in the Department of Humanities at Michigan Technological University. Her recent work focuses on social and political uses of language, the social construction of gender through discourse, and resistance to nonsexist language guidelines. Her publications have appeared in the *Journal of Women and Minorities in Science and Engineering*, *Natural Language and Linguistic Theory* and *Discourse & Society*.

Janet M. Bing is Professor of Linguistics and Women's Studies in the Department of English at Old Dominion University, Norfolk, Virginia. She also serves as an associate editor for *Women & Language*. Her publications include *Aspects of English Prosody*, *Grammar Guide*, and articles in various journals, including *Studies in African Linguistics*, *Linguistic Inquiry*, and *Women & Language*.

Mary Bucholtz, a doctoral candidate in the Department of Linguistics at the University of California at Berkeley, is completing her dissertation on European American teenagers' use of African American Vernacular English. Her research focuses on the intersection of language, identity, and power. She is co-editor of *Gender Articulated* (with Kira Hall) and *Reinventing Identities* (with Anita C. Liang and Laurel Sutton).

Deborah Cameron is Senior Lecturer in linguistics at Strathclyde University in Glasgow, Scotland. She has previously held academic posts at universities in England, the USA and Sweden. Her numerous publications on sociolinguistics and language and gender include *Feminism and Linguistic Theory* and *Verbal Hygiene*, as well as the edited volumes *Women in Their Speech Communities* (with Jennifer Coates), published by Longman, and *The Feminist Critique of Language*.

Susan Ehrlich is Associate Professor in the Department of Languages, Literatures and Linguistics, York University, Toronto, Canada. She is the author of *Point of View: a Linguistic Analysis of Literary Style, Teaching American English Pronunciation* (with Peter Avery), and the forthcoming *Language, Power and Ideology*, as well as numerous articles in discourse analysis, language and gender and second language acquisition.

Alice F. Freed is Professor of Linguistics and a member of the Women's Studies faculty at Montclair State University, New Jersey. Her research interests include discourse analysis and sociolinguistics with a focus on issues of gender. Her publications include *The Semantics of English Aspectual Complementation, The form and function of questions in informal dyadic conversation*, and *Women, men and talk: What makes the difference?* (with Alice Greenwood).

Alice Greenwood is a consultant in discourse analysis for AT&T research. She has taught at Hunter College, Vassar College, New York University, and Montclair State University. Her research interests include adolescent conversational style and group identity, and language styles and violence against women. She is co-author of *Acoustics of American English Speech: A Dynamic Approach*, and *Women, men and talk: What makes the difference?* (with Alice Freed).

Kira Hall is Assistant Professor of Linguistic Anthropology in the Department of Anthropology at Yale University. Her current research focuses on the cross-cultural study of language, gender, and sexuality. Her major publications include the co-edited anthologies *Gender Articulated* (with Mary Bucholtz) and *Queerly Phrased* (with Anna Livia).

Deborah James is Associate Professor of Linguistics in the Division of Humanities at the Scarborough campus of the University of Toronto. Her publications include two previous critical reviews of research on language and gender, dealing respectively with amount of talk (co-authored with Janice Drakich) and interruptions (co-authored with Sandra Clarke), both published in *Gender and Conversational Interaction*, edited by Deborah Tannen.

Ruth King is Associate Professor of Linguistics in the Department of Languages, Literatures and Linguistics, York University, Toronto, Canada. She is the first author of *Talking Gender*. In addition to her language and gender research, she has published in the areas of quantitative sociolinguistics and language contact.

Miriam Meyerhoff is a doctoral student in linguistics at the University of Pennsylvania, investigating the formal and social constraints on variation in Bislama (an English-based Melanesian creole). She is particularly interested in how overt patterns of variation in language can indicate underlying systems of social and cognitive organization. Her work has appeared in *Language and Society*, *Language and Communication*, the *Australian Journal of Linguistics* and *Pacific Linguistics*.

Veronica O'Donovan is Program Manager at America Online, editing the *GNN Select* best of the Internet online catalog. After receiving a fellowship for a year of linguistic and ethnographic study in Banaras, India, and completing her MA in Art History from The University of Texas at Austin, she left academia to pursue Web writing and editing projects.

Livia Polanyi is Associate Professor of Linguistics at Rice University, Houston, Texas. She was formerly a Senior Scientist in the Artificial Intelligence Department of Bolt Beranak and Newman Labs, and Associate Professor of English Linguistics at the University of Amsterdam. She is the author of *Telling the American Story*, in addition to numerous articles in computer science, formal semantics, literary theory, anthropology, economics and sociolinguistics.

Diana Strassmann is Senior Research Fellow at the Center for the Study of Cultures, Rice University, Houston, Texas. She is the founding editor of the journal *Feminist Economics* and has published widely in the areas of industrial organization, environmental policy, and economic theory. Her recent research applies insights from feminist theory, anthropology, and social studies of science to the social construction and practice of economics.

Editors' Preface

The chapters in this book, with the exception of Chapter 1, were developed from selected papers originally presented at the conference on the Language and Gender Interface: Theories and Methods for Research and Teaching. The conference, held during the 1993 Linguistic Institute in Columbus, Ohio, 16–19 July, was sponsored by the Committee on the Status of Women in Linguistics of the Linguistic Society of America. Vicky Bergvall and Janet Bing first conceived the idea for this conference while attending Sally McConnell-Ginet's and Penelope Eckert's Language and Gender class at the 1991 Linguistic Institute in Santa Cruz, in response to a perceived need for the topics of language and gender to be addressed more widely among linguists. The conference was further developed in collaboration with Alice Freed and Sally McConnell-Ginet, and was conducted with assistance from Christie Block, Kate Remlinger, Brian Joseph, Maggie Reynolds of the LSA Secretariat, and a host of willing assistants who provided crucial logistic support before and during the 1993 Institute.

This book has very much been a collaborative feminist enterprise with authors and editors exchanging ideas and learning from each other. We are grateful for the tools of modern technology (and the help of the technical experts who run them) which made these exchanges possible as we coordinated the book from Michigan, Virginia and New Jersey, with authors living in and travelling the United States, Canada, Sweden, New Zealand and Vanuatu.

We also appreciate the support – academic, technical and financial – of our departments and universities: the Department of Humanities at Michigan Technological University, the College of Arts and Letters at Old Dominion University and the separately budgeted research fund of Montclair State University.

We greatly appreciate our husbands, Craig Waddell, Charles Ruhl and Patrick Finnegan, for their continuing support during this sustained effort. They have facilitated our work by reading drafts, discussing ideas, and taking on extra domestic responsibilities far beyond the call of duty. This book would have been a very different endeavour without them.

We dedicate this book to our mothers, both biological – Ruth Bergvall, Ruth Nelson Mueller and Lillian Freed – and intellectual; the many significant contributions of the latter women are evident throughout this volume. We hope this work will inspire and encourage future generations of women and men.

Finally, we would also like to dedicate this book to our three sons, Benjamin Bergvall Waddell, Eric Whipple Bing and Marc Freed-Finnegan. We hope they will be able to live in a world where belief in gender dichotomies and stereotypes will be viewed as a historical oddity.

Victoria L. Bergvall
Janet M. Bing
Alice F. Freed

Acknowledgements

The Publishers are grateful to the following for permission to reproduce copyright material:

HarperCollins College Publishers for text and figure from *Modern Labour Economics: Theory and Public Policy*, 5th Edition, Ronald G. Ehrenberg and Robert S. Smith 1991. This material appears in our Chapter 6.

1 *The question of questions: beyond binary thinking*[1]

Janet M. Bing and Victoria L. Bergvall

The continuum of experience

Just as we rarely question our ability to breathe, so we rarely question the habit of dividing human beings into two categories: females and males. At the birth of a child we ask almost automatically, 'Is it a boy or a girl?' The question carries important messages about both biological and cultural differences; the two categories seem natural and the differences between them obvious.

However, much of our experience does not fit neatly into binary categories, and is better described as a continuum with indistinct boundaries. People relaxing at dusk experience the gradual change from day to night with no concern or precise word for the exact moment when day becomes night. Linguists travelling from village to village understand that there are no clear boundaries dividing one dialect or language from another. Berlin and Kay (1969) and Kay and McDaniel (1978) show that although basic colours have a universal biological basis, the variation across languages and individuals is so great that boundaries between colours can be identified only with fuzzy logic, a logic based on probabilities. In a study investigating how subjects distinguish between cups, bowls, mugs and vases, Labov (1973: 353) points out that although language is essentially categorical, 'in the world of experience all boundaries show some degree of vagueness, and any formal system which is useful for semantic description must allow us to record, or even measure, this property'. Because language is discrete and biased towards dichotomy and clear boundaries, the scalar values and unclear boundaries of reality are sometimes difficult to recognize and to accept; we must continually remind ourselves that reality and language can conflict. The many real-world continua hidden by language suggest a question: is our automatic division of humans into female and male as justified as we think? Are the boundaries between them as clear as the words *female* and *male* suggest?

We have reconsidered other binary distinctions that are no longer defensible. English speakers readily use categories such as Black and White (or, in the USA, African American and European American) to classify individuals with a wide range of skin colour, despite the fact that there are no definitive biological criteria for sorting human beings into races (Omi and Winant 1994). Terms such as *mulatto* or *mixed race* are rarely used, possibly because of their negative connotations and possibly because of laws stipulating that even individuals with only small percentages of 'negro blood' are classified as *Black* on their birth certificates (West and Fenstermaker 1995: 34). Even the popular press has noted the difficulty of treating all people of colour as a homogeneous group. The 13 February 1995 issue of *Newsweek* graphically illustrated its cover story 'What Color is Black?' with a series of photos showing the wide range of hues of those of African American descent. The accompanying stories note the injustice of classifying citizens by race, a practice which results in the restriction of individual rights. Despite an obvious continuum of skin colour, however, the Black–White dichotomy persists in language and in public discourse about race.

Feminist scholars have pointed out that although the majority of human beings can be unambiguously classified as either female or male, there are actually more than two sexes and/or sexualities; a binary division fails to predict purportedly sex-based phenomena such as behaviour, sexual orientation and even physiology. Because the terms *female* and *male* insufficiently categorize our experience, English also includes *tomboy, sissy, bisexual, gay, lesbian, hermaphrodite, androgyne, transvestite, transsexual, transgendered individual*, etc. The negative connotations often associated with these words suggest that although such a multiplicity exists, these are aberrations and departures from a basic dichotomy: *female* and *male*. The simple belief in 'only two' is not an experiential given but a normative social construction.

In the past, linguists have used the term *gender* to refer to grammatical word categories based on, but independent of, sex differences. The words *sex* and *gender* have traditionally referred to biological and linguistic classifications, respectively. When feminist scholars pointed out in the 1960s and 1970s that feminine and masculine behaviours were prescriptively divided into two mutually exclusive sets which do not necessarily correspond to female and male, theorists borrowed the term *gender* from linguists to refer to behaviour that was socially acquired rather than biologically innate (McConnell-Ginet 1988, Nicholson 1994). Identifying gendered behaviour as independent of biological sex has raised new questions in a number of disciplines, including psychology, sociology, anthropology and linguistics. One of these questions is, 'Can all humans be divided into only two biological categories?'

Recently, Butler (1990, 1993), J. Epstein (1990), Bem (1993), Nicholson (1994) and others have claimed that, like gender, sex is socially constructed and better described as a continuum rather than a dichotomy. In what are often called Western (meaning industrialized) countries, biological sexual variance is now surgically corrected to fit binary categories (J. Epstein 1990), in contrast to cultures that recognize more than two biological categories, as well as more than two social and linguistic categories (Jacobs and Cromwell 1992, Hall and O'Donovan this volume). Even discussions of gender have often assumed innate biological differences between females and males, but this 'biological foundationalism' (Bem 1993) is now being challenged. Butler, Bem, Nicholson and J. Epstein do not assume dichotomies in either sex or gender and their work is encouraging those in other disciplines to examine the consequences of looking for and finding dichotomies.

Traditional questions about language and gender

This book arises, in part, because the editors and contributors were troubled by many of the preconceptions and presuppositions inherent in the questions traditionally asked in research on language and gender. The contributors to this volume question the division of speech on the basis of a binary division of gender or sex. They investigate speech communities without presupposing differences between women and men and show the diverse ways in which traditional ideas about sex and gender have influenced questions asked about language. Not surprisingly, these authors raise some important new questions, including the following:

1. Why are questions that strengthen the female–male dichotomy so frequently asked, while those that explore other types of variation evoke much less interest?
2. How much of this apparent dichotomy is imposed by the questions themselves?

Although researchers studying language and gender are generally sensitive to the power of language, the traditional questions have tended to reinforce rather than to weaken the prevailing female–male dichotomy. Researchers asking the question, 'How do men and women speak differently?' (Lakoff 1975, Maltz and Borker 1982, Tannen 1990) not only presuppose that women and men do speak differently, but have too often found the language of women deficient (Jespersen 1922, Lakoff 1975), reinforcing the perception of **women** as deficient (see Cameron this volume).

A second question, 'How does language reflect, construct, and maintain male dominance?' represents another major strand of language and gender research. Feminists such as Shulamith Firestone, Catherine MacKinnon, Alison Jaggar and Mary Daly have shown how social systems limit women's freedom of choice and action (Tong 1989); feminists interested in exploring how dominance is achieved through language explore how interruptions, topic control, use of generic pronouns and nouns, polite forms and formal and informal speech all constitute evidence that language not only reflects power relationships, but helps maintain them (Zimmerman and West 1975, Fishman 1983, West and Zimmerman 1983, James and Clarke 1992, Bing 1994, etc.). Such studies challenge the rights of males to control language, but as a result of asking questions that presuppose a dichotomy, they also reinforce the predominant assumption that females and males are essentially different.

The recognition that gender roles are socially constructed has brought about a reframing of the traditional question from 'How do women and men speak differently?' to 'How are women and men **taught** to speak differently?' Those who study culture and language have always insisted that difference and inferiority are not the same, and scholars such as Maltz and Borker (1982) and Tannen (1990) emphasize parallels between gender differences and cultural differences. Although researchers adopting a cultural-difference approach do not deny male dominance nor necessarily assume an essential biological difference between women and men, those writing for a wider, popular audience, such as Gray (1992) *Men are from Mars, Women are from Venus* and Tannen (1990) *You Just Don't Understand*, emphasize differences, minimize similarities, and largely ignore unequal power or status. As Freed (1992) argues, such books reinforce stereotypes and mask the fact that female and male language and behaviour form an overlapping continuum rather than two distinct categories.

The persistence of dichotomies

Linguists have documented extensively how individual speakers command a range of styles with situationally appropriate competence (Chafe 1985, Tannen 1985, Chafe and Danielewicz 1987, Biber 1988, West 1995, Freed this volume, Greenwood this volume). Researchers such as Tannen (1981, 1982, 1984) and Labov (1972) emphasize ethnic variation and functional or social variation in some of their research but in other work seem to imply that women share a common language different from the common language of men (Tannen 1990, Labov 1991). For example, the question of why women use more prestige forms presupposes that women do use more prestige forms, despite studies that show that not all and not only women use such forms (James this volume).

There is considerable evidence that variables such as race, social class, culture, discourse function, and setting are as important as gender and not additive or easily separated (Keenan 1974, Gal 1989, 1992, hooks 1990, M. Goodwin 1980, 1991, Ochs 1992, West and Fenstermaker 1995, Freed and Greenwood 1996, Bucholtz this volume, Meyerhoff this volume, Polanyi and Strassman this volume). Eckert and McConnell-Ginet (1992a, 1992b, 1995) have argued against taking gender as natural or given and have advocated grounding the study of gender and language in investigations of the social and linguistic activities of specific groups, such as the communities of high school jocks and burnouts (Eckert 1989). The research of O'Barr and Atkins (1980) challenges the assumption that there is a women's language different from that of men, arguing that differences attributed to sex are actually differences between powerful or powerless styles of language used by both men and women. In examining how children construct arguments, Goodwin and Goodwin (1987: 205) report, 'Though there are some differences in the ways in which girls and boys organize their arguing ... the features they use in common are far more pervasive. Were one to focus just on points where girls and boys differ, the activity itself would be obscured.' Ochs (1992: 340) observes, 'In relating sociocultural constructions of gender to social meaning of language, an issue of importance emerges: *few features of language directly and exclusively index gender*' [emphasis in the original]. Evidence of this kind is often overlooked. Researchers can accept evidence that shows that gender is a social construct and that language is learned behaviour. However, because they accept a biological female–male dichotomy, they often assume that language reflects this dichotomy. Studies that reinforce female–male differences continue to capture the interest and imagination of both scholars and the general public, thus further reinforcing the presupposed dichotomy.

Certain ideas (including ideas about female–male differences) persist in the face of contradictory evidence, while other ideas just never seem to gain wide interest or attention. Facts and arguments that challenge conventional wisdom tend to be overlooked or forgotten. For example, in spite of frequent efforts to debunk the belief that Eskimos have 100 words for snow (Pullum 1989), the general public is unlikely to abandon this myth. As Pullum (1989: 277) notes, 'the lack of little things like verisimilitude and substantiation are not enough to stop a myth'. Similarly, despite the observations of researchers like O'Barr and Atkins (1980), Goodwin and Goodwin (1987) and Eckert (1989), there will probably be no decline in the number of students who begin their term-paper research with the question, 'How is the language of men and women different?' Such questions strengthen deeply held certainties that mere facts cannot dislodge. The belief that there are separate women's and men's ways of speaking reinforces the social myth that males and females are fundamentally and categorically different.

Both language and traditional social practice suggest that there are clear boundaries between biological females and males. However, if the boundaries are not problematic, it is curious that so much energy is expended to reinforce them and to render invisible large numbers of people, including homosexuals, bisexuals, eunuchs, hermaphrodites, transvestites, transsexuals, transgendered and intersexed individuals, and others who assume social and sexual roles different from those that their cultures legitimize. Anthropologists, psychologists and sociologists have long accepted the idea that gender roles are learned and arbitrary and that conventional feminine and masculine behaviour varies from culture to culture. Despite the evidence provided by Butler (1990, 1993), Bem (1993), Nicholson (1994) and many others, the claim that not only gender but the category of sex itself is also socially constructed is usually greeted with disbelief or scepticism.

Individuals who fail to fit the strict female–male dichotomy are either ignored or subject to boundary policing. Groups that inhabit or stretch the boundaries of restrictive gender roles either become taboo (unmentioned and unmentionable) or are labelled aberrant. Thus, assertive women may be nudged back into their approved roles by being labelled *aggressive bitches*, and nurturing men may be reminded of their deviance by being labelled *wimp*, *sissy*, *fag* or *pussy-whipped*. Like the dichotomies *day* and *night* and *Black* and *White*, the categories *female* and *male* are used and reinforced daily, whereas words such as *invert* or *intersexed* (words that describe hermaphrodites and ambiguously sexed individuals) are rare and likely to evoke disbelief or confusion.

The emergence of dichotomy

It is important to examine the debate between those who view sexual differentiation as innate and those who argue that both sex and gender are socially constructed. An analysis of this debate will help us understand how predominant the belief in biological essentialism is and how the female–male dichotomy helps strengthen the conviction that anatomy is destiny. By understanding how dichotomy is enforced, we may recognize that we inadvertently contribute to it. It is particularly important to look at definitions and note who does the defining. A good place to begin is with the definitions and the definers of the words *female* and *male*.

Over time, scientists have had many ways to account for differences between women and men. Citing Hippocrates, many early writers 'scientifically' accounted for sex differences as a distinction between *complexions*; that is, the balance of the qualities hot, cold, moist and dry. Because men were believed to have greater heat than women, they were judged to be superior (Cadden 1993: 171). Edward Clarke's (1873) *Sex in Education* used the concept of *vital force* to argue against the education of women, for if the nervous system has a fixed amount of energy, any energy spent in the development of a woman's brain would be diverted from her reproductive organs and, hence, would be harmful to her health (Bem 1993: 10). However, the idea that female and male bodies are fundamentally different is relatively new. Historically, women's sexual organs were believed to be the same as, but less developed than, those of men.

Thomas Laqueur (1990) identifies the historical shift in the eighteenth century from a one-sex view of the body to a two-sex view. Just as studies such as Jespersen's identified women's language as an inferior form of men's, so until relatively recently, the female body was seen as an inferior version of the male's, and the 'less-developed' female sexual organs had the same names as those of males. Prior to the eighteenth century, philosophers and physicians assumed the incapacity and dependency of women and children since both were incomplete or underdeveloped men (Cadden 1993: 181). Under this view, the fact that all embryos have tissue for both female and male genitalia and reproductive organs (Bem 1993: 23) was not problematic for defenders of the status quo.

Both the Church and Aristotle provided traditional reasons why males should rule females, but with the decline of their authority, the single-sex hypothesis became a potential threat to the social order, making it necessary to justify the limitation of women's rights by defining women as **essentially** different. If women were the same, they might ask for the same privileges enjoyed by men. The boundaries between the sexes needed to be reinforced; inter-sexed individuals ceased to be acknowledged and became redefined as a medical problem. With the shift to the two-sex view of the body, differences rather than similarities became emphasized, organs such as the vagina were given names of their own (Nicholson 1994: 87), and hermaphrodites subsequently became pseudo-hermaphrodites whose 'true' sex had to be discovered by doctors (J. Epstein 1990: 100).

Medical enforcement: fixing nature's 'mistakes'

The medical categorization of intersexed individuals shows that the distinction between female and male is an issue that is not only linguistic and cultural, but is also medical. Julia Epstein (1990: 104) quotes a 1964 medical textbook that states, 'There is no standard legal or medical definition of sex.' Biological sex results from variations in chromosome combinations (such as XX, XY, XO, XXX, and XXY), internal gonad structure, external gonad structure, hormonal dominance, secondary sexual characteristics, apparent sex, psychological sex, and sex of rearing. In the majority of human births, the combinations of these factors lead to clearly sexed males and females, but they can also result in as many as seventy different types of intersexed individuals (J. Epstein 1990: 105). Such intersexed individuals are not as rare as most people believe. Duckett and Baskin (1993: S80) report that the incidence of inter-sex is approximately 1 in 30,000 newborns, of which about 10 per cent are true hermaphrodites. The more common pseudo-hermaphroditism results from a number of causes, including hormonal variations. Although the birth of intersexed individuals is not rare, it *is* unmentionable, even in tabloids that regularly report such outrageous topics as copulation with extraterrestrials and the reappearance of Elvis.

The assignment of intersexed individuals to the categories of female and male is complex and partly dependent on the biases of particular physicians. Although chromata are often an important factor in determining sex, they are not always the deciding factor. For example, in the case of Androgen Insensitivity Syndrome (testicular feminization), individuals with XY chromatin patterns and normal androgen levels appear to be female at birth and are generally raised as females. Referring to a summary of studies on true hermaphrodites, Krob *et al.* (1993: 4–5) note that although hermaphrodites are generally 'assigned' a female sex, those with a Y chromosome are made female as often as those with an X chromosome are made male. As Kessler (1990: 12) notes, for some physicians, chromosomes are less relevant in determining sex than penis size; that is, *male* is defined neither by the genetic condition of having one Y and one X chromosome nor by the production of sperm, but by the aesthetic condition of having an appropriately large penis.

Evidence in the medical literature suggests that different physicians use different criteria for assigning sex. If the primary physician for an intersexed child is a pediatric endocrinologist, the child is more likely to be classified as female, but if the decision is made by a urologist, the same child is more likely to classified as male (Kessler 1990: 21). As one endocrinologist noted, urologists 'like to make boys' (p. 21). It is worth noting that physicians recognize and emphasize to parents of intersexed children that sex as well as gender is socially constructed, but this is rarely discussed in public domains. One pediatric endocrinologist reports '[I] try to impress upon them [the parents] that there's an enormous amount of clinical data to support the fact that if you sex-reverse an infant … the majority of the time the alternative gender identity is commensurate with the socialization, the way that they are raised, and how people view them, and that seems to be the most critical' (p. 17).

Thus, just as language and society enforce the division between genders, the medical profession enforces a binary division into two sexes, suppressing the diversity of gender positions. Intersexed individuals (who were previously treated as monsters) are now defined as 'treatable', with physicians reconstructing the body as either female or male with surgery and/or hormones. The possibility of **not** 'curing' these individuals is never considered. Although determining a true sex sometimes takes as long as two or three months, the pretence remains that all humans are born female or male, but never both, neither, or indeterminate. Despite relatively large numbers of babies born intersexed and an extensive medical literature on the subject, references to intersexed or ambiguously sexed individuals are uncommon in public discourse. Since most intersexed individuals are 'cured' as infants, even those individuals who are most affected are often unaware of their previous biological status, one enforced by silence. Similarly, until quite recently, gays, lesbians, cross-dressers, and other groups at the boundaries of gender were also treated with silence, and in many situations they still are.

Supernumerary categories

Sex and gender polarizations are widespread, but also culture-specific. The way different societies define homosexuality and intersexed individuals suggests that 'compulsory heterosexuality' (Rich 1980) is not universal. Many cultures recognize supernumerary genders, categories that describe roles other than feminine and masculine; the most widely cited are the Native American *berdache* (Martin and Voorhies 1975, Whitehead 1981). In most Native American tribes, the berdache had well-defined and sometimes respected status (Whitehead 1981). In most cases, the supernumerary terms refer to gender roles rather than to sex, as in the case of North Piegan women who became *ninauposkitzipxpe*, 'manly-hearted women' (Martin and Voorhies 1975: 101).

However, some societies also have common names for intersexed individuals. Although the Pokot of Kenya usually put intersexed individuals to death as monsters, they use a common word, *serrer*, to refer to 'male and female yet neither male nor female' (Jacobs and Cromwell 1992: 50, Martin and Voorhies 1975: 89). Similarly, the *hijras* are a visible and socially recognized part of society in India (Hall and O'Donovan this volume). The Navajo call the intersexed *nadle*, and distinguish between real *nadle* (presumably hermaphrodites) and those with either female or male genitals who pretend they are *nadle*. Both categories have well-defined and respected status in Navajo society, and the roles of both are sanctioned by Navajo mythology (Martin and Voorhies 1975: 93). The existence of four genders in tribes such as the Pima (males, females, males who act like females, and females who act like males) is a direct recognition by the society that not all people fit into just two categories. The mythologies the Navajo, Pima, Mojave and other Native American groups recognize that intersexuals, homosexuals and transgendered individuals have always existed.

The scientific basis for dichotomy: language and the brain

Scientists have abandoned many of the theories formerly used to justify the inferior status of women, including the complexion theory and the life-force theory. In place of these now-discredited hypotheses, some scientists are now asking how the brains of females and males differ. Claims based on brain research have long been used to distance privileged groups from those judged to be less worthy. As Gould (1981: 52–69) shows, nineteenth-century scientists such as Morton looked for and found 'objective' evidence to prove that whites had larger brains than Indians and Blacks. This problematic research tradition continues. J. Philippe Rushton, a psychologist at the University of Western Ontario, claims that different races have different brain sizes. Rushton (1995: 38–39) cites a number of studies correlating brain size with intelligence and claims that 'Small differences in brain volume translates [sic] into greater brain efficiency and millions of excess neurons and helps to explain the global distribution of intelligence test scores' (p. 113). Fausto-Sterling (1993) notes the consistency with which the brain research tends to mark as superior the characteristics of the researchers themselves, even if this requires some reinterpretation of the evidence. For example, in comparing the brains of deceased eminent men, turn-of-the-century scientists discovered that [male] 'scientists had some of the largest brains' (p. 35), although even their brains were not as large as those of elephants.

Current research on the brain continues to seek differences between the sexes. Shaywitz et al. (1995: 609) report 'remarkable differences in the functional organization of a specific component of language, phonological processing, between normal males and females'. In one part of this study, female and male subjects were asked to perform rhyming tasks; magnetic resonance imaging scans reportedly showed left lateralization of brain activity for all of the men and slightly less than half of the women, but bilateral activity for the remainder of the women. In a different type of brain research, Roger Gorski and his colleagues have discovered that the preoptic nuclei of male rats are significantly larger than those of female rats, and Laura Allen in Gorski's labouratory has found a similar sex difference in the human brain (Kimura 1992: 120). Doreen Kimura, one of a number of researchers studying the effects of female and male hormones, claims that 'the effects of sex hormones on brain organization occur so early in life that from the start the environment is acting on differently wired brains in girls and boys' (1992: 119).

Researchers such as Kimura say they 'don't have any ax to grind, political or otherwise' (quoted in Holloway 1990: 42), and also claim that they approach their projects with no preconceptions. However, the very questions such researchers ask and the statements they have made in interviews belie this objectivity and suggest that they are actively seeking differences. Gorski (interviewed by Stein 1990) asserts, 'Sex differences in the structure of the human brain exist. And I for one strongly believe that some of them are shaped by the sex hormone environment. My position remains: It's sexually dimorphic until you've proven it isn't' (Stein 1990: 140). In a *New York Times* article, Bennett Shaywitz is quoted as saying: 'It is a truism that men and women are different. ... What I think we can do now is to take what is essentially folklore and place it in the context of science. There is a real scientific method available to answer some of these questions' (Kolata 1995: C7). Some researchers such as Witelson find differences, but caution that 'Different is different' (Phillips 1990: 46), not better or worse; but as Gorski notes, 'What happens is that people overinterpret these things' (Kolata 1995: C7).

In reporting brain research, the popular press both overinterprets and exaggerates the results. Experiments by Bennett and Sally Shaywitz and their colleagues at Yale University (1995) found no differences on two of three language processing tasks, but they did find that slightly more than half of the women processed rhymes differently than the men. *Science News* announces this experiment with the headline 'Brain scan tags sexes as words apart' and introduces this story with 'More often than they would like, men and women have trouble talking to one another' (Bower 1995: 101). *Jet*'s cover story 'Why men and women cannot be like each other' reports that 'Researchers at Yale University recently discovered that men and women will never be like each other because they use their brains differently' and concludes, 'Many researchers agree that it's no wonder the battle between the sexes rages on as mounting evidence indicates women are more effective communicators and do better on language tests than men, who are more adept at spatial concepts' ('Why men and women cannot be like each other' 1995: 15–16).

Not only does the popular press exaggerate and overgeneralize difference, it also completely omits any mention of evidence of similarities. For example, Shaywitz *et al.* (1995) reported no differences for semantic or orthographic processing, and although eight of the nineteen female subjects showed the 'male' left lateralization, the researchers (and the popular press) create the impression of homogeneous groups by reporting that 'women' process language bilaterally. Thus, the public representation of the brain's processes as inherently different ignores 42 per cent of the female subjects and the fact that males and females performed the same way on two of the three tasks. Unfortunately, these intra-group differences and intergroup similarities often go unreported, even in the scientific literature. As C. Epstein notes, most reports obscure any similarities that might be characteristic of the majority of a sample: 'Reports of sex differences tend to gloss over the size of difference. The titles of articles that report findings convey the impression of mutually exclusive categories rather than overlap. Thus, results tend to be perceived as based on attributes that are innate or set early in life' (C. Epstein 1988: 37).

In contrast to the historical fascination with establishing the differences between females' and males' brains, research investigating other types of difference rarely captures the attention of the media or the popular imagination. For example, a number of researchers have associated different cognitive functions with different brain hemispheres and have identified left brain activity with linear analytic thinking and right brain activity with the unconscious and with creativity (Corballis 1983, Ehrenwald 1984, Springer and Deutsch 1993). Ehrenwald discusses research on professional groups predicted to have different cognitive styles and reports that 'alpha measurements show that the people from business, law and accounting professions differ from individuals in creative professions in the way their hemispheres process cognitive tasks' (Ehrenwald 1984: 10). Similarly, using Conjugate Lateral Eye Movement Tests (see Bryden 1982: 260–3), Gannett (n.d.) explores cognitive distinctions for writers and finds significant differences between the lateralization of critics and imaginative writers (fiction and poetry). Gannett's experiments suggest that when problem solving, critics tend to be left-dominant and imaginative writers either right-dominant or bilateral. Studies of cognitive style seek and find variations similar to those the media would have us believe result only from essential differences between the sexes.

Differences in brain activity have also been correlated with cultural differences, reading direction and second language learning. Obler (1981) reports right hemisphere participation in second language acquisition and diminished left-dominance for languages, such as Hebrew, which are read from right to left. Contrasting how speakers of different languages process sounds, Tadanobu Tsunoda discovered that Japanese speakers 'tend to register far more sounds in the left hemisphere than in the right. While Westerners usually process isolated vowels, animal sounds, natural sounds and non-verbal human sounds such as crying in the right hemisphere, the Japanese process them all in the left, or verbal hemisphere' (Merrill 1981: 74). This study was reported with some scepticism by Merrill, who says 'Intriguing as Tsunoda's findings are, they have not yet been replicated. ... Some scientists find his theories astonishingly elegant, while others are waiting for more data to come in' (Merrill 1981: 75). Tsunoda's work was of such interest to the Japanese, however, that '[d]espite its highly technical language, the book became a best-seller in Japan' (Merrill 1981: 74), possibly because it reinforces the belief of many Japanese that they are a unique people.

Michael Corballis (1995: 397) asks 'Why is cerebral asymmetry so relentlessly fascinating?' The on-going debate about brain lateralization is of interest partly because it encapsulates a new scientific way to explain whatever differences society is intent upon enforcing. As Fausto-Sterling (1993: 37) argues, just like the now-discredited nineteenth-century research about brain size, current research emphasizing brain differences reflects social rather than scientific arguments. Efron (1990) is also sceptical of many current claims about right and left hemispheric activity or dominance and of the 'true believers' who may speculate about hemispheric specialization. He criticizes many of the claims that have been made about the brain, including those of Kimura, and shows why they form a 'closed conceptual system' (Efron 1990: 27) which cannot be falsified. His response to speculation about hemispheric specialization, including claims about sex differences, is: 'The real problem ... is that we do not at present understand the cognitive function of **any** brain area, let alone an entire hemisphere' (p. 27).

Like Pullum's attempts to undermine the 'great Eskimo vocabulary hoax', attempts by Fausto-Sterling, Efron and others to diminish overgeneralizations about brain differences between the sexes will probably go unheeded. As Hess (1990: 81) reminds us, 'For two millennia, "impartial experts" have given us such trenchant insights as the fact that women lack sufficient heat to boil the blood and purify the soul, that their heads are too small, their wombs too big, their hormones too debilitating, that they think with their hearts or the wrong side of the brain.' The answers have changed, but the questions have not. Researchers and the media remain fascinated with any new way to pose the question: How are men and women different?

Difference is not the problem

One important fact cannot be overlooked: there are some biological differences between most women and most men. Nobody denies this, although some writers suggest that feminists do deny it and are being irrational when they criticize findings that emphasize female–male differences. Noting that in higher math, 'the topmost ranks are thronged with male minds', Nicholas Wade (1994: 32) says, 'Some feminist ideologues assert that all minds are created equal and women would be just as good at math if they weren't discouraged in school.' He discounts the effect of bias and cites an expert who 'concludes that boys' superiority at math is mostly innate'.

The issue, of course, is not difference, but oversimplification and stereotyping. One obvious oversimplification is that of using statistical differences between two groups as proof that all members of one group have certain characteristics shared by no members of the other group (and vice versa). This oversimplification has traditionally been used to limit choices and opportunities for girls and women. Contrary to what Wade suggests, the point is not that everyone is created equal, but that everyone should be allowed equal opportunity. Even if scientists were to discover some correlation between sex and innate superiority at certain math skills, this would not necessarily be problematic unless it were used as an excuse to ignore biased behaviour in the classroom (such as teachers interpreting statistical differences as categorical and telling their students that girls are no good at math). However, the average performance of a group is too often used to restrict the opportunities of individuals, such as girls who just happen to excel at math; their performance can then be labelled exceptional, thus further reinforcing lowered expectations for other girls.

Wade might have considered similar evidence from other fields. The top-ranked chefs are also mostly male; does this suggest that cooking is also an innate ability better left to men? Doreen Kimura

(1992: 125) judges females to be less suitable than men for the fields of engineering and physics. Does this suggest that colleges should train *no* female engineers or physicists, regardless of prior achievement? Does this justify the androcentric bias in engineering programmes described by Bergvall (this volume)? As Gould (1984: 7) notes, biological determinism is a 'theory of limits', and theories which treat all members of a group as identical impose real limits on real people.

The issue is not difference, but *gender polarization*, 'the ubiquitous organization of social life around the distinction between male and female' (Bem 1993: 2). Bem observes:

> It is thus not simply that women and men are seen to be different but that this male–female difference is superimposed on so many aspects of the social world that a cultural connection is thereby forged between sex and virtually every other aspect of human experience, including modes of dress and social roles and even ways of expressing emotion and experiencing sexual desire. (p. 2)

As Bem shows, the problem with gender polarization is not that there are differences, but that these differences define mutually exclusive scripts for being female and male (p. 80).

Gender polarization makes it easier to limit opportunities and exclude girls and women from education, public office and the military and easier to deny them legal protection and highly paid positions. For example, in a court case claiming employer discrimination against women, representatives defending the retail corporation, Sears, argued 'that "fundamental" differences between the sexes (and not its own actions) explained the gender imbalances in its labor force' (Scott 1988: 39). The plaintiff's attorneys provided statistical evidence to show that women were not being hired in commission sales jobs. Sears contended that differences could be accounted for not by discrimination against women, but by **natural** difference. By treating women as a homogeneous group and establishing this group as **different**, Sears won its case. Apparently 'women' did not want the more lucrative positions, in spite of the fact that it was women who sued.

The issue is not difference, but the denial of any differences within or across groups. In the United States, individual rights are fiercely defended, so it is ironic that women are so often treated as members of a group and not as individuals. Exclusion on the basis of sex is not uncommon. For example, in the United States, women have been excluded from some state-supported military academies (the Citadel and the Virginia Military Institute) despite outstanding achievement of women at others; the top graduate from West Point in 1995 was Rebecca Elizabeth Marier.

The case of Debra DiCenso, an amateur bodybuilder, provides another reminder of how much variation there is within the categories *women* and *men*, as well as a striking example of how strongly gender polarization is still enforced. Ms DiCenso was arrested for working out in the men's weight room in a Boston gym. She was there because the heaviest dumbbells in the women's weight room were 34 pounds too light for her workout. This would not be a problem for most women, but for the 'crime' of working out in the men's weight room (not forbidden by any gym rules) and for refusing to leave when asked, this woman was 'handcuffed, driven to the police station and booked' (Associated Press 1995: A6). Debra DiCenso's 'crime' was that of disobeying the unspoken rules of gender polarization. For her, the problem was not difference; she's different not only from most men but also from most women. For Debra DiCenso, the problem was inequality of opportunity.

Difference, diversity and gender polarization

Some aspects of difference are positive. Feminists have sometimes emphasized difference in order to show that women's speech, bodies and work are valuable (Scott 1988, Hess 1990, Tannen 1990, West and Fenstermaker 1995). But for many feminists, the word *difference* is a problem because, when it is used, the power differential between groups is usually ignored. Attempts to prove difference are often attempts at gender polarization and one way to rationalize limiting the opportunities of women. For those who perceive no inequality of opportunity, *difference* does not signal an underlying pattern of dominance. Trudgill (1974: 95), for example, states: 'Thus geographical, ethnic group and social-class varieties [of language] are, at least partly, the result of social *distance*, while sex varieties are the result of social *difference*.' Many feminists would disagree, arguing that sex, class and ethnicity all involve social distance (difference in status) and not simply difference (McIntosh 1988, Bing 1994).

The word *diversity* also has different meanings for different people. For many feminists and people of colour, the word *diversity* implies equality of opportunity for traditionally excluded groups and the recognition of individual differences within groups. Gender polarization is a failure to accept diversity. As Scott (1988:45) says of gender polarization:

> In effect, the duality this opposition creates draws one line of difference, invests it with biological explanations, and then treats each side of the opposition as a unitary phenomenon. Everything in each category (male/female) is assumed to be the same; hence, differences within either category are suppressed.

For members of privileged groups, *diversity* is often unwelcome. Although *difference* can be used to justify the status quo, *diversity* challenges it. To some people, *diversity*, like *affirmative action*, does not suggest equal opportunity, but another false dichotomy: They ask, do we give a woman an opportunity, or do we choose the best candidate, that is, someone who is qualified? The simplifications of such dichotomies not only hide the genuine complexities of experience, but also provide justification for the exclusion of individuals. Critics, such as Wade (1994), who chastise 'feminist ideologues' for pointing out the dangers of emphasizing difference, should address the question of what it is that they find so threatening about diversity. After all, isn't diversity just a more complex and accurate understanding of difference?

Beyond dichotomy

It would be ironic if *feminists* interested in language and gender inadvertently reinforced gender polarization and the myths of essential female–male difference. By accepting a biological female–male dichotomy and by emphasizing language which reflects the two categories, linguists may be reinforcing biological essentialism, even if they emphasize that language, like gender, is learned behaviour. Unfortunately, there are indications that this is exactly what happens. In a chapter called 'Speculations on the Evolution of Mind, Woman, Man, and Brain', Joseph (1992) cites the work of a number of linguists, including Tannen (1990) to underscore what he believes are essential female–male differences. Linguists must realize that when they publish answers to the question, 'How do women and men speak differently?', their discoveries of difference may be co-opted for the purpose of strengthening gender polarization.

Deborah Cameron recognizes this problem. Her chapter begins

with a question previously asked by Sally McConnell-Ginet (1988: 75), 'Why have linguists been relatively inactive in the growing area of research on language and gender?' This question leads Cameron to explore why the *socio-* in *sociolinguistics* is devalued. She classifies the work of language and gender scholars into deficit, difference, and dominance models and suggests that a majority of linguists are most comfortable with the difference model. As Cameron notes, linguists are trained to work with descriptive paradigms and to be non-judgemental about differences. However, she cautions that although **linguists** may be impartial about difference, the general public is not. Cameron illustrates the ways in which the press has (mis-)used language and gender research to promote what she calls *verbal hygiene* and to provide advice to women about how to become more successful in business by sounding more like men. She charges language and gender researchers to be more aware of the logical extensions of their work and urges them to ask new questions: 'Instead of "How do women and men behave linguistically", we can ask how particular language practices contribute to the production of people as "women and men".'

Despite a growing body of evidence challenging assumptions about differences between the speech of women and men, many language researchers still assume that female and male are unproblematic categories. Building on previously published work with Alice Greenwood, Alice Freed explores an experimental situation in which other variables prove to be more important than sex. She asks '[W]hy [do] the language patterns of the women and men who participated in this project turn out to be so similar despite the fact that other researchers have so often found differences in the speech characteristics of women and men?' Freed challenges the widespread assumption that where there are sex differences there will also be language differences. She shows that setting and communicative tasks rather than sex can be the index to what has been described as a gendered style of speech. Unlike previous researchers who presuppose that sex is the basic category to be investigated, Freed examines the data and finds that sex is not a relevant variable. She argues that in order to fully understand differences, it is important to control many potentially intersecting variables and not simply assume the categories female and male. She demonstrates that one way to do this is with the use of carefully constructed research settings.

In investigating a series of conversations within one particular community of practice – a group of adolescent siblings and their friends – Alice Greenwood provides further evidence that sex is an insignificant variable for explaining who holds the floor or who interrupts or is interrupted. The young people in the dinner conversations analysed by Greenwood reported that the reason they were talking was to entertain and amuse themselves. Speakers who accepted the group's purpose and norms and who were, in turn, accepted by the group, interrupted family members and were interrupted in ways that expressed solidarity, sometimes failing and sometimes succeeding in gaining the floor, but never spoiling the fun. One speaker who failed to accept the established group norms protested what he perceived as frequent interruptions of his talk and, to some extent, was able to control the discourse, but he never felt comfortable and was perceived to be acting like an outsider. Greenwood offers evidence that, even within a single family group, the rules for establishing a topic of conversation or interrupting others are complex. However, she found no evidence that the sex of the speakers was ever a significant variable in this setting. As she points out, in order to prevent overgeneralization and distortion, we have to ask exactly which group is under investigation, 'under what circumstances are they speaking, in the role of what, in relation to whom, with what background, and so on.'

Sociolinguists have often asked 'Why do women use more prestige forms than men?', a question that presupposes that they always do. Such presuppositions encourage researchers to undervalue cultural, status and situational differences in an attempt to simplify complex variables. Deborah James's survey of the literature reveals that the use of prestige forms by women is not universal and that market forces, social networks, status and types of discourse are all relevant variables. The assumption of only two relevant categories, female and male, reinforces gender polarization and encourages researchers to overlook other possibly relevant factors. James raises interesting new questions for future researchers. In what kinds of communities are particular factors likely to be salient? What kinds of factors can outweigh and nullify other factors, and in what circumstances will they do so? The answers can only come from 'careful and detailed analyses of the social structures of particular communities', and the close examination of specific discourse contexts and cross-cultural comparisons of different communities. It is clear that the answers will never devolve simply into women's versus men's strategies.

Livia Polanyi and Diana Strassmann illustrate how abstraction, oversimplification and stipulation of gender roles serve political ends in the field of economics. They examine and find wanting the stereotypes and assumptions about social class and gender roles found in a popular introductory economics textbook. In economics texts, people in illustrative examples are idealized as economic agents who make decisions based only on economic factors, that is, 'constrained optimization'. In the illustrative stories of the texts, idealized women fulfil stereotypical gender and class roles (cooking, raising children, growing their own food), but the authors of these stories imply that these same hypothetical women possess all of the choices, personal resources and characteristics of educated, privileged white males. Thus, poverty, misfortune and unhappiness can be attributed to poor choices and bad judgement, rather than to a system of unequal privilege. The oversimplifications and stereotypes not only misrepresent, but also help maintain and perpetuate an unjust economic system. Those whose personal histories enable them to recognize the classist and sexist assumptions within the textbooks may question whether they are an intended audience or have any potential as future economists. This analysis provides a model for others who wish to question the premises behind the gatekeeping strategies by which a discipline reproduces itself.

Susan Ehrlich and Ruth King provide an excellent example of the power of definition and redefinition. In reporting on the hearings that result from an accusation of sexual harassment (more accurately, date rape), Ehrlich and King illustrate the power of questioners and the power of questions that define and control discourse and 'do ideological work'. The questions of the university disciplinary tribunal described by Ehrlich and King control the discourse and reframe the testimony of the victims, reconstructing the events in question as consensual sex. While the chapter does not overtly address the issues of the social enforcement of gender expectations, it does make clear that the defendants in the hearings are submitted to the (re-)construction of their 'appropriate' social roles via the questions of the review board. Differences between the language styles of the less powerful female defendants in contrast to that of a more powerful female tribunal member again show why a unified notion of 'woman's language' can be misleading.

Victoria Bergvall shows how language reflects the conflicts between professional and traditional gender expectations of women studying to be engineers. The demands of the technological university of Bergvall's study overtly require adherence to a gender-neutral, androgynous standard of academic conduct, but the forces of heterosexual attraction push women into traditionally assigned gender roles. Although the women perceive and report gender-neutral conditions in their classes, academic expectations in engineering classes are, in fact, androcentric rather than androgynous, partly because of the military origins of the field of engineering and partly because it is still primarily a male-dominated field. Thus, women in engineering are expected simultaneously to meet both traditional female social role expectations and male professional role expectations. The data illustrate how these women resist and are resisted, and accede and accommodate to the conversational and social demands of peers and profession. From the double bind of these women, new questions arise: What verbal and non-verbal acts support and enforce gender polarization? How can these be resisted through language?

Miriam Meyerhoff addresses the question of how best to describe and represent the complexity of multiple identities. Drawing from research in social psychology and her previous work on pidgins and creoles, Meyerhoff provides the metaphor of a sphere for the presentation of identity, one different from the 'additive' and 'multiplicative' metaphors that have been proposed in the past (see West and Fenstermaker (1995) for a review). Meyerhoff shows how speakers signal the predominance of different identities in different situations depending on their motives and opportunities, using the image of a sphere which is spun to foreground salient group or personal identifications and links. Like Eckert and McConnell-Ginet (1995), Meyerhoff emphasizes that gender is only one of many social identities and cannot be analysed independently of others.

Kira Hall and Veronica O'Donovan's chapter on shifting gender positions among Hindi-speaking hijras describes the language use of the hijras, who have been called India's 'third sex'; although they are socially acknowledged in India, they are feared and marginalized. The hijras are feared because their presence and very existence provides a constant reminder that gender roles and even sex itself can be arbitrary. As the authors show, what little power the hijras have is partially gained through their fluency and control over both masculine and feminine grammatical markers. Rejected even by their own families, the hijras' only choice of community is with other hijras. Although they live outside of the traditional female–male dichotomy, their employment of linguistic gender is still influenced by a traditional, dichotomous notion of sex roles. As Hall and O'Donovan point out, 'men and women of many communities manipulate linguistic expectations of femininity and masculinity in order to establish varying positions of solidarity and power.' Paradoxically, this includes even India's hijras, with their alternative gender identities. One question arising from their study is whether a system of dichotomies can be successfully challenged.

Mary Bucholtz suggests that it can. Her analysis reveals what happens when linguists take seriously the implications of feminist theory. The African American women whom she observed were able, successfully, to challenge the authority of a radio panel discussion moderator and redefine the conventions of public discourse. Reflecting ideas expressed by African American feminist theorists, such as hooks (1984) and Collins (1990), these women successfully restructured the talk on a radio panel discussion in a number of ways, including reframing the position of the moderator, challenging the moderator's right to control the discourse, and insisting on the personal accountability of all members of a group ('you white people'). They even challenge the type of language used by introducing African American vernacular into a formal public forum. The success of these African American women in the situation described by Bucholtz shows that women do not have to accept the roles and identities conventionally allotted to them, and, in fact, can succeed in redefining and reframing what is being said. They can make themselves heard by not simply accepting the system as given, but by consciously changing it to achieve their own goals.

Asking new questions

The chapters in this volume raise new questions about language which challenge rather than reinforce gender polarization. If we are to abandon traditional dichotomies and binary questions, we must ask new questions and discover new metaphors which help us think about gender, sex and language. Nicholson (1994: 100) suggests that we compare *women* to a tapestry unified by 'overlapping threads of color', noting that 'no one particular color is found throughout the whole'. This metaphor suggests a 'complicated network of criss-crossing intersecting similarities and differences' (Nicholson 1994: 100). Nicholson also borrows the well-known game metaphor from Wittgenstein; just as there is no single feature common to all games, there is also no characteristic common to all women, but any two individuals in a group will share some common trait. West and Fenstermaker (1995) suggest a visual metaphor to account for interactions of gender, class and race; they propose a number of intersecting circles to capture the fact that different members of groups share some, but not all, characteristics.

To comprehend the complexity of experience, most people need some way to simplify it, and these new metaphors suggest ways to simplify without ignoring individual differences within or across groups. All of these ways of thinking about groups emphasize diversity rather than dichotomy. By refusing to allow oversimplification and by asking new questions, we can abandon the tired and repressive old dichotomy, 'How do women and men speak differently?', remembering that every time we seek and find differences, we also strengthen gender polarization. The old binary models of deficit, difference and dominance all emphasized difference by overlooking similarities and overlapping categories. These problematic binary models suggest dichotomies separated by clear boundaries. Although, in one sense, these boundaries exist more in language than in reality, in other ways they can raise or maintain very real social barriers for women and people of colour.

In order to move beyond binary thinking to an acceptance of diversity, we need to examine the presuppositions that underlie our questions, seek new metaphors and new models, and study different communities of practice without preconceived ideas about language and gender. We need to understand that 'innocent' questions, such as 'Is it a boy or a girl?', reveal a great deal about our value systems. Can we now move on to other questions?

Note

1. We would like to thank John Broderick, Mary Bucholtz, Susan Ehrlich, Alice Freed, Dana Heller, Charles Ruhl and Craig Waddell for their helpful comments on earlier versions of this chapter and Anita Fellman, Ethel Pollack and Kathy Pearson for helping us find sources. Any inaccuracies or misrepresentations are, of course, our own.

References

Associated Press 1995 (3 June) Woman is arrested for not being a guy. *Virginian Pilot-Ledger Star* p A6.

Bem Sandra 1993 *The lenses of gender: transforming the debate on sexual inequality*. Yale University Press, New Haven.

Berlin Brent, Kay Paul 1969 *Basic color terms: their universality and evolution*. University of California Press, Berkeley.

Bergvall Victoria this volume: Constructing and enacting gender through discourse: negotiating multiple roles as female engineering students.

Biber Douglas 1988 *Variation across speech and writing.* Cambridge University Press, Cambridge.

Bing Janet 1994 Friendly deception: status and solidarity. In Bucholtz Mary, Liang A C, Sutton Laurel A, Hines Caitlin (eds) *Cultural performances: proceedings of the third Berkeley women and language conference.* Berkeley Women and Language Group, Berkeley, CA pp 44–9.

Bower Bruce 1995 (18 Feb.) Brain scans tag sexes as words apart. *Science News* 147: 101.

Bryden M P 1982 *Laterality: functional asymmetry in the intact brain.* Academic Press, New York.

Bucholtz Mary this volume: Black feminist theory and African American women's linguistic practice.

Butler Judith 1990 *Gender trouble: feminism and the subversion of identity.* Routledge, New York.

Butler Judith 1993 *Bodies that matter: on the discursive limits of 'sex'.* Routledge, New York.

Cadden Joan 1993 *Meanings of sex difference in the middle ages: medicine, science, and culture.* Cambridge University Press, Cambridge.

Cameron Deborah this volume: The language–gender interface: challenging co-optation.

Chafe Wallace 1985 Linguistic differences produced by differences between speaking and writing. In Olson David, Torrance Nancy, Hildyard Angela (eds) pp 105–23.

Chafe Wallace, Danielewicz Jane 1987 Properties of spoken and written language. In Horowitz Rosalind, Samuels S Jay (eds) *Comprehending oral and written language.* Academic Press, New York pp 83–113.

Clarke Edward H 1873 *Sex in education, or, a fair chance for girls.* J R Osgood, Boston.

Collins Patricia Hill 1990 *Black feminist thought.* Unwin Hyman, Boston.

Corballis Michael C 1983 *Human laterality.* Academic Press, New York.

Corballis Michael C 1995 (2 Feb.) Dividing the mind. *Nature* 373, p 397 (Review of Davidson Richard J, Hugdahl Kenneth (eds) 1995 *Brain asymmetry.* MIT Press, Cambridge, MA).

Duckett John, Baskin Laurence 1993 Genitoplasty for intersex anomalies. *European Journal of Pediatrics* 152 [Suppl 2]: S80–S84.

Eckert Penelope 1989 *Jocks and burnouts: social categories and identity in the high school.* Teacher's College Press, New York.

Eckert Penelope, McConnell-Ginet Sally 1992a Communities of practice: where language, gender, and power all live. In Hall Kira, Bucholtz Mary, Moonwomon Birch (eds) pp 89–99.

Eckert Penelope, McConnell-Ginet Sally 1992b Think practically and look locally: language and gender as community-based practice. *Annual Review of Anthropology* 21: 461–90.

Eckert Penelope, McConnell-Ginet Sally 1995 Constructing meaning, constructing selves: snapshots of language, gender and class from Belten High. In Hall Kira, Bucholtz Mary (eds) *Gender articulated: arrangements of language and the socially constructed self*. Routledge, London and New York pp 469–507.

Efron Robert 1990 *The decline and fall of hemispheric specialization*. Lawrence Erlbaum Associates, Hillsdale, NJ.

Ehrenwald Jan 1984 *Anatomy of genius*. Human Sciences Press, New York.

Ehrlich Susan, King Ruth this volume: Consensual sex or sexual harassment: negotiating meaning.

Epstein, Cynthia Fuchs 1988 *Deceptive distinctions: sex, gender and the social order*. Yale University Press, New Haven.

Epstein Julia 1990 Either/or–neither/both: sexual ambiguity and the ideology of gender. *Genders* 7: 99–142.

Fausto-Sterling Anne 1993 (Oct.) Sex, race, brains, and calipers. *Discover* 14: 32, 35–7.

Fishman Pamela 1983 Interaction: the work women do. In Thorne Barrie, Kramarae Cheris, Henley Nancy (eds) pp 89–101.

Freed Alice 1992 We understand perfectly: a critique of Tannen's view of cross-sex communication. In Hall Kira, Bucholtz Mary, Moonwomon Birch (eds) pp 144–52.

Freed Alice F this volume Language and gender research in an experimental setting.

Freed Alice, Greenwood Alice 1996 Women, men and type of talk: what makes the difference? *Language in Society* 25.1: 1–26.

Gal Susan 1989 Between speech and silence: the problematics of research on language and gender. *Papers in Pragmatics* 3.1: 1–38.

Gal Susan 1992 Language, gender, and power: an anthropological view. In Hall Kira, Bucholtz Mary, Moonwomon Birch (eds) pp 153–61.

Gannett Cinthia Lee n.d. Writers and appositionality. University of New Hampshire, Durham, N.H., unpublished ms.

Goodwin Marjorie Harness 1980 Directive-response speech sequences in girls' and boys' task activities. In McConnell-Ginet Sally, Borker Ruth, Furman Nelly (eds) *Women and language in literature and society*. Praeger, New York pp 157–73.

Goodwin Marjorie Harness 1991 *He-said–she-said*. Indiana University Press, Bloomington.

Goodwin Marjorie Harness, Goodwin Charles 1987 Children's arguing. In Philips Susan, Steele Susan, Tanz Christine (eds) *Language, gender and sex in comparative perspective*. Cambridge University Press, Cambridge pp 200–48.

Gould Stephen Jay 1981 *The mismeasure of man*. W.W. Norton, New York.

Gould Stephen Jay 1984 (12 Aug.) Similarities between the sexes. (Review of Bleier, Ruth 1984 *Science and gender: a critique of biology and its theories on women.* Pergamon Press, New York.) *The New York Times Book Review* p 7.

Gray John 1992 *Men are from Mars, women are from Venus: a practical guide for improving communication and getting what you want in your relationships.* Harper Collins, New York.

Greenwood Alice this volume: Floor management and power strategies in adolescent conversation.

Hall Kira, Bucholtz Mary, Moonwomon Birch (eds) 1992 *Locating power: proceedings of the second Berkeley women and language conference.* Berkeley Women and Language Group, Berkeley, CA.

Hall Kira, O'Donovan Veronica this volume: Shifting gender positions among Hindi-speaking hijras.

Hess Beth 1990 Beyond dichotomy: drawing distinctions and embracing differences. *Sociological Forum* 5.1: 75–93.

Holloway Marguerite 1990 (Oct.) Profile [Doreen Kimura]: vive la différence. *Scientific American* 263: 40, 42.

hooks bell 1984 *Feminist theory: from margin to center.* South End Press, Boston.

hooks, bell 1990 (Jul./Aug.) Feminism and racism: the struggle continues. *Z Magazine* 3.7: 41–3.

Jacobs Sue-Ellen, Cromwell Jason 1992 Visions and revisions of reality: reflections on sex, sexuality, gender, and gender variance. *Journal of Homosexuality* 23.4: 43–69.

James Deborah this volume: Women, men and prestige speech forms: a critical review.

James Deborah, Clarke Sandra 1992 Interruptions, gender, and power: a critical review of the literature. In Hall Kira, Bucholtz Mary, Moonwomon Birch (eds) pp 286–99.

Jespersen Otto 1922 The woman. In *Language: its nature, development and origins.* Allen & Unwin, London pp 237–54.

Joseph Rhawn 1992 *The right brain and the unconscious: discovering the stranger within.* Plenum Press, New York.

Kay Paul, McDaniel C K 1978 The linguistic significance of the meanings of basic color terms. *Language* 54: 610–46.

Keenan Elinor Ochs 1974 Norm-makers and norm-breakers: uses of speech by men and women in a Malagasy community. In Bauman Richard, Scherzer Joel (eds) *Explorations in the ethnography of speaking.* Cambridge University Press, New York pp 125–43.

Kessler Suzanne J 1990 The medical construction of gender: case management of intersexed infants. *Signs: Journal of Women in Culture and Society* 16.1: 3–26.

Kimura Doreen 1992 (Sept.) Sex differences in the brain. *Scientific American* 267: 119–25.

Kolata Gina 1995 (28 Feb.) Man's world, woman's world? Brain studies point to differences. *New York Times* pp C1, C7.

Krob G, Braun A, Kuhnle U 1994 True hermaphroditism: geographical distribution, clinical findings, chromosomes and gonadal histology. *European Journal of Pediatrics* 153: 2–10.

Labov William 1972 The isolation of contextual styles. In *Sociolinguistic patterns*. University of Pennsylvania Press, Philadelphia, PA pp 70–109.

Labov William 1973 The boundaries of words and their meanings. In Bailey Charles-James, Shuy Roger (eds) *New ways of analyzing variation in English*. Georgetown University Press, Washington, DC pp 340–73.

Labov William 1991 The intersection of sex and social class in the course of linguistic change. *Language Variation and Change* 2.2: 205–54.

Lakoff Robin 1975 *Language and woman's place*. Harper & Row, New York.

Laqueur Thomas 1990 *Making sex: body and gender from the Greeks to Freud*. Harvard University Press, Cambridge, MA.

Maltz Daniel, Borker Ruth 1982 A cultural approach to male–female miscommunication. In Gumperz John J (ed) *Language and social identity*. Cambridge University Press, Cambridge pp 196–216.

Martin M Kay, Voorhies Barbara 1975 *Female of the species*. Columbia University Press, New York.

McConnell-Ginet Sally 1988 Language and gender. In Newmeyer Frederick J (ed) *Linguistics: the Cambridge survey. Vol IV: language; the sociocultural context*. Cambridge University Press, Cambridge pp 75–99.

McIntosh Peggy 1988 White privilege and male privilege: a personal account of coming to see correspondences through work in women's studies. *Wellesley College working paper no. 189*. Wellesley College Center for Research on Women, Wellesley, MA.

Merrill Sally 1981 (Nov.) The Japanese brain. *Science Digest*: 74–5.

Meyerhoff Miriam this volume: Dealing with gender identity as a sociolinguistic variable.

Nicholson Linda 1994 Interpreting *gender. Signs: Journal of Women in Culture and Society* 20.1: 79–105.

Ochs Elinor 1992 Indexing gender. In Duranti Alessandro, Goodwin Charles (eds) *Rethinking context: language as an interactive phenomenon*. Cambridge University Press, Cambridge pp 335–58.

O'Barr William, Atkins Bowman K 1980 'Women's' language or 'powerless' language? In McConnell-Ginet Sally, Borker Ruth, Furman Nelly (eds) *Women and language in literature and society*. Praeger, New York pp 93–110.

Obler Loraine 1981 Right hemisphere participation in second language acquisition. In Diller Karl (ed) *Individual differences and universals in language learning aptitude*. Newbury House, Rowley, MA pp 53–64.

Olson David, Torrance Nancy, Hildyard Angela (eds) 1985 *Literacy, language, and learning: the nature and consequences of reading and writing*. Cambridge University Press.

Omi Michael, Winant Howard 1994 *Racial formation in the United States: from the 1960s to the 1990s.* Routledge, New York.

Phillips Kathryn 1990 (Oct.) Why can't a man be more like a woman … and vice versa. *Omni* 13: 42–6, 68.

Polanyi Livia, Strassmann Diana this volume: Storytellers and gatekeepers in economics.

Pullum Geoffrey 1989 The great Eskimo vocabulary hoax. *Natural Language and Linguistic Theory* 7: 275–81.

Rich Adrienne 1980 Compulsory heterosexuality. *Signs* 5: 631–60.

Rushton J Philippe 1995 *Race, evolution, and behavior.* Transaction Publishers, New Brunswick, NJ.

Scott Joan 1988 Deconstructing equality-versus-difference: or, the uses of poststructuralist theory for feminism. *Feminist Studies* 14.1: 33–50.

Shaywitz Bennett, Shaywitz Sally, Pugh Kenneth, Constable R Todd, Skudlarski Pawel, Fulbright Robert, Bronen Richard, Fletcher Jack, Shankweiler Donald, Katz Leonard, Gore John 1995 (16 Feb.) Sex differences in the functional organization of the brain for language. *Nature* 373: 607–9.

Springer Sally, Deutsch Georg 1993 *Left brain, right brain.* W H Freeman, New York.

Stein Douglas 1990 (Oct.) Interview: Roger Gorski. *Omni* 13: 70–6, 132–4, 138–40.

Tannen Deborah 1981 New York Jewish conversation. *International Journal of the Sociology of Language* 30: 133–49.

Tannen Deborah 1982 Ethnic style in male–female conversational style. In Gumperz John (ed) *Language and social identity.* Cambridge University Press, Cambridge pp 217–31.

Tannen Deborah 1984 *Conversational style: analyzing talk among friends.* Ablex, Norwood, NJ.

Tannen Deborah 1985 Relative focus on involvement in oral and written discourse. In Olson David, Torrance Nancy, Hildyard Angela (eds) pp 124–47.

Tannen Deborah 1990 *You just don't understand: women and men in conversation.* Morrow, New York.

Thorne Barrie, Kramarae Cheris, Henley Nancy 1983 *Language, gender, and society.* Newbury House, Rowley, MA.

Tong Rosemarie 1989 *Feminist thought: a comprehensive introduction.* Westview Press, Boulder, CO.

Trudgill Peter 1974 *Sociolinguistics: an introduction.* Penguin, Harmondsworth.

Wade Nicholas 1994 (12 June) Method and madness: how men and women think. *New York Times Magazine* p 32.

West Candace 1995 Women's competence in conversation. *Discourse & Society* 6.1: 107–31.

West Candace, Fenstermaker Sarah 1995 Doing difference. *Gender & Society* 9.1: 8–37.

West Candace, Zimmerman Don 1987 Doing gender. *Gender & Society* 1.2: 125–51.

West Candace, Zimmerman Don 1983 Small insults: a study of interruptions in cross-sex conversations between unacquainted persons. In Thorne Barrie, Kramarae Cheris, Henley Nancy (eds) pp 102–17.

Whitehead Harriet 1981 The bow and the burden strap: a new look at institutionalized homosexuality in native North America. In Ortner Sherry B, Whitehead Harriet (eds) *Sexual meanings: the cultural construction of gender and sexuality*. Cambridge University Press, Cambridge pp 80–115.

Why men and women cannot be like each other 1995 (3 April) *Jet* 87: 15–16.

Zimmerman Don, West Candace 1975 Sex roles, interruptions and silences in conversation. In Thorne Barrie, Henley Nancy (eds) *Language and sex: difference and dominance*. Newbury House, Rowley, MA pp 105–29.

2 The language–gender interface: challenging co-optation

Deborah Cameron

Interfaces

In her review of language and gender studies for the 1988 Cambridge survey of linguistics, Sally McConnell-Ginet poses a crucial question about the language–gender interface (and its alter ego, the linguistics–feminism interface). Noting in paragraph one that the feminist intellectual revolution 'has been little felt by most linguists', she goes on in paragraph two to enquire:

> Why have linguists been relatively inactive in the growing area of research on language and gender? One reason is that most of the initial impetus for investigation of this area derived from feminist thinkers' concern to understand gender ... and not from interest in language as such. This emphasis made the early research of limited professional interest to linguists though often of considerable personal and political interest to many of us as participants in the women's movement. (McConnell-Ginet 1988: 75)

McConnell-Ginet is not saying the two things cannot be combined. Her review goes on to make a case for recent work in the field as a genuine and significant contribution to our understanding of language and language use. This is an obvious point to stress to the mainstream audience of the Cambridge survey, and there is no doubt it is justified, at least if we take structured variability to be among the properties of language systems which mainstream linguistics aims to characterize. Yet in another context one might equally want to pose the question from the opposite side of the language–gender interface. Where linguists *have* actively pursued research on language and gender, why has that work apparently contributed little to the growing area of interdisciplinary feminist theory about gender? Why does it draw little from the most recent and most sophisticated expressions of that theory? Has our 'interest in language as such', the interest that qualifies us for inclusion in the Cambridge survey, led us away from 'feminist thinkers' concern to understand gender'? And if so, at what cost?

Analogous questions could be asked about other kinds of socio- or variationist linguistics. As McConnell-Ginet also notes, the perception of conflicting loyalties arises from the way linguistics is constituted as a discipline (and the hierarchies that are one consequence of that constitution). 'Hyphenated' disciplines may perceive a conflict between their two elements, and they may also feel pressure to resolve that conflict by explicitly aligning themselves with a more prestigious 'core' discipline.

In 1978, for example, Peter Trudgill wrote an introduction to a collection of British work in the quantitative paradigm to which he gave the rather curious title, 'Sociolinguistics and sociolinguistics'. He argued that while there were many ways to approach the study of 'language in society', the term *sociolinguistics* – or *sociolinguistics proper* – should be reserved for those approaches that share with all linguistics the goal of discovering inherent properties of language systems. 'All work in this category', he comments, 'is aimed ultimately at improving linguistic theory and at developing our understanding of the nature of language' (Trudgill 1978: 11). Trudgill wants to distinguish his notion of sociolinguistics 'proper' from two sets of things he feels it might be confused with. One set, which he mentions explicitly, contains the approaches to questions about language and society that are taken by disciplines other than linguistics, such as psychology and sociology. The second set, however, consists of alternative paradigms whose adherents would certainly locate themselves *within* linguistics. Although he does not say so explicitly, Trudgill wants to differentiate 'sociolinguistics proper' from traditions like functionalism and integrationalism, which do not accept the postulate of language as an autonomous object whose nature is independent of and separable from other social phenomena. For linguists working within these non-autonomous traditions the opposition between language as a social phenomenon and language 'as such' does not make sense. For Trudgill by contrast it is central to the definition of 'sociolinguistics proper'.

There are political as well as intellectual reasons why variationist linguists might wish to argue for this particular definition. One motive might be to escape the all-too-common categorization of work that deals with 'language in society' as sociology or politics rather than 'proper' linguistics – a categorization to which work outside the autonomous paradigm is particularly liable, since it often has an explicitly 'committed' political agenda.[1] Trudgill must also be aware, however, that for some linguists in his own preferred autonomous paradigm, even what he calls 'sociolinguistics proper' is regarded with similar suspicion – it too is sometimes accused of not being 'serious' linguistics. That perception puts pressure on sociolinguists within the autonomous tradition not only to assume but actually to emphasize the separation of the socio- and the linguistic, and to privilege the linguistic. As Suzanne Romaine (1984) has pointed out, however, the trouble with this response is that sociolinguistics by definition requires some account of the 'language–society interface'. However sound the linguistics, if social phenomena are treated in a naive or cursory way it weakens the whole enterprise of sociolinguistics, leaving it with little explanatory power.

In this chapter I want to argue that language and gender studies, like other subfields within sociolinguistics, has tended to neglect theoretical questions about its 'socio' side (in this instance, gender). Moreover, I want to argue that if this is a problem for sociolinguists generally, it is a particularly acute one for language and gender researchers. Apart from Romaine's point that inadequate social theory leads to inadequate sociolinguistic explanation, there are a number of reasons why I believe we urgently need to develop more sophisticated theories of gender than those which have been common in our field since the mid-1970s.

Modern gender scholarship is an interdisciplinary enterprise. For linguists to be excluded from the conversations going on about gender among philosophers, literary theorists, historians, sociologists, psychologists, etc., is in my view an unfortunate thing for all parties. The linguists are cut off from insights that would be relevant to their work, while feminists in other disciplines can continue to talk about language in ways that are not accountable to the specialized knowledge linguistics makes available.

Our isolation from feminist theorists elsewhere would be one thing if linguistics itself provided a perfectly satisfactory set of conceptual tools for our work, but this is very far from being the case. Even where it does not fall into crude stereotyping, the sociological apparatus of mainstream sociolinguistics does not begin to address the complexity of gender, which has turned out to be an extraordinarily intricate and multilayered phenomenon – unstable, contested, intimately bound up with other social divisions. 'Women' and 'men' cannot usefully be treated as analogous to the geographically, ethnically and socially defined communities our frameworks were designed for (and this remains so even when our 'women' and 'men' are not global categories but members of a single local community). The category of gender does not lend itself well to the models of speech community, social identity and social differentiation that are the stock-in-trade of sociolinguistics. Not only does this mean that language and gender researchers need alternative models, perhaps it means other sociolinguists could benefit from them too.

For feminists, the need for more sophisticated models is a political matter as well as a theoretical academic one. If the subject you work on is sensitive or contested, and the standpoint you work from a committed one, it becomes necessary to calculate the effect of your theoretical interventions on real-world perceptions and practice. Language and gender research, no less than other kinds of discourse on gender, *has* had effects outside the academy (whether or not these were always intended by scholars). Oversimplified notions of the relation between language and gender are increasingly having an impact on women's lives, as academic research findings are taken up in popular media, and applied institutionally for practical purposes (such as communication training in the workplace). Before I return to theoretical issues, I want to consider in a little more detail this question of how language and gender research is being used in the 'real world'.

Co-optation?

I begin with a text which has undoubtedly had an impact outside the academy, and which has also caused considerable controversy among language and gender researchers: Deborah Tannen's *You Just Don't Understand* (Tannen 1990). Tannen's popular success has drawn unprecedented public attention to our field, but a number of her colleagues in that field have been less than positive in their assessment of her work. Tannen herself seems to regard critical reviews as evidence of scholarly prejudice against popularization. But the content of the reviews in question suggests that popularization *per se* is not the issue: rather, the issue is *co-optation*.

For example, a much-cited review by Senta Troemel-Ploetz (1991) charges that *You Just Don't Understand* is yet another sign of the anti-feminist 'backlash', and turns feminist linguistics into a branch of the self-improvement industry. Certainly the book follows many of the conventions of the self-help genre, and it has been widely read as a guide for women to improving communication with men. The paperback cover quotes a *Washington Post* review that says, 'People are telling Tannen that the book is saving their marriages.' *Cosmopolitan*'s excerpt in 1991 was headed 'Here, the secrets of mantalk – and how to decode it', while, in 1993, *Elle* magazine asked, 'Are men and women doomed to speak different languages? Experts say there's hope – and you don't even need Berlitz.' It is obvious why this sort of thing might give cause for intellectual and political concern. Feminists have criticized the self-help genre both for reducing the complexities of gendered behaviour to crude generalizations, and for glossing over systemic problems of gender inequality, urging that those problems be addressed through individual adjustment rather than collective political action. Saving a woman's marriage is a far cry from producing a critique of marriage itself.

In my view, however, the problem of feminist work being co-opted by popular advice discourse is too general and deep-seated to be dealt with at the level of criticizing individual authors. Research findings on language and gender, whether their authors are aware of it or not, have been playing a part in various self-help enterprises for some years. Because of its extraordinary success in the marketplace, *You Just Don't Understand* has turned the spotlight on this phenomenon, but it is neither the first example nor the most egregious. Moreover, it might be said that the authors of self-help texts about language and gender are not just harnessing linguistics to reactionary trends outside the academy: they are carrying certain trends in language and gender studies to what is arguably their logical conclusion.

For my purposes here, this last point is the most significant, and I will return to it in detail below. But before I develop the argument that popular advice literature shares important assumptions with at least some scholarly work in language and gender studies, I want to substantiate my first point, that Deborah Tannen's book is only one example of a much larger phenomenon – in other words, that we are dealing with a syndrome and not just an isolated symptom. This brings me to my own recent work on the topic of 'verbal hygiene'.

Verbal hygiene

'Verbal hygiene' is my collective term for a diverse set of normative metalinguistic practices based on a conviction that some ways of using language are functionally, aesthetically or morally preferable to others.[2] These practices include what we usually call 'prescriptivism', that is, the authoritarian promotion of élite varieties as norms of correctness, but they also include activities with very different ideological underpinnings: for instance, campaigns for Plain English, spelling reform, dialect and language preservation, non-sexist and non-racist language, Esperanto and the abolition of the copula, as demanded by the International Society for General Linguistics in San Francisco. They also include self-improvement activities such as elocution and accent reduction, Neurolinguistic Programming, assertiveness training and communication skills training.

This last category of verbal hygiene, linguistic self-improvement, has become noticeably more visible in recent years. At one end of the social spectrum we have more and more public figures, like Margaret Thatcher, Bill Clinton and most recently Princess Diana, employing consultants to help them with their verbal self-presentation. At the other end, we have more and more workplaces encouraging or requiring employees to undergo some form of communication training. This is partly related to long-term shifts in advanced Western economies, where service industries are overtaking manufacturing and manufacturing itself is being reorganized with emphasis on teamwork and problem solving. These developments make interactional skills important for increasing numbers of workers at all levels (Fairclough 1992). Women are particularly affected because of their predominance in the service and new light industrial sectors. Outside the workplace, we also have a growth in participation in more personalized forms of self-help, such as the 'recovery' movement ('twelve-step' programmes modelled on Alcoholics Anonymous, which have proliferated in recent years). Again, women are major consumers of the literature and other materials associated with these programmes.

It is, therefore, not surprising that in the past five or ten years a genre of verbal hygiene advice has emerged, addressed specifically to women and purporting to deal with their particular problems of communication.[3] This advice comes in various forms: one-on-one consultancy, group training courses and seminars both in workplaces and outside them, training manuals and videotapes, mass market books, articles in women's magazines and items on daytime TV. I have been researching this development by reading texts, interviewing and observing practitioners and consumers of the new verbal hygiene for women. And I have found that much of it draws clearly, if selectively, on the scholarly literature about language and gender. The work of linguists on gender differences in language use has apparently provided a rationale for submitting women, or persuading them to submit themselves, to a series of practices which, in my opinion, are at best of little use and at worst quite oppressive.

Verbal hygiene for women comes in two varieties which are strikingly contradictory: career advice, which aims to improve the linguistic effectiveness of professional women, and relationship advice, which deals with communication difficulties in male–female interaction, particularly in the context of heterosexual relationships. Let us briefly examine these two subgenres in turn.

Career advice tells women that scientific research suggests they are not fulfilling their potential because of the way they use language, and if they want to get ahead at work they should therefore learn to adopt the verbal strategies this same research has associated with men. A typical example of the genre is a training manual titled *Leadership Skills for Women: Achieving Impact as a Manager* (Manning and Haddock 1989). The manual contains such observations as: 'men typically use less body language than women. Watch their body language to see how they do it' (p. 7). Another comment glosses well-known research findings in the following cavalier manner: 'Speak directly and stand firm when you are interrupted. Statistics show that women allow themselves to be interrupted 50 % more often than men. Don't contribute to those statistics' (p. 15). Training materials in this genre make use of a 'deficit' model suggesting that women are their own worst enemies in professional and public settings. SkillPath, Inc., a US training and consultancy business, advertises a one-day seminar on 'Power-packed communication skills for women' in which, for $49, delegates will learn how 'unconscious credibility-robbing speech habits and mannerisms can all work against you ... how to avoid the 14 common language mistakes that can sabotage your credibility ... how to eliminate power-robbing speech habits, words and gestures that say "I'm a lightweight!"'.

The same sort of thing also appears regularly in women's magazines. *Cosmopolitan*, for instance ran an article in 1990 headed 'Why Not Talk Like a Grown-Up?' – though it should have been called 'Why Not Talk Like a Man?' This piece informed readers that women often fail to gain respect in the workplace because of the way they talk. Certain characteristics of female speech – tag questions, rising intonation, whiny, breathy or high-pitched voices – must be scrupulously avoided. Obviously, much of this laundry list of alleged female linguistic offences comes straight from Robin Lakoff (1975), whose negative interpretation of them is presented as fact. *Options* magazine in 1992 included 'tentative language' – again defined in terms drawn from Lakoff – as one of the 'Ten Classic Career Mistakes All Women Make'. Overdependence on Lakoff is not the only problem with career-oriented verbal hygiene, however. *Glamour* (June 1990) ran a piece which translated Tannen's rather different arguments into a set of handy hints – for example, to avoid making indirect requests to male subordinates because 'women shy away from giving blatant orders, but men find the indirect approach manipulative and confusing'.

Tannen herself is an exponent of the other kind of advice, which focuses on personal, particularly heterosexual, relationships. This genre is based not on the idea that women are *deficient* compared to men, but on the idea that they are *different*, and that this causes misunderstanding. Because it avoids positing a deficit, relationship advice appears less overtly sexist than career advice. It seeks to explain the underlying reasons why men and women have such trouble communicating, and usually ends up recommending not that women should emulate men, but that both genders should practise mutual tolerance and adjustment. As a number of critics have argued, though, covertly it is *women* who are being urged to accept as merely 'different' the forms of male verbal behaviour they find distressing and/or disadvantageous.

Most language and gender researchers will be familiar with the thesis of *You Just Don't Understand*, and I will not rehearse it in detail here. It is probably worth pointing out, though, that there are a significant number of other titles in much the same vein. Some predate Tannen (for example, Naifeh and Smith 1984), while others may have been inspired by her runaway success (my favourite recent example has a title that is a fine *reductio ad absurdum* of Tannen's argument that men and women are linguistically alien to one another: John Gray's 1992 bestseller, *Men are from Mars, Women are from Venus*).

There is more to be said about the range of verbal hygiene currently on offer to women (for a detailed account see Cameron 1995), but the discussion above is meant only to establish that linguistic advice literature for women is widespread, and that it draws heavily (though selectively) on research in the field of language and gender. It uses that research to argue either that women's ways of speaking are inherently problematic (a deficit model), or that the differences between women and men are problematic (a difference/miscommunication model), and goes on from this to recommend either that women should change their verbal behaviour or that they should adjust in certain ways to men's.

But what about my other claim, that this kind of self-help material does not just represent a cynical appropriation of feminist linguistic scholarship but is in some sense a logical extension of it? Let me make clear that I do not believe language and gender researchers share either the commercial or the ideological interests of the self-improvement industry. Indeed, linguists are likely to feel particularly compromised by the material presented above, because it breaches the injunction of our discipline to be 'descriptive not prescriptive'. Self-help is nothing if not prescriptive. This anti-prescriptive line of criticism is something of a red herring, however, for while feminist scholars share a general scientific commitment to observing and understanding the world, we also want to change it. What should worry us is rather the possibility that our own models of the relationship between language and gender, conceived as a means of promoting both understanding and change, have left our work far too vulnerable to being appropriated or co-opted for questionable purposes.

Paradigms: deficit, dominance and difference

A historical-typological account of feminist linguistic approaches over the past 20 years would probably distinguish three main models of language and gender. One is a *deficit* model in which women are seen as disadvantaged speakers because of their early sex-role socialization: the obvious example is Robin Lakoff's *Language and Woman's Place* (Lakoff 1975). The second is a *dominance* model in which women are seen, often through an ethnomethodological frame, as negotiating their relatively powerless position in interaction with men: male social privilege is made manifest in recurrent patterns of language use. This model could be exemplified by the work of Candace West on interruptions and floor apportionment (Zimmerman and West 1975, West 1984) or by Pamela Fishman's studies of heterosexual couples' talk (1980, 1983). Finally, there is a *cultural difference* model in which analogies are made between gender and other social divisions like ethnicity; segregation of the sexes during childhood and adolescence produces marked differences in their conversational goals and styles. A major reference point for this model is the work of Gumperz and his associates (e.g. Maltz and Borker 1982); Tannen's work also exemplifies it.

As I have already intimated, the verbal hygiene advice described above makes use of two out of these three approaches. Career-oriented advice is typically based on the deficit model, relationship advice on the cultural difference model.[4] Self-help texts do allude to research done within the dominance model (e.g. early findings on interruptions), but these are reinterpreted to fit the framework of either deficit ('don't contribute to those statistics!') or difference.

It is clear, then, that self-help draws *selectively* on scholarly work, and the explanation that comes most readily to mind for its selectivity is political: the dominance model is too explicitly feminist to sell books to a mass audience. Yet there may be more to it than that. During the 1980s, it would be fair to say that cultural difference models of language and gender gained ground over other models in scholarly as well as popular literature. It is interesting that the popular preference for difference over dominance models (though not the preference for deficit models) mirrors developments in language and gender studies.

Some feminist linguists would say that the scholarly turn to difference is itself politically motivated, part of the same backlash advice literature exemplifies. For example, Nancy Henley and Cheris Kramarae (1991) have argued that the recent interest of so many researchers in studying male–female 'miscommunication' is a retreat from issues to do with power, and therefore represents a watering down of feminism. But again, I suspect there is more to it than this. The difference approach is no doubt attractive to some politically moderate researchers because it neither disparages the way women speak nor casts men as oppressive villains. Beyond these considerations, however, the gradual ascendancy of difference was almost inevitable given the ideology of twentieth-century linguistics.

Difference, and not inequality, is what the framework of structural linguistics is designed to deal with. Indeed, for the linguist, inequality is typically conceived as resulting not from difference itself but from intolerance of difference. Thus linguists have insisted it is wrong to label languages 'primitive' or dialects 'substandard'; it is wrong to force people to abandon their ways of speaking, or to judge them by the yardstick of one's own linguistic habits. Throughout this century, the norm in linguistics has been linguistic and cultural relativism – 'all varieties are equal'. It has always been an honourable position, and sometimes an outright radical one. In applying it to the case of male–female differences, it might be said that Tannen and others have only reasserted the historical logic of the discipline they were trained in.

One could draw a parallel at this point between the logic of linguistics and the logic of self-help, and use it to explain why the dominance model is out of favour with both. Self-help – as its name suggests, a discourse on modifying the attitudes and behaviour of one individual, the 'self' – cannot handle a model based on interactively produced and context-dependent social relations; it can only handle one based on individual characteristics. And it might well be argued that sociolinguistics, including language and gender studies, has typically offered an account of the relationship among individuals, the groups they belong to and their behaviour that shares this limitation.

Both the deficit and the difference models have at their centre the idea of individuals who speak as they do because of who they are (i.e. have been socialized to be), and not because of the way they are positioned in interaction with others in various contexts; this is what enables us to talk so globally about 'women's' or 'men's' language'. The language is an attribute of the person, the woman or man. Of course, the two models contrast on the axis of *evaluation* – one says women are deficient, the other that they are merely different from men. But in other respects the models are two sides of the same coin, and their currency is as good in self-help as in sociolinguistics.

Does this mean that our best strategy for avoiding co-optation lies in a return to the dominance approach? I do not believe we can return, given what we now know about the complexities of gender, which is not *only* a relation of power (and the power involved in it is in any case more complicated than early analyses of male dominance would suggest). Historically, dominance and difference represented particular moments in feminism: dominance was the moment of feminist outrage, of bearing witness to oppression in all aspects of women's lives, while difference was the moment of feminist celebration, reclaiming and revaluing women's distinctive cultural traditions. It would be foolish to suggest that these responses are no longer applicable, but I do think the theories which underpinned them are no longer sufficient. We need new ways of conceptualizing the relation between women and men; and most important of all, we need to consider more carefully what it means to talk about 'women' and 'men' in the first place.

That we *can* talk unproblematically about women and men is something that has long been taken for granted. In the study of language and gender – again, following the practice established in sociolinguistics more generally – it is *language* that is taken as the phenomenon to be explained, and gender which has been seen as constituting the explanation. In the static common-sensical world-view of sociolinguistics, there are women and there are men, bearers of the attribute we call gender: our task is to catalogue the ways they mark this attribute in their linguistic behaviour. Then, we may seek to explain the effects of gender on language use by talking about the socialization of women and men, the inequality between women and men or the social segregation of women and men. What we cannot so easily do is ask more searching questions about these crucial constructs 'women' and 'men'. Gender has been taken as a given, an attribute that exists prior to the behaviour we are interested in. Thus our work gets used to validate a worldview that treats gender difference as a 'natural' phenomenon, where feminism would want to deconstruct it.

In this discussion I have tried to draw attention to two problems which I believe are built into the general assumptions of sociolinguistics, and which make language and gender research more vulnerable to co-optation than it might otherwise be. The first problem is the axiom of linguistic and cultural relativism; the second is the notion of gender as a pre-existing demographic correlate which accounts for behaviour, rather than as something that requires explanation in its own right. Each of these problems merits more detailed examination.

Relativism: are some varieties more equal than others?

As I noted above, it is traditional in linguistics to suppose that difference itself is neutral, while inequality results from the suppression or stigmatizing of difference. Thus there is nothing wrong with non-standard dialects, only with the prejudice against them. Linguistic diversity is good: only the suppression of diversity is bad. This approach works well enough when the difference in question is a relatively superficial matter of linguistic form. But when we are dealing with the sort of discourse strategy that interests many language and gender researchers today, the questions become more complicated, because they relate not just to the forms but also the functions of language – what language users are *accomplishing* through the use of a particular communicative strategy or speech style.

Different discourse strategies arise in distinct social contexts, and they are used to accomplish different tasks, rather than simply to do the same task in a different way. A common version of this, unexceptionable as far as it goes, is that girls and boys in their peer groups are not engaged in the same activities, or motivated by the same goals: therefore they evolve different norms of interaction. Another way of looking at it is to say that even quite young girls and boys already occupy differing positions in a given social formation. The behavioural differences associated with these positions cannot convincingly be passed off as neutral, accidental or arbitrary – nor, indeed, as purely linguistic. They are rooted in, and they help to maintain, a larger social and political order, in which women and men are destined not simply to differ from one another (in the way that Japanese culture, say, differs from Navajo culture) but in important respects to *complement* one another, to be ideally what 'the opposite sex' is not (e.g. nurturant where he is aggressive, intuitive where he is logical). The gender system prescribes a rather deliberate division of labour between women and men, offering them different opportunities and different rewards. It should also be noted that in the case of gender, complementarity does not mean equality. On the contrary, gender relations are predicated on the subordination of one group to another.[5]

If this analysis is taken seriously, the relativist argument that differing speech styles should be treated axiomatically as 'equally valid' appears superficial and naive. Equally valid for what? We need to ask not just *how* men and women differ, nor even just *why* they differ (i.e. 'because of what local conditions'), but also *for what larger purpose* they differ. As MacCannell and MacCannell aptly remark (1987:208), 'Institutionalized separation and segregation of the sexes is not the cause of gender disorders, but only a part of the system, its maintenance equipment.' If we accept that differences in speech style cannot be understood in isolation from differences in speakers' social positioning – the activities they are expected to undertake, the personal characteristics they are encouraged to develop, the sources of satisfaction available to them – the question becomes whether those who typically use a particular style of discourse are thereby being excluded from (or, conversely, are monopolizing) not only certain verbal practices but, more significantly, a range of *social* practices. (Eckert and

McConnell-Ginet (1992: 95) make what I take to be a similar suggestion in their remarks on the reproduction of gender and gender
inequality through differential participation in 'communities of
practice'.) If so, the issue is not so much whether this way of speaking is as good as that, as whether the division of labour has
significant political consequences, systematically empowering some
groups at the expense of others. To be sure, it makes little sense to
argue about whether 'status' is better than 'intimacy' or vice versa.
Nevertheless, if there is a gender-specialization whereby girls learn
to seek intimacy and boys to seek status, that is hardly arbitrary in
terms of the larger social structure. It could be characterized as a
training of boys for public and girls for private life; or as a training
for boys in the exercise of power and for girls in its abdication.

This argument implies that inequality can give rise to difference,
rather than the other way around. The fact that different discourse
strategies often appear in single-sex peer groups in no way detracts
from the important point that *the difference arises in a context of
unequal gender relations*. To suppose that the problem is intolerance of difference, and that if only we valued women's styles as
highly as men's there would be no problem, is reminiscent of that
brand of right-wing pseudo-feminism which enjoins us to honour
the housewife and mother for doing the most important job in the
world, glossing over the fact that her gendered occupation is itself
a product of inequality and exploitation. Feminism is not about
giving housewives their due, it is about changing the conditions of
domestic labour altogether. Similarly, feminism cannot stop at val-
idating the linguistic strategies typical of women; it must also ask
why women find some communicative practices more accessible
and more relevant than others: a question, as Eckert and
McConnell-Ginet argue, of what social practices they are permit-
ted/enabled/encouraged to participate in.

Gender: rethinking 'acts of identity'

Earlier I suggested that sociolinguistics has taken gender for granted by treating it as a demographic category that is given in advance,
whereas research in other disciplines has increasingly called it into
question. The most important insight this work can offer us is that
gender is a problem, not a solution. 'Women talk like this, men talk
like that' – the assertion to which so many research papers in our
field ultimately boil down – is not only overgeneralized and stereotypical, it fails utterly to address the question of where 'women'

and 'men' come from. Feminists must take it as axiomatic that this is indeed a question worth asking. As Simone de Beauvoir said, 'One is not born, but rather becomes a woman.' The question is, how?

Both difference theorists of language and gender and those working in the deficit tradition of Lakoff are dependent on a sex-role socialization model in which 'becoming a woman' is something accomplished at an early stage of life – either in the pre-school years within the family or slightly later in the single-sex peer group. They suggest that gender identities and divisions precede and give rise to linguistic practice; later on they invoke the idea of an already-fixed gender identity with certain linguistic reflexes firmly attached to it as the solution to the problem of why adult women and men behave as they do.

But perhaps it is the practices people engage in that produce their identities, and not the other way around. People's patterns of linguistic behaviour arise, in Eckert and McConnell-Ginet's view, from their habitual engagement in certain practices and their membership of the relevant communities. If women and men differ on that level, their language use will tend to differ; this is not a direct relationship, but one mediated by the crucial variable of practice. (This argument gains support from Alice Freed's finding that men and women performing the same, highly controlled series of tasks did *not* display the typical patterns of gender-related linguistic variation (Freed, this volume).) If we take Eckert and McConnell-Ginet's account seriously, it might imply that gender itself is a sedimentary effect of participating in particular social practices, and not in others. This would cast doubt on socialization models in which the child is mother to the woman or father to the man. Throughout our lives we go on entering new communities of practice: we must constantly reproduce our gendered identities by performing what are taken to be the appropriate acts in the communities we belong to – or else challenge prevailing gender norms by refusing to perform those acts.

Recent feminist theory emphasizes that no one is ever finished becoming a woman, or a man. Each individual subject must constantly negotiate the norms, behaviours, and discourses that define masculinity and femininity for a particular community at a particular point in history. From this point of view, it would be desirable to reformulate notions like 'women's language' or 'men's style'. Instead of saying simply that these styles are produced by women and men as markers of their pre-existing gender identities, we could say that the styles themselves are produced as masculine and feminine, and that individuals make varying accommodations to those styles in the process of producing *themselves* as gendered subjects. In other words, if I talk like a woman this is not just the inevitable outcome of the fact that I am a woman; it is one way I have of becoming a woman, producing myself *as* one. There is no such thing as 'being a woman' outside the various practices that define womanhood for my culture – practices ranging from the sort of work I do to my sexual preferences to the clothes I wear to the way I use language. The complexities of on-going gender construction cannot be satisfactorily accounted for within a framework that takes behaviour as the simple and direct reflex of a once-and-for-all identification with a particular gender group.

Kira Hall and Veronica O'Donovan (this volume) provide a striking example of speakers producing themselves as gendered subjects in their study of the hijras of Banaras in India, who are viewed as a 'third sex', and who habitually switch between the masculine and feminine markers that are obligatory on Hindi verbs and adjectives to construct themselves as 'masculine' or 'feminine' from moment to moment. In their case the constructional work involved is unusually obvious, since it flouts the norm that gender should be invariant and congruent with anatomical sex. Yet in an important sense we are all like the hijras. Even when we take gender for granted as an integral and invariant part of our identity, we still have to enact it. And, conversely, the hijra example implies that it is possible in principle for women (and men) to produce ourselves in *different* ways; to vary (as most of us do routinely) our gendered self-presentation in different contexts, or, more radically, to defy, subvert or deliberately seek to redefine gender norms.

A particularly thorough-going version of this line of argument, which I think has potential as a theoretical framework for research on gender and linguistic behaviour, is put forward by the philosopher Judith Butler in her book *Gender Trouble: Feminism and the Subversion of Identity* (1990). Butler argues, using a term that will be familiar to linguists, that gender is 'performative': that is, 'constituting the identity it is purported to be' (p. 25). She describes gender as 'the repeated stylization of the body, a set of repeated acts within a highly rigid regulatory frame that congeal over time to produce the appearance of substance, of a natural sort of being. A political genealogy of gender ontologies ... will deconstruct the substantive appearance of gender into its constitutive acts and locate and account for those acts within the compulsory frames set by the various forces that police the social appearance of gender' (1990: 33).

Many sociolinguists have emphasized the idea of language using as an 'act of identity', by which they mean a conscious or unconscious linguistic marking of an identity that exists prior to the act – people use language to mark their gender, class, ethnicity, membership in a local network or a tight-knit peer group (see especially Le Page and Tabouret-Keller 1985). Butler turns this on its head: where the sociolinguists say that how you act depends on who you (already) are, she says that who you are, and are taken to be, depends on your repeated performance over time of the acts that constitute a particular identity. These acts, Butler notes, are neither automatically determined nor freely chosen, but produced or resisted in relation to normative pressures, forces that 'police' what is permissible, intelligible and normal.

Although Butler refers to 'the repeated stylization of the *body*', her notion of performance is highly applicable to language use. Language using is obviously a repeated act, and also one subject to social norms and regulatory practices. The kind of verbal hygiene I have been looking at is a striking example of a practice that 'police[s] the social appearance of gender'. Women attending courses in communication skills or assertiveness training are essentially being shown how to construct, through repeated and stylized verbal performances, a certain kind of gender identity which contrasts with (and is preferred to) other possible identities.

It is important to stress here that deconstructing gender into its constitutive acts is not a denial of its existence or of its social salience. Most people do experience gender as an inalienable part of who they are, and the treatment they get reflects who others think they are. It is *because* gender is so salient that so much work goes into its production and reproduction. For linguists, what follows from the deconstructive approach is not the wholesale abandonment of language and gender studies, but a change in the question we begin with: instead of 'how do women and men behave linguistically?' we can ask how particular linguistic practices contribute to the production of people as 'women and men'. If we regard gender as a set of constitutive acts (different ones in different communities and different periods of history), rather than seeing the acts themselves as an outcome of gender, we will be able to acknowledge the complexity of the gender-work language users do, while also leaving open the possibility that gender itself could be transformed.

Back to the interface

Judith Butler's work, and other work that takes a critical approach to categories like gender and identity, can make a useful contribution to our reflections on the language–gender interface. Such critical approaches allow us to reinterpret the notion of language using as an 'act of identity', so that language use is seen as something that constitutes rather than just reflects pre-given gender identities; but unlike some forms of poststructuralist theory (Lacanian approaches, for example, where the term 'language' is often used in such an abstract and figurative sense that it is hard to connect statements about it to observations of actual speech), the 'performative' model still permits language to be described concretely in terms of specific acts and norms. In this regard linguistics has something valuable to offer feminist theory. Feminist scholars in a number of disciplines have identified language as an important concern, and it can only enrich feminist scholarship if we find ways to combine the sophisticated theories of gender developed outside linguistics with the detailed and sophisticated descriptions of language in which linguists specialize.

In addition, the deconstructive approach may assist feminist linguists who would like to break the connection I have described between linguistic scholarship and verbal hygiene – a development that turns scholarship into a part of the regulatory framework that polices gender norms. To resist this form of co-optation effectively we must begin from an understanding of why it happens and what makes it possible. One interpretation is that researchers' ideas get distorted through a process of selective reading and oversimplification: in other words, by non-linguists' or popularizers' failure to apply proper scholarly standards. But in the case we are concerned with here, I do not believe this to be the fundamental problem. Our critique of ill-founded and reactionary verbal hygiene practices will not be effective if we confine ourselves to criticizing their poor scholarship. The justification I offer in support of this assertion takes us back to the main theme of this chapter: the need to treat gender as rigorously and as critically as we treat linguistic phenomena.

My research suggests that the single most important factor in the popularity of the verbal hygiene discussed above is people's eagerness to believe certain common-sense propositions *about gen-der*.[6] Their desire to believe that 'women are thus and men are so' is strong enough to compensate for what, from a purely academic standpoint, are obvious shortcomings or contradictions in the evidence presented. And indeed, academic discourse itself is not immune from a milder form of this tendency to interpret all evidence in accordance with certain foregone conclusions. Many of the same propositions we find in popular discourse (and the same eagerness to believe them) can also be discerned in the work of sociolinguists who may not be feminist, but whose scholarly credentials are not in doubt.[7]

The central problem, then, is not so much a lack of linguistic scholarship as a lack of any alternative to prevailing common sense about gender. Unless such an alternative is articulated explicitly, anything we say about language and gender is liable to be interpreted through the models people already have in their heads. It is only by adopting a deconstructive approach to gender – in other words, by refusing to take common-sense assertions of the form 'women are thus and men are so' at face value – that feminist linguists can hope to avoid co-optation.

Sociologists studying the reception of self-help literature have concluded that its main function for those who regularly read it is not to change their ideas, let alone their lives, but to put a quasi-academic gloss on their existing folk-knowledge by gathering scattered insights into a more systematic form and attaching suitably 'scientific' labels to them (Lichterman 1992, Simonds 1992). This may be a dependable formula for selling self-help books, but for feminists whose goal is social change, it is woefully unambitious. We need theories of gender, and of the language–gender interface, that are not just academic renditions of received wisdom, but are capable of challenging people's customary ways of thinking. Sociolinguistics has not provided us with such theories (though it is welcome to use any that we pick up elsewhere), and from that fact we might draw one additional conclusion. In order to challenge our co-optation for verbal hygiene purposes, we may also have to challenge our co-optation by those within our discipline who would set narrower agendas for 'sociolinguistics proper' than we at the interface can afford.

Notes

1. I am thinking particularly of the functionalist paradigm associated with the work of M.A.K. Halliday and his followers. Outside the USA this approach remains a salient alternative to the Chomskyan paradigm, and it is no doubt relevant that Trudgill was writing for a primarily British audience.

2. I should add that 'verbal hygiene' is intended as a descriptive label for the practices it applies to; it is not intended to imply a negative evaluation of them. One reason I choose to avoid the term 'prescriptivism' is that it has come to be treated in linguistics as a term of condemnation; whereas I argue that normative practices are an inevitable concomitant of language using, and that such practices should be evaluated case by case, with arguments *pro* and *con* focusing not on their mere existence but on their actual substance, the values underlying them and the goals they are meant to achieve. For example, one might judge movements for the suppression of minority languages or non-standard dialects rather differently from movements for plain language or non-discriminatory language. Obviously, the basis for this sort of judgement is not purely scientific or technical, which is why many linguists regard it as illegitimate. One might observe, however, that to condemn all normative linguistic practices in principle is not an objective and value-neutral stance either – it plainly entails evaluation of what I would argue is a very authoritarian kind, since the criteria are not open to discussion. (See Cameron 1995 for a fuller exposition of this line of argument.)

3. Actually, verbal hygiene advice for women is not a phenomenon of the last ten years, or even of the last 100 years; it can be traced as far back as medieval conduct books, and found in such well-known early-modern texts as Castiglione's *The Courtier* (see Armstrong and Tennenhouse (1987) for a survey of conduct literature and many examples of its verbal hygiene content). The 'genre' to which I am alluding here is novel, however, in being based on recent language and gender research, and also on new bourgeois gender norms (e.g. women as well as men should have career ambitions; marriage is ideally a relationship of equals).

4. Since the first draft of this chapter was written, career advice and workplace training programmes based on the cultural difference/miscommunication model have begun to emerge: I have seen or been told about examples in the UK, the USA and Sweden. Since I have not so far been able to study their content in detail, however, no more will be said about them here.

5. This is, of course, also true of other social relations, notably those of race and class within one social formation. The analogy that cultural difference theorists often make between gender differences and ethnic differences is not only unconvincing because gender is not the same as

ethnicity; it is also suspect insofar as ethnic differences may themselves arise in a context of institutionalized inequality. The Japanese/Navajo example given earlier is not, to my mind, directly comparable to (let us say) the example of white and black Americans. In the former case there has been no historical contact, let alone a relationship of dominance and subordination, between the groups in question; their cultural norms have developed quite separately. In the latter case things are very different: the forms of contact and separation between the two groups have been structured by racism, and it is inconceivable that this has not played some part in shaping their notions of ethnic identity and their distinctive forms of social organization.

6. For an extended argument to that effect, based on interviews with participants in verbal hygiene practices as well as on textual analysis, see Cameron (1995). Briefly, the beliefs to which books like *You Just Don't Understand* seem to appeal are: (a) that gender is a fixed attribute that lies at the core of every person's sense of self; (b) that women and men, though equal, are irreducibly different from one another; (c) that 'gender troubles' are caused by innocent misunderstanding, not by malice or deep-rooted conflicts of interest; and (d) that women and men can become less damagingly alien to one another *without* losing their essential femininity or masculinity. These beliefs contain elements of both gender egalitarianism and gender conservatism, and as such they reflect the preoccupations of the main target audience for self-help books about relationships, i.e. educated white middle-class heterosexual women aged 25–45. These women have been influenced by liberal feminist ideas and do not want to return to traditional gender roles, but they are extremely threatened by the more radical notion of gender difference itself becoming blurred or irrelevant.

7. Pertinent illustrations of gender stereotypes which the evidence does not support being adduced repeatedly in the scholarly as opposed to popular work of sociolinguists may be found, for example, in Cameron and Coates (1989) and Eckert (1989).

References

Armstrong Nancy, Tennenhouse Leonard (eds) 1987 *The ideology of conduct: essays on the literature and the history of sexuality*. Methuen, New York.

Butler Judith 1990 *Gender trouble: feminism and the subversion of identity*. Routledge, New York.

Cameron Deborah 1995 *Verbal hygiene*. Routledge, London.

Cameron Deborah, Coates Jennifer 1989 Some problems in the sociolinguistic explanation of sex differences. In Coates Jennifer, Cameron

Deborah (eds) *Women in their speech communities*. Longman, London pp 13–26.

Eckert Penelope 1989 The whole woman: sex and gender differences in variation. *Language Variation and Change* 1: 245–67.

Eckert Penelope, McConnell-Ginet Sally 1992 Communities of practice: where language, gender and power all live. In Hall Kira, Bucholtz Mary, Moonwomon Birch (eds) *Locating power: papers from the second Berkeley women and language conference*. Berkeley Women and Language Group, Berkeley, CA. pp 89–99.

Fairclough Norman 1992 *Critical language awareness*. Longman, London.

Fishman Pamela 1980 Conversational insecurity. In Cameron Deborah (ed) 1990 *The feminist critique of language*. Routledge, London pp 234–41.

Fishman Pamela 1983 Interaction: the work women do. In Thorne Barrie, Kramarae Cheris, Henley Nancy (eds) *Language, gender and society*. Newbury House, Rowley, MA pp 89–102.

Freed Alice F this volume: Language and gender research in an experimental setting.

Gray John 1992 *Men are from Mars, women are from Venus*. Harper Collins, New York.

Hall Kira, O'Donovan Veronica this volume: Shifting gender positions among Hindi-speaking hijras.

Henley Nancy, Kramarae Cheris 1991 Gender, power and miscommunication. In Coupland Nikolas, Giles Howard, Wiesmann John M (eds) *'Miscommunication' and problematic talk*. Sage Publications, Newbury Park, CA pp 18–43.

Lakoff Robin 1975 *Language and woman's place*. Harper & Row, New York.

Le Page Robert, Tabouret-Keller Andrée 1985 *Acts of identity: creole-based approaches to language and ethnicity*. Cambridge University Press, Cambridge.

Lichterman Paul 1992 Self-help reading as a thin culture. *Media, culture and society* 14: 421–47.

MacCannell Dean, MacCannell Juliet Flower 1987 The beauty system. In Armstrong Nancy, Tennenhouse Leonard (eds) pp 206–38.

McConnell-Ginet Sally 1988 Language and gender. In Newmeyer Frederick (ed) *Linguistics: the Cambridge survey. Vol. IV: language; the sociocultural context*. Cambridge University Press, Cambridge pp 75–99.

Maltz Daniel, Borker Ruth 1982 A cultural approach to male–female misunderstanding. In Gumperz John J (ed) *Language and social identity*. Cambridge University Press, Cambridge pp 195–216.

Manning Marilyn, Haddock Patricia 1989 *Leadership skills for women: achieving impact as a manager*. Crisp Publications, Menlo Park, CA.

Naifeh Stephen, Smith Gregory White 1984 *Why can't men open up? Overcoming men's fear of intimacy*. Frederick Muller, London.

Romaine Suzanne 1984 The status of sociological models and categories in explaining linguistic variation. *Linguistische Berichte* 90: 25–38.

Simonds Wendy 1992 *Women and self-help culture: reading between the lines*. Rutgers University Press, Brunswick, NJ.

Tannen Deborah 1990 *You just don't understand*. Ballantine Books, New York.

Troemel-Ploetz Senta 1991 Selling the apolitical. *Discourse & Society* 2.4: 489–502.

Trudgill Peter (ed) 1978 *Sociolinguistic patterns in British English*. Edward Arnold, London.

West Candace 1984 When the doctor is a 'lady'. *Symbolic Interaction* 7.1: 87–106.

Zimmerman Don, West Candace 1975 Sex roles, interruptions and silences in conversation. In Thorne Barrie, Henley Nancy (eds) *Language and sex: difference and dominance*. Newbury House, Rowley, MA pp 105–29.

3 Language and gender research in an experimental setting[1]

Alice F. Freed

The search for female and male speech differences

Since the beginning of this century, linguists and social scientists from a variety of disciplines have sought to uncover the causes of the supposedly mysterious differences in the speech of women and men; in the process, far too many inaccurate generalizations about female and male speech have been made. From Jespersen's work in 1922, to Lakoff's pioneering 1973 article, to Tannen's popularized 1990 depiction of women's speech, we can trace a well-established pattern of widely read and frequently cited writings about women, men, and their language differences based on introspection and anecdotal information but for which there is little empirical foundation. I single out these three works because of their historic value: although Jespersen's portrait of women was extremely stereotyped, his work was unique in devoting an entire chapter of a book on the nature of language to a discussion of the characteristics of women's speech. The publication of Lakoff's work legitimized the study of women's language within sociolinguistics and simultaneously provided a political context for the interpretation of women's speech. The release of Tannen's book, for better or for worse, brought the topic of potential differences between women and men's speech to the attention of an enormous general public.

Each of the above-mentioned scholars described women and men as belonging to socially and linguistically distinct groups and each portrayed the groups as internally homogeneous. These researchers largely disregarded the multitude of social and cultural differences among women and among men that have long been recognized as affecting speech.[2] Unfortunately, the quantitative studies of such notable sociolinguists as Labov (1972) and Trudgill (1972), while empirically based, provided no meaningful correction to this historic trend and did little to advance us beyond a conventional and traditional view of the sexes. (See Cameron and Coates 1989 for a critique of the sociolinguistic paradigm for language and gender research.) Due to the notoriety and importance attributed to the work of Jespersen, Lakoff, Tannen, Labov and Trudgill, and despite the significant diversity of approaches used by these five linguists, most people outside of language and gender studies accept the conclusions that these researchers present about the speech of women and men and most trust the interpretations that they provide of their research results. People generally persist in believing that women are more conservative in their speech than men (Jespersen 1922), that women are more polite than men (Lakoff 1975), that women seek more verbal intimacy than men (Tannen 1990), that women are less secure and more status-conscious in their speech than men (Labov 1972), and that women use standard ('correct') speech more than men (Trudgill 1972).

In contrast, relatively few non-specialists are familiar with the many more significant studies which explicate the specific social or discourse conditions which motivate the language choices of particular groups of women and men. Among these are Gal (1978), Brown (1980), Milroy (1980), Nichols (1983), Holmes (1986), Eckert (1989) and M. Goodwin (1990). An excessive amount of research energy has been devoted to testing and/or refuting a relatively small number of claims about the language of women put forth by a few prominent individuals. That the academic community is still discussing unsubstantiated statements about women's language made more than 20 years ago is quite disturbing. Still more troubling is the fact that researchers are still responding to stereotypic representations of women as essentially (and primarily) conservative, nurturing, hesitant and status conscious.

To begin anew, researchers need to treat as archaic the frequently asked questions: 'How do women talk? How do men talk? What differences exist between women's and men's speech?' As interesting as these questions may be to individuals attracted to a discussion of sex differences of any kind, it is now evident that such queries are basically misguided and naive. The error lies in viewing sex and gender as simple bipolar distinctions and in believing in the existence of natural and inherent differences between women and men (Butler 1990, Bem 1993, Bing and Bergvall this volume). As applied to language research, the mistake is more subtle and perhaps more complex; it resides additionally in the overgeneralizations that are drawn about women's and/or men's verbal behaviour based on language samples taken from specifically situated speech and in the stereotyped interpretations that continue to be offered about such data. (See above.) The problem may also result from what Cameron (this volume) describes as the 'inadequate sociological apparatus of mainstream sociolinguistics' that does not begin to address the complexity of gender. Researchers need to exert extreme caution before generalizing about any characteristics garnered from specific women's or men's verbal interactions and should hesitate before attributing to sex or gender linguistic differences which can more accurately be accounted for by economic privilege, subcultural phenomena, setting, activity, audience, personality, or by the context-specific communicative goals of the particular speakers who are being studied.

While there is a growing consensus among language and gender researchers that we must cease partitioning the world into two simple populations composed of either all women or of all men, there remain a significant number of unresolved issues about how to attain the research goals to which we are committed. In the discussion which follows, I outline some of what I believe we need to examine and I attempt to articulate the sorts of questions which I think we should be addressing. The discussion illustrates how a laboratory setting, often scorned as unnatural, artificial and socially without value, holds some unexpected merits for language and gender research. I will provide details of a research project that a colleague and I recently conducted in an experimental setting that illustrate the social symbolism carried by particular ways of speaking and demonstrate the socially constructed nature of what others have called 'gendered speech styles'. It will be seen that the character of the experimental situation and the nature of the verbal tasks performed by the participants are more critical variables for explaining the language that occurs than the sex or gender of the speakers.

The research value of an experimental setting

Several years ago, my friend and colleague Alice Greenwood and I embarked on a research project which had as its goal the linguistic analysis of informal conversations between pairs of female friends. The first major stumbling block was that we saw no reliable and ethical way of gaining access to such conversations. We were not interested in investigating our own interactions or the limited samples which we could gather by studying the conversations which each of us had with other close friends. We wanted to collect a large sample of conversations so that we might carry out a systematic study of specific linguistic features and pragmatic devices which others had asserted existed in the speech of women.

Since we sought to collect a fairly large sample of private interactive speech from people who knew each other but with whom we, ourselves, would not be interacting, a device had to be created that would bring friends together in our presence. While we knew that data collected in a laboratory setting risked being inauthentic, we believed that if the project were designed properly, the problems and constraints associated with this type of data could be minimized and turned to our advantage. We decided to proceed as if doing a study of friendship and solicited volunteers from linguistics and women's studies classes at Montclair State University in New Jersey and from among women we knew in the local community. We invited individuals who wished to participate to come with a friend of the same sex (from inside or outside the university community) to a specified location at a prearranged time. Since three male students volunteered, we decided to include them in our sample. (A fourth pair of men was invited to participate by one of the women who volunteered.) All together, 30 conversations were recorded. The research described here focuses on the conversations of the four pairs of male friends and four pairs of female friends. The four female pairs used for this study were selected so that their ages and lengths of friendship roughly matched the ages and lengths of friendship of the male participants. No analysis of the conversations was undertaken until after the eight pairs had been identified.

The location which we chose for our data collection was a room in the university's Psycho-education Center. The room, equipped with a one-way mirror, was designed as a nursery school classroom and was normally used to evaluate the behaviour of young children. This physical arrangement allowed us to video-tape our participants unobtrusively through the one-way mirror; all had been informed in advance that they were to be audio- and video-taped. We eventually settled on a research design which divided the conversations into three different time periods. When the participants first arrived, we told them that we were not completely ready to begin and we left them alone, encouraging them to relax and enjoy the juice and doughnuts which we had provided. Microphones and a tape recorder were in full view on the table at which they were asked to sit; they were informed that the tape was running before we left them alone. We call this first part of the conversation the 'spontaneous' talk segment because, although the participants were aware of the recording equipment, they alone controlled the conversation and they were under the impression that the study had not yet formally begun. Each pair spoke about matters unrelated to the subject of the study.

After 10 minutes, we re-entered the room, apologized for the delay and then spent several minutes talking with the participants. We presented ourselves as women's studies faculty and told them that we wanted to know what they thought about friendship between women as compared to friendship between men. We explained that an interview with each of them separately would not be as interesting as a conversation on the subject between friends. We intentionally employed a casual and personal style while talking, joked together and asked whether they thought that men and women had the same kinds of close friendships and whether they thought that a woman and a man could be close friends if they did not have a sexual relationship. We related a funny male-bonding story that a male student in one of our classes had told; the story, which was recounted complete with off-coloured language, produced a good bit of laughter from everyone. Following this four-way interaction, the participants were left alone to talk. The series of questions that we asked and the story that we related successfully elicited fairly natural conversation from everyone, although some of the speakers seemed somewhat more self-conscious during this second part of the conversation than they had in the first segment. We label this second part of the conversation 'considered' speech since the speakers were focused on a specific assigned topic of conversation.

At the end of 15 minutes, we interrupted the participants, thanked them, and asked them each to fill out an anonymous demographic questionnaire and a form granting us permission to use the taped conversations. Since the documents had to be filled out individually, no conversation was required. Nonetheless, there was usually a good deal of verbal interaction between the speakers. Most of the participants appeared more relaxed knowing that the formal part of the study was over; they made jokes about the questions, read them aloud to each other, decided together on answers to some of the questions and engaged in general commentary about filling out the questionnaires. This segment, which lasted between 6 and 13 minutes, provided us with an opportunity to observe what we decided to call 'collaborative' talk.

The terms 'spontaneous', 'considered', and 'collaborative' do not describe the conversational style used by the participants but refer instead to the 'type of talk' (Freed and Greenwood 1996) exchanged by the speakers. The terms focus on the fact that in the first part of the conversation, the participants **spontaneously** chose what to talk about; in the second part they **considered** an assigned topic and, in the third part, they **collaborated** on the answers to a questionnaire that each speaker could have completed individually and in silence. These terms have been used elsewhere (Greenwood and Freed 1992, Freed 1994, and Freed and Greenwood 1996) to describe 'the types of talk' in these conversations.

The data generated by this project are considerable; the corpus consists of more than 15 hours of conversation between 30 pairs of same-sex friends. Yet the speech samples recorded probably do not represent the type of conversational exchanges which were initially sought. Instead we collected three different sorts of conversational samples from each of thirty pairs of friends. Each part of the conversation (the spontaneous, considered and collaborative talk segments) constituted a somewhat different speaking situation for the participants and each elicited a different kind of verbal interaction. While the conversations are of varying degrees of intimacy with different amounts of self-consciousness evident from speaker to speaker and from pair to pair, for the most part there are great similarities in the conversational dyads. Of greatest significance was the fact that in analysing the phrase *you know* and the use of questions, we discovered a striking quantitative and qualitative difference in distribution of these forms across the three separate segments of the conversation for all of the speakers (Freed and Greenwood 1996). Thus, the original purpose for which the samples were collected became subordinated to the research possibilities which presented themselves as a result of the data collection techniques and the data themselves. We began to understand the power of the laboratory setting for the collection of natural language samples.

Detailed discourse-based findings

The present discussion is centred on an analysis of two discourse features that have been regularly associated with a female speech style, the occurrence of *you know* and the use of questions. Over the past 20 years, these two language forms have been continually described as signals of women's conversational style. The expression *you know* has been characterized as a female hedging device and interpreted as a marker of hesitancy, insecurity and/or of powerlessness (Lakoff 1973, 1975, Fishman 1978, 1980, O'Barr and Atkins 1980, Ostman 1981, Coates 1986). Question use has also been stereotypically associated with the conversational style of women (Lakoff 1973, 1975, Hirschman 1973, 1994, Fishman 1978, 1980, Tannen 1990). Lakoff (1973), among the first to claim that women used more questions than men, declared that women used tag questions as a hedging device and that women had a greater tendency to use rising intonation on declaratives, thereby turning their statements into questions. As with *you know*, this usage was interpreted as a sign of women's hesitancy and societal powerlessness. By examining the use of these forms in comparable conversations of four pairs of female friends and four pairs of male friends, Greenwood and I (Greenwood and Freed 1992, Freed and Greenwood 1996) have been able to determine that it was the discourse requirements associated with the three different types of talk in the conversations studied and not the sex or gender of the speakers that explained the distribution and the function of *you know* and of questions in these conversations. Our analysis revealed that the women and men in this study displayed remarkably similar language behaviour.

The corpus examined contained 612 instances of *you know* from approximately four and a half hours of informal conversations between the eight same-sex pairs of friends. Of the total 612 tokens of *you know*, women used the expression 310 times and men 302 times. The frequency of occurrence of *you know* varied widely with the type of talk of the three different parts of the conversation and all the speakers in the sample, female and male, varied their usage of *you know* in identical ways in accordance with the three types of talk. Furthermore, in every conversational pair, one speaker used the expression more frequently than the other. (See Freed and Greenwood 1996 for further detail.)

More specifically, the distribution of *you know* changed dramatically across the three parts of the conversation. We found that a startling 89 per cent (546 tokens) of the total 612 instances of *you know* occurred in part two, the 'considered talk' segment of the conversations as compared to only 9 per cent (56 tokens) of *you know* in part one of the conversations and a mere 2 per cent (10 tokens) in part three. (Adjusted for the time differences among the three parts of the conversations, 13 per cent of the instances of *you know* occurred in part one, 84 per cent in part two and 3 per cent in part three.) The only change that took place in moving through these conversations, where the setting remained constant and the relationship between the participants was unaltered, was the requirements of the various tasks presented to the speakers. This distribution of the occurrence of *you know* was nearly identical for the female and male speakers.[3]

In part one of the conversation, when the speakers were becoming accustomed to their physical surroundings and to talking to each other in this new environment, and when, furthermore, the participants thought that the actual research project had not officially begun, a fairly wide range of topics was discussed. The participants sometimes commented on the nature of the classroom they were in, speculated on the purpose of the research project, talked about what they had been doing earlier in the day or the night before, discussed school-related topics and miscellaneous events in their own lives. The interactions were marked by natural sounding speech, a good bit of eating and drinking, and relatively little self-consciousness about talking. There were some signs of physical awkwardness from some of the speakers while they adjusted to the surroundings. Some fidgeted and some participants got up and walked around the room inspecting the toys they saw and then proceeded to talk about the toys; in contrast, others just sat down and picked up a conversation that seemed to have begun earlier. There were a greater number of questions uttered in this part of the conversation than in either of the following two parts and there was usually a fairly disjointed series of topics discussed. As stated above, only 9 per cent of the total number of all occurrences of *you know* took place in this part of the conversation.

It was in part two of the conversation that the speakers were asked to discuss their thoughts on the nature of friendship between women as compared to the character of friendships between men; thus, it was in this part that the participants were asked to jointly develop an assigned topic of conversation. The process of responding in tandem to an assigned topic produced a subtle change in the demeanor and the manner of speaking of the participants. This was exhibited by longer speaker turns, slower speech, increased phatic communication through question use, greater attention to a single topic – the assigned one – and a greater use of such discourse devices as *you know*. The relative frequency of *you know* in this part of the conversation clearly tied speaker-turns together, allowed the speakers to check in with one another, and reinforced the joint production of conversation. These discourse functions can be seen in the following examples of *you know* from part two of the conversation.

1. *Female pair*
   A: um, I know. It's good. I don't know. It's different like there's a lot of kinds of friendships, **you know,** like
   B: like when I talk to my best friend Jen, it's interesting. Because the two of us, **you know,** we can talk about guys, we can talk about stuff that's going on in our life, we can talk about, **you know,** soaps and school. It's, **you know,** it's just something I can, I feel like I can relate more to her than I do to
   A: anyone else.

2. *Male pair*
   A: Two people I know of, two guys that, **you know** if I don't talk to them for two years, I could call them up and **you know** it would
   B: it would still be the same
   A: no big deal.
   B: Yeah.
   A: We're still friends. It doesn't matter if you don't keep in touch all the time. It doesn't matter this; it doesn't matter that. And that's, that's kind of **you know** like my friend Mike. **You know.** He's lived in town. There's no reason I, I just
   B: Yeah.
   A: We just haven't gotten together for a long time.

In part three, during which only ten instances of *you know* occurred, still another speaking pattern became apparent. Speakers were noticeably more relaxed and consulted with one another while answering the questions on the demographic survey. They joked about the questions, sometimes explained them to one another ('What does sexual orientation mean?'), collaborated on their answers ('How long have we known each other?'), and though they talked together, they were more superficially involved in the conversation than they had been earlier since talking was not the main activity (Freed and Greenwood 1996).

The investigation of question use also unearthed patterns of usage related to the different discourse requirements of the three parts of the conversation and, as with *you know*, failed to reveal a different distribution of forms for women as compared to men. Using syntactic and intonational criteria to identify utterances as questions, we identified six types of questions in the corpus: (1) Yes/no questions characterized by simple subject–auxiliary inversion; these included reduced yes/no questions where the auxiliary is deleted and alternative questions; (2) wh-questions; (3) full declaratives and other syntactic phrases with a final phrase rise; (4) tag questions including both canonical (or auxiliary) tags, e.g. *They didn't hit you, did they?* and invariant (or lexical) tags, e.g. *That's where you lived, right?*; (5) wh-questions, followed by a phrase with a final rise in tag position, *What's today's date? the 25th?*, sometimes called 'wh-questions plus guess' constructions (Norrick 1992); and (6) questions of the form *how/what about ...* , e.g. *What about when women get older, like when they get married and stuff?*

The corpus contained 787 questions used by the sixteen different speakers. Of the total number of questions uttered, women used 404 questions and men 383. The frequency of occurrence of questions varied with the type of talk of the three different segments of the conversation and all the speakers in the sample varied their usage of questions in comparable ways in accordance with the three types of talk. (See Freed and Greenwood 1996 for further detail.) In five out of eight of the conversational pairs, one speaker asked noticeably more questions than the other.

As with *you know*, the distribution of questions changed across the three parts of the conversation. While questions were used in all parts of the conversation by all speakers, it was evident that the differing discourse requirements of the three parts elicited a different frequency of questions for all speakers. The pattern is a non-random distribution with 42 per cent of all questions occurring in the first 10-minute segment, 33 per cent in the second 15-minute segment, and 25 per cent in the third segment that lasted between 6 and 10 minutes. (Adjusted for time, the distribution is 45 per cent in part one, 24 per cent in part two and 31 per cent in part three.) The women and men in the sample responded to the differences in exactly the same way. Again, the only change that took place in the conversation, where the setting remained constant and the relationship between the participants was unaltered, was the nature of the talk exchanged.

By analysing the discourse function of each question in the corpus as it occurred in context, we were able to establish a taxonomy of question functions (Greenwood and Freed 1992, Freed 1994). We determined that not only did the number of questions vary per segment, but that the functional types of questions used were different from segment to segment. Questions that sought factual information about the lives and activities of the two speakers (e.g. *Did you watch* 90210 *last night?*) as well as metalinguistic questions that focused on the 'talk' of the conversation (e.g. *What did you say?*) predominated in part one of the conversation. That is, it was in this segment that the women and men alike asked a large proportion of questions that either sought factual information of a personal nature or sought clarifications, repetitions and confirmations about preceding utterances. In part two, these two types of questions occurred significantly less often than in part one. Instead there was a very high proportion of two other classes of questions. Speakers used questions that asked for agreement, phatic communication and for elaboration of comments made (e.g. *Do you know what I mean?*; *So what do you talk about?*); alternatively, they conveyed their own feelings through the use of self-directed questions, rhetorical questions, and questions used for humour, etc. (e.g. *Why'd I say that?*; *Who knows?*).[4]

Part three of the conversation, during which the participants were filling out questionnaires, showed a still different pattern of question usage. In this segment, questions that were used to elicit specific factual information (e.g. *What's today's date?*) occurred more than twice as often as any other type of question. The sorts of questions that were characteristic of the other parts of the conversation were noticeably absent; questions that sought elaboration, those that were used for phatic communication, and those that asked for repetitions and clarifications occurred infrequently. Once again, the female and male speakers were remarkably similar in their use of questions. From the analysis of these data, Greenwood and I concluded that it was the requirements of the different types of talk of the three segments that produced the varying question patterns and not the sex or gender of the speakers or their relationship to each other.

Taken together, these findings indicate that the women and men under investigation in this study responded in like ways to the discourse requirements of the talk situations and that it was these demands that controlled the frequency of occurrence and the function of *you know* and of different sorts of questions. These results are significant since they provide concrete evidence about the effect on discourse of variables internal to the speech situation itself when sex (or gender) and the relationship between speakers remain constant. Furthermore, these results illustrate the valuable theoretical lessons which can emerge from the collection of data and from the analysis of speech samples obtained in a controlled environment, even when such outcomes are not anticipated in the original research design. This point is reminiscent of the one made by Edelsky (1981) when she describes the process by which 'both variables and hypotheses ... [can] emerge from the data' (1981: 384) in a piece of sociolinguistic research.

Interpretation of data

In musing about these data and the implications of this research, I find that the most provocative question to ponder is why the language patterns of the women and the men who participated in this project turn out to be so similar despite the fact that other researchers have so often found differences in the speech characteristics of women and men. When I contemplate this question, I am led to two seemingly contradictory conclusions. On the one hand, I am prepared to conclude that this work verifies what I have long suspected, that the notion of 'gendered speech styles', that is, styles uniquely associated with just women or just men, is a myth. Indeed, these data strengthen the belief that it is specific social circumstances, particular types of activities that people are engaged in, various sorts of daily occupations, together with the artificial constructs created in our gender-differentiated society that are responsible for the way people conduct themselves verbally. On the other hand, I am tempted to argue that the experimental conditions created by this particular research design may themselves be responsible for the men's using language in a manner that others have claimed are characteristic of a female speech style (Hirschman 1973, 1994, Fishman 1978, 1980, Coates 1989, Tannen 1990). (Recall that the features under discussion have been previously identified as characteristic of women's language and that here the women and the men follow nearly identical patterns of usage for the forms analysed.) Perhaps when social conditions are reproduced in a laboratory setting, the conditions themselves generate particular communicative styles for both female and male speakers.

In other words, do these data provide the much sought-after verification that women and men do not necessarily (and automatically) have different speech styles? Perhaps all that was needed to detect this was an experimental setting that sufficiently controlled the appropriate variables. Or is it rather that, as researchers, Greenwood and I created a particular 'community of practice' through the process of recruiting students from particular sorts of classes to participate in a college-centred research project on friendship? The speakers in this study certainly appear to share a wide range of conversational features (only two of which have been analysed in detail) which may be characteristic of their age group, their regional variety of speech and representative of this student population, or, more interestingly, may be a by-product of the structure of the experimental setting. These two apparently contradictory viewpoints, which would lead to fairly different conclusions about the relationship between women, men and language, need to be explored.

The limited demographic data that were collected from the participants could potentially shed light on their language use and direct my thinking. However, a review of the material provided by the speakers on their demographic surveys (see Appendix) reveals little that is relevant to solving the question of why the female and male speakers showed such closely parallel speaking styles despite the fact that other language and gender research would predict greater linguistic divergence between the groups. There is not a significant amount of social diversity either within or across the female and male groups (although a slightly greater degree of heterogeneity was present among the male speakers). If we reject the belief that sex and gender can alone be responsible for speech differences, then the parallel speaking patterns of the women and men are not surprising given the general similarities among the participants aside from sex and gender. So, other aspects of the sociolinguistic context in which these language samples occurred need to be examined in order to move the focus of the analysis away from anything inherent to the speakers themselves towards an examination of the linguistic context and the activities in which the speakers were engaged.

One area that calls for investigation is the experimental design itself. As Cameron *et al.* (1992) remind us in their discussion of research techniques, since it is impossible to completely remove the researcher from the research setting, perhaps in the process of establishing a format conducive to natural conversation between pairs of female friends, Greenwood and I inadvertently created an experimental space which is *symbolic* of what our society views as a 'female space'. This in turn may have produced the sort of talk which is associated in our society with the speech of women speaking in private, a speech style which itself has become *symbolically* (and stereotypically) associated with women.

By designing an experimental setting that placed women and men in symmetrical social relations and by compelling them to undertake identical tasks, we have drawn attention to two crucial facts: first, participating in the same practice produced in the women and men the same kind of talk; second, outside of this experimental setting, it is possible that women and men would be less likely to find themselves in such similar settings, given the sex- and gender-differentiated society in which we live – that is, given a choice among the vast number of communicative settings, and different 'communities of practice' (Eckert and McConnell-Ginet 1992a, 1992b) that exist as a matter of custom, men may less commonly choose the sort of community space created in this experiment than women. Thus language and gender studies conducted in natural settings may often find differences not similarities in women's and men's speech simply because women and men are frequently engaged in different activities (see M. Goodwin 1990) and not because of any differences in women and men themselves. Since it is increasingly clear that speech patterns are products of the activities that people are engaged in and not inherent to the participants, we can conclude that communicative styles are not 'speech habits' or styles appropriately associated with one sex or gender over another but are customs related to actions, activities and behaviours differentially encouraged for women and men.[5]

It appears that the specific conditions which were produced in this laboratory setting – including the nursery school classroom complete with children's toys, juice and doughnuts, two female women's studies researchers purposely using informal nurturing conversational tones, as well as the types of tasks given to the speakers, may themselves be responsible for the particular sort of talk which occurred. I am suggesting that the setting and associated communicative tasks became an index of a 'gendered style' (Ochs 1992). If this is the case, then not only can a particular linguistic feature be an index of a social meaning (which in turn is attached to gender), but certain social activities may themselves be indexed for certain types of talk. These activities and practices may then themselves become symbolically gendered if they are regularly and consistently associated with either women or men. (Similarly, certain activities and practices become symbolically associated with adults or children, with members of certain professions or particular ethnic groups, based on the frequency or regularity with which individuals, possessing some externally identifiable characteristic, participate in that activity.) The speech situation created here, consisting as it did of sitting face-to-face with a friend in a fairly fixed posture to discuss the nature of friendship, may encourage a particular language style. In our culture, this activity and the language style associated with it may be conventionally connected to women simply because women have participated in this sort of activity more frequently than men. This language style should not be construed, however, as a simple behavioural habit of women. Individuals consciously choose to construct, signal, emphasize and even de-emphasize gendered identities by participating (or refusing to participate) in practices associated with one group or another (see Hall and O'Donovan this volume). It should be clear that there is nothing about any particular activity or communicative task (or communicative style) that is itself inherently female or male, nor are the speaking patterns of individuals mindless habits that exist as disembodied linguistic reflexes.

We seem to have come full circle. We can substantiate the claim that the language used by the speakers in this study was affected by the conditions under which they were speaking and by the communicative tasks which they were assigned. We can, in addition, document the similarity of the speech of the women and the men and hypothesize that the setting and related speaking activities themselves were responsible for the sameness in language. We see that the male participants were not without the skills needed to participate in the assigned tasks (see Freed 1992). What we learn most emphatically from the results of this study is that gender was not a significant variable and that, therefore, the linguistic patterns which emerged cannot be described or characterized as female language; at most, we can characterize the style as one which has become symbolically associated with activities in which women commonly participate. The idea that sex difference brings with it specific gendered behaviours is thus seriously challenged as we conclude that the notion of binary gender categories, in and of themselves, have little to do with the findings.

Conclusion

I am compelled to ask why, if neither sex nor gender is a salient feature here, should we expect these to be significant features in other sociolinguistic research? The results of this study certainly call into question any easy assumptions about sex and gender being universally basic or salient. And if they are not consistently proved to be significant, why do we pursue this line of research? The answer lies in the role that gender continues to play in society. When I assert that gender is not salient, I do not intend any general claims about the insignificance of gender in our lives. Rather, I wish to emphasize the degree to which gender has been imposed on us as a 'lens' (Bem 1993) through which we view the world. I want to underscore the extent to which gender has been over-used as a unitary theoretical construct. And I want to stress what Bem (1993) so eloquently explains: the imposition of gender polarization on our world reinforces similarities among women where differences actually exist, creates the impression of difference between the sexes where little would otherwise be found, supports and strengthens androcentrism by fostering an essentialist view of male and female styles of thinking, of speaking, of playing, of dressing, etc., which is accompanied by a view of maleness as the norm, and finally 'turns men and women into gender caricatures' (1993: 194) whereby women and men acquire the 'the idea of being a "real" man or woman as opposed to a merely biological man or woman' (194).

As researchers, we now realize, perhaps with some reluctance, that we need to abandon a number of our early and fairly simplistic feminist ruminations about the role of gender in language research. As we gain additional sophistication about the construction of social identities (Ochs 1992), the overriding significance of context (Duranti and C. Goodwin 1992), the nature of talk as social organization (M. Goodwin 1990) and the notion of communities of practice (Eckert and McConnell-Ginet 1992a, 1992b), we must concede that sex and gender, as straightforward dualistic categories for sociolinguistic investigation, are unsatisfactory. We are beginning to understand that instead, we need to embark on a close examination of different communities and settings and of the various individuals who move in and out of these communities as they engage with one another in talk. We must abandon, as Eckert and McConnell-Ginet (1992a: 91) say, the idea that 'gender works independently of social identity and relations, that it "means" the same across communities, and that the linguistic manifestations of that meaning are also the same across communities'.

We might consider the relation of language to gender suggested by Ochs (1992). Ochs correctly asserts that particular language features do not simply represent women's or men's speech but rather that language features operate as indexes of 'certain social meanings (e.g. stances, social acts, social activities, etc.), which in turn help to constitute gender meanings' (p. 341). Since, unfortunately, there continues to exist in every society a well-organized set of social expectations about who, women or men, will convey which social meanings, then it follows that in most societies, women and men are seen as having differential access to the enactment of specific social roles, activities, etc. It follows also that our very perceptions of one another are related to our expectations of who should convey which social meanings and these expectations and resultant preconceptions are part of the well-entrenched gender stereotypes which many of us have sought to fight. When the language behaviour of individual women (or men) does not conform to society's expectations, a set of judgements is formed about them. Their language is seen as marked (Ochs 1992: 343) and they themselves are often seen as deviant. Thus Ochs' characterization of language and gender does not assist in the description of the changing roles of women (and men); nor does it describe the resistance mounted by members of both sexes to rigid gender-assignments and to the stereotyped expectations which may themselves result in part from indexical relations between language and social meaning (see Bergvall this volume).

When I contemplate the role of gender in our lives, I realize that what connects women to one another in our culture (and no doubt in cultures all over the world) is most irrefutably the persistent perception of women – by other women and by men – as women, despite significant heterogeneity among women. It is this view of women, so long ago described by Simone de Beauvoir (1952) as 'other', that ultimately drives our research and fuels our need to focus on sex and gender even after we realize the error of viewing these as independent, unitary categories of social scientific research. Whether this gender-determined perception is tied to the androcentric norm of most societies (Bem 1993) and facilitates the perpetuation of women as a separate underclass of humans, or whether the perception is merely connected to predetermined sex and gender-expectations and is symbolic of societal gender stereotypes matters little. For as long as individuals in society feel the need to emphasize sex and gender differences and to profess the existence of static unchanging gender-identities, overgeneralizations and prejudice will persist. And as long as gender dichotomies persist, researchers will be obliged to consider gender (as a variable that interacts with other social variables) in the process of analysing the interaction of language and social life. But we will need a much clearer understanding of the concept of gender itself. As Saville-Troike (1989: 182) explains (referring also to Hymes 1966), social differences that exist (or that may be created) influence our attitudes about language. The linguistic differences that emerge from these social differences become symbolic of the social dimensions themselves and can be used to discriminate against certain people and to control them as they are categorized and 'ke[pt] ... in their place'. When language styles are identified as symbolic of the social nature of women, it is these very associations that can then be used to perpetuate the unequal treatment of women in our world.

Appendix: Demographic profile of participants

The participants ranged in age from 19 to 28. Two of the women (ages 23 and 24) and three of the men (ages 24, 28 and 28) were older than the traditional college student. Two pairs of women and two pairs of men had been friends for only 5 or 6 months. One female and one male pair had been friends for 2 to 3 years. The oldest pair in each group were friends of long-standing; the female pair had been friends for 13 years; the male pair reported an 18-year friendship.

Seven of the eight female speakers were Montclair State students; only four were students who had ever been in class with one of the researchers. (All four of these were from women's studies classes.) The eighth female participant was not a student. In contrast only four of the male speakers were students at Montclair State University. Two were students at other institutions and two were not students at all. Of the four Montclair students, three knew one of the researchers: one was a graduate student in linguistics and two were from women's studies classes.

All the participants described themselves as single and hetero-sexual. Twelve of fourteen stated that they were middle-middle class; one male participant stated that he was upper-middle class and one female said that she was lower-middle class. (These answers were based on a subjective question in which the speakers were asked to choose from a range of social classes without any specifics about financial status. Two students left the question blank, one declaring herself as being financially independent and surviving on $6,000 a year.)

Of the males, six stated that their family was Catholic; six females also named Catholicism as their family's religion. There were two Protestants among the female speakers; there was one Protestant and one Jew among the male participants. Twelve of the speakers grew up in New Jersey; one listed Brooklyn, New York, as his hometown and one participant simply wrote 'Italy'. One female failed to give a hometown and another said that she had moved around too much to have a hometown. All of the participants appeared white; one male and one female each listed their ethnic identity as Hispanic. Two other males wrote 'Italian' for their ethnic identity.

Seven women reported that English was spoken in their homes; one of these seven said that Spanish and English were used. One other woman listed only Spanish as the language spoken at home. Six of the men said that their families used English at home; of these six, one said that English, Italian and Spanish were spoken and another indicated that both English and Spanish were spoken. One man said that Italian was spoken at home. (None of the speakers had a non-native accent that either researcher detected. It was only upon reviewing the demographic surveys that information about the participants' language backgrounds became known.)

The educational background of the speakers' parents differed considerably from speaker to speaker. Overall, the parents of the male speakers had attained a slightly higher educational level than parents of the female speakers. The eight men described their sixteen parents as follows: five had a high school education; three had some college but no degree; seven had a college degree and one had a graduate degree. Of the female speakers, two had less than a high school education; five had finished high school; one had a few years of college; four had graduated from college and one had a graduate degree. The educational level of three of the women's parents was unknown.

Fifteen of the participants stated that they worked at least part time. The women were employed as waitresses, as food preparers, one as a baby-sitter, others in 'retail sales' (one as a retail manager), and in a library. The men were in retail sales, in the insurance business, one worked with international exchange visitors; two of the students said that they were in a band together and two others listed 'actor, musician, employee playwright' as their secondary occupations.

Four women and four men said that they did not spend a lot of time talking on the telephone. Three men said that they talked on the phone frequently and one said that he sometimes did. By coincidence, the women's responses were identical.

Notes

1. I would like to thank Vicky Bergvall, Janet Bing, Deborah Cameron and Alice Greenwood for their helpful comments on earlier drafts of this chapter. I valued all of their suggestions, even if I did not always follow them. This work was partially supported by a grant from the Separately Budgeted Research Fund at Montclair State University.

2. In some of her other work, Tannen emphasizes the interplay of ethnicity, regional difference, culture and conversational style (Tannen 1981, 1982, 1992); however, in her 1990 publication, she focuses on women and men as homogeneous groups without regard for the importance of the interrelatedness of sex and gender with these various other social phenomena.

3. As another part of the same research project, Greenwood and I studied the use of *you know* and the occurrence of questions in the conversations of four pairs of women who ranged in age from 39 to 52 years. These women used *you know* somewhat less frequently than did the younger women and young men (207 tokens as compared to 310 for the younger women and 302 for the young men) but the pattern of usage across the three parts of the conversation still showed a substantial increase in moving from part one to part two. The change was, however, far less dramatic than shown for the eight pairs of young speakers. These women used *you know* 56 times in part one, 137 times in part two and 14 times in part three. Adjusted for the time difference of the three parts, 34 per cent of the tokens of *you know* occurred in part one, 56 per cent in part two and 10 per cent in part three.

4. Women and men showed a slight difference in part two, with men using more questions that expressed their own opinions and women asking more questions that sought elaboration. But more significant than the small difference was the distinct and parallel pattern of question usage for each group in moving from one part of the conversation to the next (Freed and Greenwood 1996).

5. The belief that women and men participate in very different sorts of communicative events during which they display, respectively, cooperative versus competitive speech styles, is widely held in white middle-class America. I, personally, do not believe that the type of verbal behaviour used by the men in this study is as uncommon as has been suggested. (See also Freed and Greenwood 1996.) It is my view that the findings that report extensive verbal competitiveness among men are an artefact of our research techniques and are a product of the limited access that we have to private conversations between men in a wide range of situations.

References

Bem Sandra Lipsitz 1993 *The lenses of gender*. Yale University Press, New Haven.

Bergvall Victoria L this volume: Constructing and enacting gender through discourse: negotiating multiple roles as female engineering students.

Bing Janet M, Bergvall Victoria L this volume: The question of questions: beyond binary thinking.

Brown Penelope 1980 How and why are women more polite: some evidence from a Mayan community. In McConnell-Ginet Sally, Borker Ruth, Furman Nelly (eds) pp 111–36.

Butler Judith 1990 *Gender trouble: feminism and the subversion of identity*. Routledge, New York.

Cameron Deborah this volume: The language–gender interface: challenging co-optation.

Cameron Deborah, Coates Jennifer 1989 Some problems in the sociolinguistic explanation of sex differences. In Coates Jennifer, Cameron Deborah (eds) pp 13–26.

Cameron Deborah, Frazer Elizabeth, Harvey Penelope, Rampton M B H, Richardson Kay 1992 *Researching language: issues of power and method*. Routledge, London and New York.

Coates Jennifer 1986 *Women, men and language* (first edition). Longman, London.

Coates Jennifer 1989 Gossip revisited: language in all-female groups. In Coates Jennifer, Cameron Deborah (eds) pp 94–121.

Coates Jennifer, Cameron Deborah (eds) 1989 *Women in their speech communities*. Longman, London.

de Beauvoir Simone 1952 *The second sex*. Bantam Books, New York.

Duranti Alessandro, Goodwin Charles (eds) 1992 *Rethinking context: language as an interactive phenomenon*. Cambridge University Press, Cambridge.

Eckert Penelope 1989 The whole women: sex and gender differences in variation. *Language Variation and Change* 1: 245–67.

Eckert Penelope, McConnell-Ginet Sally 1992a Communities of practice: where language, gender and power all live. In Hall Kira, Bucholtz Mary, Moonwomon Birch (eds) pp 89–99.

Eckert Penelope, McConnell-Ginet Sally 1992b Think practically and look locally: language and gender as community-based practice. *Annual Review of Anthropology* 21: 461–90.

Edelsky Carol 1981 Who's got the floor? *Language in Society* 10: 383–421.

Fishman Pamela 1978 Interaction: the work women do. *Social Problems* 25: 397–406. (Reprinted as Fishman Pamela 1983 Interaction: the work women do. In Thorne Barrie, Kramarae Cheris, Henley Nancy (eds) pp 89–102.)

Fishman Pamela 1980 Conversational insecurity. In Giles Howard,

Robinson W Peter, Smith Philip (eds) *Language: social psychological perspectives*. Pergamon Press, New York pp 127–32.

Freed Alice F 1992 We understand perfectly: a critique of Tannen's view of cross-sex communication. In Hall Kira, Bucholtz Mary, Moonwomon Birch (eds) pp 144–52.

Freed Alice F 1994 The form and function of questions in informal dyadic conversation. *Journal of Pragmatics* 21: 621–44.

Freed Alice F, Greenwood Alice 1996 Women, men and type of talk: what makes the difference. *Language in Society* 25.1: 1–26.

Gal Susan 1978 Peasant men can't get wives: language change and sex roles in a bilingual community. *Language in Society* 7: 1–16.

Goodwin Marjorie Harness 1990 *He-said–she-said: talk as social organization among Black children*. Indiana University Press, Bloomington.

Greenwood Alice, Freed Alice F 1992 Women talking to women: the function of questions in conversation. In Hall Kira, Bucholtz Mary, Moonwomon Birch (eds) pp 197–206.

Hall Kira, Bucholtz Mary, Moonwomon Birch (eds) 1992 *Locating power: proceedings of the second Berkeley women and language conference*. Berkeley Women and Language Group, Berkeley, CA.

Hall Kira, O'Donovan Veronica this volume: Shifting gender positions among Hindi-speaking hijras.

Hirschman Lynette 1973 Female-male differences in conversational interaction. Paper presented at the annual meeting of the Linguistic Society of America, San Diego, CA.

Hirschman Lynette 1994 Female-male differences in conversational interaction. *Language in Society* 23.3: 427–42.

Holmes Janet 1986 Functions of *you know* in women's and men's speech. *Language in Society* 15: 1–22.

Hymes Dell 1966 Two types of linguistic relativity. In Bright William (ed) *Sociolinguistics*. Mouton, the Hague pp 114–67.

Jespersen Otto 1922 The woman. *Language: its nature, origin and development*. George Allen & Unwin, London pp 237–54.

Labov William 1972 *Sociolinguistic patterns*. University of Pennsylvania Press, Philadelphia.

Lakoff Robin 1973 Language and woman's place. *Language in Society* 2: 45–80.

Lakoff Robin 1975 *Language and woman's place*. Harper & Row, New York.

Milroy Lesley 1980 *Language and social networks*. Basil Blackwell, Oxford.

McConnell-Ginet Sally, Borker Ruth, Furman Nelly (eds) 1980 *Women and language in literature and society*. Praeger, New York.

Nichols Patricia 1983 Linguistic options and choices for Black women in the rural south. In Thorne Barrie, Kramarae Cheris, Henley Nancy (eds) pp 54–68.

Norrick Neal R 1992 Wh-questions with guesses in tag-position. *Journal of Pragmatics* 18.1: 85–9

O'Barr William, Atkins Bowman K 1980 'Women's' language or 'powerless' language? In McConnell-Ginet Sally, Borker Ruth, Furman Nelly (eds) pp 93–110.

Ochs Elinor 1992 Indexing gender. In Duranti Alessandro and Goodwin Charles (eds) *Rethinking context: language as an interactive phenomenon.* Cambridge University Press, Cambridge pp 335–59.

Ostman Jan-Ola 1981 *You know: a discourse functional approach.* John Benjamins, Amsterdam.

Saville-Troike Muriel 1989 *The ethnography of communication.* Blackwell, Oxford.

Tannen Deborah 1981 New York Jewish conversational style. *International Journal of the Sociology of Language* 30: 133–49.

Tannen Deborah 1982 Ethnic style in male–female conversation. In Gumperz John (ed) *Language and social identity.* Cambridge University Press, Cambridge pp 217–31.

Tannen Deborah 1990 *You just don't understand: women and men in conversation.* William Morrow, New York.

Tannen Deborah 1992 Rethinking power and solidarity in gender and dominance. In Kramsch Claire, McConnell-Ginet Sally (eds) *Text and context: cross-disciplinary perspectives on language study.* D.C. Heath, Lexington, MA pp 135–47.

Thorne Barrie, Kramarae Cheris, Henley Nancy (eds) 1983 *Language, gender, and society.* Newbury House, Rowley, MA.

Trudgill Peter 1972 Sex, covert prestige and linguistic change in the urban British English of Norwich. *Language in Society* 1: 179–95.

4 *Floor management and power strategies in adolescent conversation*

Alice Greenwood

Introduction

When Penelope Eckert and Sally McConnell-Ginet call for grounding language and gender research in 'local communities of practice' (1992), their challenge is to move away from global generalizations and stereotyped conclusions about language and about gender. Actual instances of language use must be considered as part of a complex of interlinking cultural, social, political, psychological and linguistic systems. Earlier analytic categories, such as the unified, dichotomous notion of 'gender' and theoretical frameworks like the 'difference' and 'dominance' models (Thorne and Henley 1975, Thorne *et al.* 1983), have proved to be rigid and unyielding; such formulations are unable to account for the vast array of phenomena that occur when people, in all their diverse and fuzzy categorizations and situated in particular political climates, speak to each other. We need to develop a methodological and theoretical approach to issues of language and gender that allows for the integration of varied, complex, even disparate information.

Contemporary research has shown that gender is a fluid, dynamic and constructed notion, and not at all a self-evident or *a priori* designation (Cameron this volume). Our sense of ourselves as gendered beings occurs in varying degrees and is dependent on complicated social, psychological and interactive processes (Rhode 1990a). As research has become more sophisticated, we realize that we have to ask ourselves exactly which group of women is under investigation, in what circumstances are they speaking, in the role of what, in relation to whom, with what background, and so on. We have learned that attempting to extract something called a 'female style' (Lakoff 1975) from this mass of information leads to very overgeneralized, oversimplified, and finally distorted conclusions. Moreover, the social and linguistic occasions when gender displays and distinctions are not relevant are every bit as interesting and important as those which encourage distinction (Thorne 1990, Freed this volume).

Interruption

Just as the concept of gender has been enlarged and is now considered a highly complex social category, our understanding of what 'conversation' entails has also undergone change. Accordingly, descriptions and analyses of conversational strategies need to be modified. Examining a discourse function like interruption, for example, provides a good illustration of the kinds of complexities that should be addressed in any discussion of interactive conversation. As a discourse behaviour, interruption is especially intriguing because it is has been generally accepted as having a definite form – intruding into a speaker's turn space – and a particular function – taking away the conversational floor. Yet upon analysis, both definition and function have been shown to be highly inadequate representations of what actually occurs when people converse. Further, interruption has been associated with verbal enactments of power and dominance and with stereotyped gender distinctions (James and Clarke 1992).

Much early research in language and gender was driven by social and political concerns. The pervasive sexism of a patriarchal society was found to be enacted in the microcosm of daily conversations between women and men. Thus, when Zimmerman and West (1975) and others (Esposito 1979, West and Zimmerman 1983) found that men were violating women's speaking turns with inappropriate intrusions into their turn space, their conclusions (and their metaphors) felt entirely adequate and were satisfying to many researchers. Indeed there are many conversational situations where women feel bullied and insulted by men, and interruption, the wresting of conversational space, seemed a likely place to look for instances of domination and control. Yet defining interruption is not straightforward and requires the same acceptance of complexity as is necessary for definitions of gender or conversation.

For instance, the structural definition of interruption used by

Zimmerman and West is based on a particular model of conversation, the one-at-a-time turntaking framework developed by Sacks *et al.* (1974) that was assumed viable for all conversations. However, subsequent empirical research has shown that this turntaking model does not in fact account for all conversational exchanges. In friendly and casual speech, and among women in particular, the conversational floor may be managed by several speakers at once (Edelsky 1981); or, within a single conversation, there may be different kinds of floor management, single or multiple, depending on the subject and the emotional involvement of the participants (Coates 1989). Conversation, we have come to realize, is no more static and unidimensional than any other aspect of language use. In order to analyse conversation, and conversational events like interruption, we must take into account the size and kinds of groupings involved in the conversation, the relationship among the speakers, the topic of the talk, and the interactional goals of all the participants.

Interruption cannot be defined solely as a turntaking problem because interruption is often considered an instance of linguistic and social rudeness; and the notion of rudeness involves a violation of appropriate standards of behaviour. Such standards of behaviour are based on the rights speakers feel entitled to, and these may vary from one speech community to another and indeed from one conversational encounter to another within a speech community (Murray 1985). If interruption is defined as a violation of appropriate behaviour rather than simply of speaking turn, then it may be a complex psychological or social phenomenon and not a linguistic one at all (Bennett 1981, Tannen 1989). Beattie's (1981) examination of interruption in non-dyadic competitive groups of university tutorials, for example, illustrates that conversational strategies may differ according to the intentions and strategies individual speakers have, and may vary on the basis of self-presentation and social goals (see also Brown 1980). The complex interaction of social, linguistic, psychological, political and other factors that may be involved with interruption has yet to be identified. Clearly, though, simple formulations that declare that men interrupt women are inadequate and have to be rethought.

A recent review of the interruption literature (James and Clarke 1992) shows that there are no consistent findings across all situations and groupings as to the relationship between interruption, regardless of how it is defined, and power differentials among speakers. Nor is there any one-to-one correspondence between interruption styles and the gender of the speakers. Studies that investigate the social and personal characteristics of the interrupter (whatever definition is adopted) offer inconsistent and peculiar findings as well. There is research that shows that less intelligent speakers interrupt more than more intelligent speakers (Rim 1977); extroverts interrupt more than introverts, relaxed and independent women interrupt more than dependent and anxious women (Feldstein and Welkowitz 1978). Speakers who have a high need for social approval interrupt more than others (Natale *et al.* 1979); the more male-like a person's self-identity is, regardless of biological sex, the more overlaps in speech (Drass 1986). The more socially powerful a speaker, the more interruptions occur (West 1979); the less socially powerful a speaker, the more interruptions (Beattie 1981). Such contradictory findings belie the notion that there is a straightforward link between a linguistic form like simultaneous speech and either a social variable, such as gender or power, or a personality trait, like insecurity or independence. As frustrating as this may be, the task of defining and interpreting interruption forces us away from global generalizations and broad categorizations to careful examination of specific interactions.

Who holds the floor?

I use data from three conversations of a group of adolescents to illustrate how inadequate and misleading it can be to correlate a discourse strategy like interruption with specific social variables such as power and gender. Further, these data suggest an alternative model for interpreting variation in discourse behaviour, one based on the social psychological principles of group identification. Speech Accommodation Theory (Thakerar *et al.* 1982) describes how speakers may vary their discourse behaviour in accordance with their desire to signal allegiance to or divergence from other members of the group.

The following conversations are excerpted from a larger study of adolescent discourse styles (Greenwood 1989). Three siblings, Dara, her twin brother David, age 13, and Stephanie 11, were recorded over a period of months when they were having dinner with various friends. Although all the children involved knew they were being recorded, the tape recorder was out of sight and their conversation sounds unconstrained and natural. There were no adults present during these exchanges. Thus the same speakers were observed in almost identical situations. Some of these data have been cited (Tannen 1989, 1990) as illustrative of either non-hostile or non-domineering interruption styles. Yet an even more important aspect of this study is that it allows us to explore how individual speakers vary their conversational style, how conversational style defines power relations and friendship, and if and when gender is a salient feature in conversation (Freed and Greenwood 1996).

It may be tempting to use traditional stereotypes of gender styles in language to explain the variation of verbal behaviour seen in these conversations. Following the dominance model, we could say that Max in (I) is a conversational bully, who won't 'play' if he can't control the game. We might say that Stephanie in (II) is passive and compliant, and because she has been trained to wait her turn rather than aggressively claim it, she is acting like a typical girl. Following the difference model, we might say that in the all-female exchange (III), there was a much more inclusive and collaborative style than in the mixed-sex encounters. But neither of these theoretical frameworks accounts for the complexity of the verbal and social alliances and behaviours that are represented by these data. Dara dominates Stephanie in (II), although they are both female, and she aligns herself with Jihad. In (I), Max attempts to control the floor through interruption, and Dara won't allow it to happen; she is tenacious in her desire to have her verbal agenda completed. In (II), Dara invites Jihad to share control of the floor with her, at Stephanie's expense. In (III), all three girls manage the floor together, and although this conversation is full of simultaneous speech, there is no sense of dominance or rudeness. In each of these conversations, David, male, is extremely quiet and withdrawn, even when his friends are present.

In order to examine interruption and floor management strategies in this or any specific conversational context we need to allow definitions of appropriate conversational behaviour to evolve from *within* the situation. The members of the group should, if possible, be interviewed because speakers are capable of formulating and articulating their social and verbal goals. They can explain what they are doing when they talk, and what they are hoping to achieve socially in interactions. When I interviewed this group of young people about their social goals in the situations cited, they all said the same thing: they wanted to have fun, to laugh and make jokes and do silly routines, tell stories, etc. Other social situations, no doubt, have other social goals. Talk for this group in this situation is a medium of play, a way to entertain and amuse themselves

(Greenwood forthcoming). The children also reported that they wanted to feel liked and accepted and not be on their guard or worried about being judged by others in the group.

Adolescent speakers offer a largely unexplored and particularly rich field for analysis because their conversational needs are often explicitly and not very subtly expressed. For example, when they want each other's attention, they don't engage in tempting conversational openings; rather they repeatedly say, 'watch, look, watch, watch', and 'listen listen', until they are sure that they are being attended to. Or, when a joke is coming, they announce, 'this is soooo funny'. Similarly, when there is trouble or discomfort, they state it explicitly as well, as the first example shows.

As individual membership in the group changed, so did the discourse style of the three stable members. That these speakers varied their conversational strategies when they were speaking to different people is hardly a novel idea in sociolinguistics. Discourse strategies, like other linguistic forms, are context sensitive. What is less obvious and more in need of analysis is what motivated the style switch since the setting, formality, social agenda, etc., remained constant.

In this first excerpt (I) the three family members are having dinner with Max, a school friend of David's, who had only met Dara and Stephanie recently. Max, 14, is a year older than David and Dara, and much taller than the other three children. He is the only child of actor parents and has been performing on stage for several years; his speech style is unusually self-possessed and confident. The dinner table conversation, up to this point, has been somewhat strained; the children seem to be having trouble finding a comfortable subject. The following excerpt occurs about 5 minutes after the children have started dinner. They have been talking about the upcoming presidential election and Michael Dukakis. Max has been bragging that his family is 'best friends' with actress Olympia Dukakis. Dara changes the subject away from the Dukakis family and attempts to engage Max in a verbal routine which the family members think is funny. The joke involves unnatural voices, set dialogue, with a rapidly spoken tongue twister as the punchline. They signal the onset of the routine by the change from their ordinary speaking voice to an obvious 'play' one.[1]

(I)
    1 Dara: Betty what?
    2 Steph: ((in her Betty voice)): Betty Boop.

3 ((Steph giggles))
4 Dara: I hear Mrs Rosenblum.
5 Max: Sooooo?
6 Dara: Are you Betty?
7 Max: Do you know what, uh, whatever his name is Dukakasises.
8 Dara: But that's not half as important as who//
9 Max: [Katie
10 Dara: That's not half as important as uh who drop//ed out of
11 Max: [I know
        that too.
12 Dara: So why did you say 'more importantly'?
13 Max: Because it is more important.
14 Steph: To Dukakis maybe.
15 Max: I told you, they dropped out of the race. Who cares
        about them any more?
16 Dara: It's important to know who was in it.
17 Steph: It's more important to //Dukakis who's who
18 Max: [What? You're afraid I'm gonna
        vote for someone who dropped out or something.
19 Dara: ((screechy)): Nooo. I don't vote. I'm sorry. //I'm not
        eighteen yet but
20 Max: [You look it.
21 Dara: Ah. Thank you. That // is the highest compliment. I
        look more like it than
22 Max: [Yeah, actually.
23 Steph: There's a nice relation going between six and eighteen.
24 Dara: ((funny voice)): Yes. Six times three. Ya know and uh,
        uh
25 Dara: Stephanie, do it!
26 Max: **It used to be fun here. You guys didn't beat up on me.**
27 Dara: Stephanie, come on. **Before he gets mad at us.**
28 David: ((in a special voice of another routine)): Come on. Don't
        be such a stupid idiot.
29 Dara: Listen to this. Max, listen.
30 Dara: ((in Betty voice)): Stephanie, are you Betty?
31 Steph: I am not Betty.
32 Dara: Stephanie. Do it!
33 David: No. Come on. Do it, Steph.
34 Steph: You say to me: 'Stephanie, are you Betty?'
35 Dara: ((in Betty voice)): Ste- No. Are you Betty?
36 Steph: ((in Betty voice)): No.
37 Dara: Stephanie, do it.
38 Steph: No.
39 Dara: Come on.
40 Steph: No.

41 Dara : ((whining)): Stephanie.
42 David: It's so funny, Steph.
43 Dara: It's sooo funny. Listen.
44 Steph: All right. All right.
45 Dara: All right.
46 Dara: Watch this.
47 Max: Is it as funny as a
48 ((David laughs))
49 Dara: Our piano teacher is named Betty. She's an idiot. She's prim and proper. So I go ((in Betty voice)), Excuse me, are you Betty?
50 Steph: ((in a voice from another routine)): Yes.
51 Dara: Stephanie, don't talk like Clu.
52 Steph: Oh, yes.
53 Dara: ((in Betty voice)): Betty who?
54 Steph: ((in Betty voice)): Bettybitabitofbitterbutterbutter.
55 ((David, Dara, and Stephanie laugh))
56 Max: **Whaaaat?**
57 ((David, Dara and Stephanie laugh))
58 Dara: I said, Betty who, like you say Betty Cohen. Then she says, Bettybit//abitofbitter
59 David: [Did anyone eat from this yet?
60 Max: No. Actually, what I was going to say was can I try that soup? It looks quite good.
61 Dara: **Listen, listen, listen, listen.**
62 Max: Say it in slow motion, okay?
63 Steph: Betty bought a bit of bitter butter and she said this butter's bitter. If I put it in my batter, it will make my batter bitter. So Betty bought a bit of better butter //to
64 Dara: [You never heard that before?
65 Max: No. Never.
66 Dara: Max, seriously?
67 Max: Seriously.
68 Dara: It's like the fa//mous to-
69 Steph: [tongue twister.
70 Max: No. The famous tongue twister is: Pe//terpiperpicked pickeda
71 Dara: [Same thing. It's like that. It's like that one.
72 Max: **You keep interrupting me.**
73 Dara: It's like saying, it's like saying, Peter Who? Peter piper picked. ... It's like her last name.
74 Max: It doesn't make any sense at all.
75 Dara: It's funny.

76 Max: What is Peter? Who is anything?
77 ((David and Steph laugh))
78 Dara: Listen to this. We'll do it in slow motion. Come on.
           Watch.
79 ((David laughs))
80 Dara: David, shut up!
81 ((David laughs))
82 Max: Stephanie who?
83 Dara: Stephanie, just Stephanie.
84 ((Dara, David, and Stephanie laugh))
85 Dara: Stephanie is pretending to be our piano teacher, Betty,
           and I'm pretending to be someone who doesn't know
           her last name. So I say ((in Betty voice)): Excuse me.
           Are you Betty?
86 Steph: ((in Betty voice)): Yes.
87 Dara: ((in Betty voice)): Betty who?
88 Max: But if you don't know who she is, how are you asking
           her name?
89 Steph: Maybe I have a nameplate on me that says 'Betty'.
90 Max: Okay.
91 Dara: Okay. Watch.
92 Dara : ((in Betty voice)): Excuse me. Are you Betty?
93 Steph: ((in Betty voice)): Yeees.
94 Dara : ((in Betty voice)): Betty who?
95 Steph: It's no fun in slow motion.
96 David: It's not good in slow motion.
97 Dara: Okay. ((in Betty voice)): Are you Betty?
98 Steph: ((in Betty voice)): Yes.
99 Dara: ((in Betty voice)): Betty who?
100 Steph: ((in Betty voice)): Bettyboughtabitofbitterbutterbut
101 ((Dara laughs))
102 David: ((laughing)): I love it.
103 Dara: ((in Betty voice)): I thought you were Betty.
104 Steph: ((in Betty voice)): No. That's my sister.
105 ((pause))
106 Dara: **Do you get it?**
107 Max: ((fake loud laughter)) **Ha! Ha! Ha! Ha! Ha!**
108 ((Steph laughs))
109 David: **Max, you don't seem to be //enjoying**
110 Max: [Oh, it's real fun.

In this conversation, the three family members have trouble
engaging Max in their family routine. He ignores Dara's initial
attempt to enlist Stephanie in doing the joke (1–5) and takes the
floor and returns to a previous topic: 'Do you know what … ' (7).

From lines 8–22, Max, Dara and Stephanie speak about Max's topic. However, although the topic is of his choice, and not theirs, Max frequently interrupts both Dara and Stephanie; that is, he begins talking while they are speaking, in a non-supportive way:

```
 8 Dara:  But that's not half as important as who//
 9 Max:                              [Katie
10 Dara:  That's not half as important as uh who drop//ed out of
11 Max:                                         [I know
          that too.
...
17 Steph: It's more important to //Dukakis who's who
18 Max:                          [What? You're afraid I'm gonna
          vote for someone who dropped out or something.
19 Dara:  ((screechy)): Nooo. I don't vote. I'm sorry. //I'm not
          eighteen yet but
20 Max:                                      [You look it.
21 Dara:  Ah. Thank you. That // is the highest compliment. I look
          more like it than
22 Max:                       [Yeah, actually.
```

Neither Dara nor Stephanie protests his action, either explicitly or by pausing or through silence (in contrast to the findings of Zimmerman and West 1975). At line 25, Dara returns to her opening gambit, and asks Stephanie to 'do it'. Max's response to this is curious. He says that he feels attacked, 'beat up on' by the others; he implies that he is not happy, not having 'fun' when 'it used to be fun' being with them (26). Dara responds to what she senses as his anger and with more urgency implores Stephanie to do this routine 'before he gets mad at us' (27).

Although Dara and Stephanie proceed with the routine, Max is clearly not a good audience. His attention wanders; Dara says, 'Listen to this. Max, listen' (29). Stephanie is reluctant to continue and both David and Dara try to convince her to 'do it'.

```
32 Dara:  Stephanie. Do it!
33 David: No. Come on. Do it, Steph.
...
37 Dara:  Stephanie, do it.
...
39 Dara:  Come on.
```

and they both remind her that this is 'so funny' (42, 43). After the tongue twister is accomplished and the three family members are laughing, Max says 'what?' (56), not participating in the joke. Dara keeps trying to engage him, and Max continues to be a reluctant audience. He and David talk about the food. Dara, tenacious, again tries to get him to 'listen, listen, listen, listen' (61). When she tries to explain the humour, he denies that it is funny, saying, 'it doesn't make sense' (74).

When Dara interrupts Max for the first time to clarify what she means, he protests immediately and explicitly.

> 70 Max: No. The famous tongue twister is: Pe//terpiperpicked
>   pickeda
> 71 Dara: [Same thing. It's
>   like that. It's like that one.
> 72 Max: **You keep interrupting me.**

Max says that Dara 'keeps interrupting' (72) him. Through this protest Max signals that he feels his rights as a conversational interactant have somehow been violated, that he has not been allowed his conversational space. He feels continually interrupted ('keep'), although there has been no previous instance of a structural interruption; his talk turn has not been intruded on. By observing Max and his reaction to Dara, it is clear that Max's definition of interruption is something other than a simple turn-taking violation and is related to an inability to control the conversational floor. In some way, Max's interactional needs are not being addressed, and his protest at being interrupted may be his way of calling attention to the problem.

It has been widely accepted that successful communication depends on the shared interpretation of what is going on in a conversation (Gumperz 1982, Tannen 1990). But here we see that Max knows exactly what is going on. Two of the family members have announced to him that their routine is 'sooo funny' (42, 43, 75). When after repeated attempts to engage Max in the fun, Dara asks 'do you get it?' (106), Max says 'ha! ha! ha! ha! ha!' (107), signalling that he realizes that laughter is the goal. He knows what is being asked of him; he just refuses to join in the game with them.

This was an unsuccessful conversation and social interaction for all the participants involved. After this dinner, Dara said she didn't like Max at all; in fact, she said he was a 'rude pig', and David and Stephanie agreed. Max never asked to come over again and David and Max stopped being friends. Since there was no pre-existing antipathy among the children before this dinner, it was probably the verbal and social interaction that led to their subsequent social trouble.

The lack of success of this interaction cannot be explained by interpreting the problematic conversation in terms of different sub-cultural styles for girls and boys. In fact, the difference model of cross-sex misunderstandings (Maltz and Borker 1982) would have David and Max's style similar to each other and different from the girls'. The two boys were raised in the same neighbourhood, went to the same elementary school, played together after school, had sleepovers at each other's houses, etc. But in this instance family style is more salient than gender group style. Our social identities are constructed in many different arenas. Sometimes peer group is the most influential; other times not (Meyerhoff this volume).

The lack of success of this conversation arises because Max does not share the conversational goals of the other members of the group, or, alternatively, the other members of the group are unwill-ing to change their goal to accommodate his. However we frame the problem, Max and the others are unable to establish themselves as belonging to the same group. We see that Max is unwilling to participate in the family's desire to amuse him, although he clearly recognizes and understands what they are trying to accomplish. His separateness from them is underlined by his discourse style. Max interrupts Dara and Stephanie with no protest from either girl. By protesting when Dara interrupts him, he implies that they have unequal and non-reciprocal conversational rights and obligations to each other. The disparity of their rights, rather than his inter-ruptions, is unfriendly, in fact, rude, to Dara and the others. By holding himself apart and aloof, both in his lack of engagement in the subject and in his lack of reciprocity of style, he made himself an outsider.

Example (II) shows how a similar conversational situation can be interpreted by the same participants in an alternative way, resulting in a different social outcome. In this exchange the three family members are having dinner with another friend of David's, Jihad, 14. Like Max, Jihad and David are friends from school, but Jihad has been a very good friend to David for many years and has been at the children's home frequently. Both Dara and Stephanie know him well and like him very much. In the following conversational exchange, Stephanie cannot get control of the floor to pursue her conversational agenda and the others do not grant her reciprocal speaking rights. However, unlike Max, Stephanie does not separate herself from the rest of the group, either explicitly by not joining in the conversation or by her verbal style. When I interviewed her later, she said she had no sense of any conversational trouble or social conflict. We have to assume that, for Stephanie, floor control is not related to interruption or rudeness, at least not in this conversation.

(II)

1	Steph:	We were talking about recycling paper because we have this thing in our school about recycling paper.
2	Dara:	Ah!
3	Steph:	**[And]**
4	Jihad:	[So] does my mom.
5	David:	Really? Really?
6	Jihad:	Um hum.
7	Dara:	Oh, recycling. We put all our cans in one garbage and (x) of our boxes.
8	Jihad:	You do?
9	Dara:	You have to put all your tin or aluminum in one garbage can.
10	Steph:	**You know what? You know what?**
11	Jihad:	We throw it down the table and whatever can it goes to.
12	Dara:	Where do you sit?
13	Steph:	**Listen!**
14	Jihad:	At a long table at the end, so I just slide it down.
15	Dara:	It's at the door, right at the door. There's two yellow garbage cans.
16	Jihad:	But I don't do that.
17	Dara:	Oh, well, usually people don't have cans. Why was it so full of soda the other day? Were they selling soda? The whole thing was full of lots and lots of soda.
18	Jihad:	Maybe it's from a few weeks.
19	Dara:	Maybe it's from the teachers.
20	Steph:	**Well, anyway,** so he was telling us what we could put in it and what we couldn't and he said we could put tissues ((and she tells a long story)).

Stephanie introduces the topic of recycling on line 1 and is unable to develop it. When Jihad and Dara take over the floor, Stephanie is unable to reclaim it. She tries, asking, 'you know what? you know what?' (10) but is ignored by the others. She repeats her attempt, saying, 'listen' (13), but she is unsuccessful; no one attends to her and she withdraws from the talk until they grant her turn at line 20. She resumes, 'well anyway', and continues where she left off twenty lines earlier.

In this exchange Dara and Jihad assume that they have equal and
reciprocal conversational rights. They both ignore Stephanie and
speak to each other, building the topic together. Stephanie is not
granted equal rights to the floor by the others. She is unable to pursue her stated topic; they take it over. Nonetheless this dinner
conversation is evaluated as successful by all the participants,
including Stephanie.

These two excerpts illustrate that the relative success or lack of
success of a verbal interaction, from the point of view of the participants, has to do not only with a sense of equality of
conversational rights but also with the response of the individual to
the group. Holding oneself aloof and apart signals hostility, a lack
of identification with the group. Max held himself apart and was
thought unfriendly, even 'rude'. Stephanie, in contrast, passively
accepted the norms of the group and was felt to be part of it, not
out of it, even though she was treated unequally.

Excerpt (III) shows Dara and Stephanie in yet another interaction, this time with Dara's best friend Sarah, age 14. Sarah has been
involved with the family since the children were babies. She has
spent many nights sleeping over, eating with the family and joining
in their activities. This conversation illustrates the wide range of
discourse behaviour these girls have at their command. The following exchange takes place about 10 minutes into the dinner;
Stephanie has just spilled her carrots and peas on her lap. The conversation is full of laughter, singing, funny voices, caricatures of
other speakers, and extremely rapid and simultaneous and overlapping speech. All three girls are involved in playing with the pun
on 'pea/pee' which they find tremendously entertaining.

(III)
1 Steph: ((funny voice)): I don't appreciate this predicament.
2 Dara: She's got carrots in her crotch now.
3 Steph: (laughing)): Carrots.
4 Sarah: =I always have //carrots in MY
             crotch.
5 Steph: ((funny voice)):   [carrots in the
             crotch, ya know.
6 Sarah: =a bio//logical
7 Dara: [phenomenon.
8 Sarah: Yeah.
9 ((laughter))

```
10 Sarah:   Phenomenonenomenomenom//
11 Steph:                              [this looks
            really dis//gusting, doesn't it?
12 Sarah:                   [enomeneon
13 Dara:    ((singing)): [Stephanie went to the bathroom.
14 Sarah:   She went carrot. I have to carrot. Excuse me, but I have
            to go carrot.
15 Steph:   Oh yes, go 'head. Don't //mind us.
16 Dara:                            [eat every carrot and pee on your
            plate.
17 Sarah:   ((tapping her mouth)): Aaaaaaaaaah!
18 Steph:   Eat every carrot and pee on MY plate.
19 ((laughter))
20 Dara:    Eat all your carrots and //pee
21 Steph:                             [eat all the carrots on your plate
            and pee on my plate//
22 Dara:                              [eat all the carrots and pee on his
            plate.
```

The three girls are frequently intruding into each other's turns, which seems to be the way the fun is created. They are playing with the joke together. There is no protest, no sense of being 'beat up on' (as in (I)) or ignored, no pleas to 'listen' or calls for attention (as in (II)). Dara, Stephanie and Sarah are equally involved in collaboratively managing the floor and constructing the topic. They encourage each other in their silliness by each ratifying the game. They repeat each other's phrases and speak simultaneously. Dara and Stephanie accept Sarah's bathroom joke about the spilled carrots ('She went carrot. I have to carrot. Excuse me, but I have to go carrot' (14)) and contribute their own extension of the joke with a collaboration on the 'eat every carrot and pea [pee] on your plate' routine. In this interaction, unlike the previous two, Dara, Sarah and Stephanie have formed a single group, all with the same conversational rights and opportunities as the other.

Discussion

Comparing the discourse style of Dara and Stephanie across these three conversations reveals how dynamic and varied style can be for a single speaker, even in the same social context. Each of these interactions is independent from the others, and group identification for the individual members is very flexible. The specific social context and the salient group identification inform the language style of the speaker. For Dara, in (I), the family was her group. The three siblings functioned as the in-group to Max's 'other'. In (II), the in-group was the older age group, the three who were in the same grade. Stephanie, the younger, was the outsider. And in (III), no distinction was made between an in-group and an outsider or 'other', although there certainly might have been. Dara and Stephanie could have aligned as family members, or Dara and Sarah could have aligned as older, as indeed occurs in other situations with these same three speakers.

These three examples illustrate how a discourse strategy, like interruption, even within a single community of practice like this small group of adolescent friends at dinner, is best analyzed by looking both within and across several interactions. Using multiple conversations as data, we are able to get a sense of how a specific group interprets a particular strategy, as well as the variety in discourse repertoire available to individual speakers. Observing only one conversation might well lead to confusing a *particular* use of a discourse strategy, arising from the needs of a *specific* social context, with a speaker's so-called style. What interruption means and how it is used in the first conversation is quite different from the other two. It may well be that Dara at her most relaxed is a frequent simultaneous speaker, but when she feels less socially secure, as with Max, she is more careful about intruding into another's turn. After Max called her to account, she never interrupted him again. She understood that he considered interruption a conversational rudeness. Yet with Sarah, Dara's use of simultaneous speech was not thought rude by either girl, or even as an interruption. These girls share a reciprocal sense that joint control of the floor is friendly. With Sarah, Dara doesn't have to watch her conversational manners.

Explanations that depend on gender, particularly simple stereotyped formulations, are quite unhelpful here. We are forced to admit that not all interactions encourage gender distinctions; some situations actually mute them (Deax and Major 1990). How, then, can we understand and interpret the variation of style evinced in these examples? A useful and largely unexplored connection can be made between discourse style variation and speech accommodation theory (SAT), from the perspective of the social psychology of language (Giles and Robinson 1990). Social psychology relies on the premise that individual identity is composed of multiple group identifications and associations. A person is a member of a family, a neighborhood, a group of friends, with an economic, social and cultural background, etc. Depending on the social needs of a particular social encounter (and it should be remembered that conversation, especially friendly conversation, is a social encounter), an individual is identified with one group or another. Sociolinguistics has concentrated on establishing that variation occurs with some degree of predictability. SAT makes an attempt to go one step further and explores explanations for the underlying reasons of speech variation. Speech accommodation theory posits that when speakers want to signal solidarity and in-groupness, they will adopt a style similar to the members of the group they feel most allied with. And when they want to signal separateness and out-groupness, their style will move away from those members of the group with whom they want to contrast themselves. A convergence or divergence of speaking styles, then, can encode information about both an individual's psychological motivation and that individual's relationship to the group at the time of the specific encounter (Thakerar *et al.* 1982). The use of particular discourse strategies is thus seen as governed (even if unconsciously) by social, psychological and political factors.

In terms of SAT, friendliness would be signalled by a reciprocity of conversational rights and a convergence of discourse styles. Lack of friendliness would be marked by a divergence of style and a lack of reciprocity of conversational rights. In these examples, having fun, feeling liked, being friends, was the articulated social goal. In the first example, Max and Dara were unable to negotiate symmetrical speaking rights, as to topic and floor control, and rights of simultaneous speech. Each felt that the other was rude, and the result was that they were unable to interact in a friendly way. Neither of them would defer to the other. In the second example, Stephanie was unable to negotiate her rights, but Dara, Jihad and David signalled in-groupness with each other. Because Stephanie seemed to accept their norms and not challenge them, there was no overt conversational tension, and everyone thought it was a happy and successful exchange. They had fun being together. In the third example, both Stephanie and Dara participated in the conversation with equal and reciprocal rights, and again, the result was that they said they had a good time.

But more than friendship alliances are being negotiated and enacted in these conversations. Power and status positions are being defined as well. Speech accommodation theory is able to provide us with a useful theoretical model for defining dominance in conversation as well as friendship. If one person or group has its style accommodated to much more than another's – that is, sets the norm for the characteristics of the in-group style – that group is acknowledged as powerful by the other members of the interaction (Mulac et al. 1986). If, over many interactions with the same participants, an asymmetrical accommodation always occurs, we have an index with which to measure more or less dominant speech styles within the group (Bilous and Krauss 1988). We saw in example (II) that Stephanie seemed to acquiesce to the more powerful and controlling style of the older three kids. But in example (I), neither Max nor Dara would adopt the other's norms, and there was no consensus about status. The SAT model offers a principled way to understand how power, dominance, status and friendship are mutually constructed by all the members of a conversational group.

Conclusion

Enlarging the concepts of speech accommodation theory to encompass discussions of discourse variation enables us to link the psychological motivations and the social goals of speakers to specific discourse choices. Such a framework is much more appealing and explanatory than others that interpret conversation uniquely on the basis of power politics or cultural stereotypes. We need to give more respect to speakers' capacity to choose from among alternative forms, and need to understand the motives behind such choices. If we do not think of some speakers as passive conversational victims, then our analyses of conversational interaction will necessarily be more complex and informative.

Note

1. The transcription conventions used for these conversations are:

//	double slashes indicate point of interruption
(( ))	used for descriptions, not utterances
? , .	punctuation for intonation, not grammar
noooo	repeated vowel for elongation
[ ]	indicates simultaneous speech
(x)	indicates something was spoken but was unintelligible
=	indicates 'latched' speech; one speaker follows the previous one with no break

References

Beattie Geoffry W 1981 Interruption in conversational interaction and its relation to the sex and status of the interactants. *Linguistics* 19: 15–35.

Bennett Adrian 1981 Interruptions and the interpretation of conversation. *Discourse Processes* 4.2: 171–88.

Bilous Frances R, Krauss Robert M 1988 Dominance and accommodation in the conversational behaviours of same- and mixed-gender dyads. *Language and Communication* 8.3/4: 183–94.

Brown Penelope 1980 How and why are women more polite: some evidence from a Mayan community. In McConnell-Ginet Sally, Borker Ruth, Furman Nelly (eds) *Women and language in literature and society*. Praeger, New York pp 111–36.

Cameron Deborah this volume: The language-gender interface: challenging co-optation.

Coates Jennifer 1989 Gossip revisited: Language in all-female groups. In Coates Jennifer, Cameron Deborah (eds) *Women in their speech communities*. Longman, London and New York pp 94–122.

Deax Kay, Major Brenda 1990 A social-psychological model of gender. In Rhode Deborah L (ed) *Theoretical perspectives on sexual difference*. Yale University Press, New Haven pp 89–99.

Drass Kriss 1986 The effect of gender identity on conversation. *Social Psychological Quarterly* 49.4: 294–301.

Eckert Penelope, McConnell-Ginet Sally 1992 Think practically and look locally: language and gender as community-based practice. *Annual Review of Anthropology* 21: 461–90.

Edelsky Carole 1981 Who's got the floor? *Language in Society* 10: 383–421.

Esposito Anita 1979 Sex differences in children's conversation. *Language and Speech* 22: 213–20.

Feldstein Stanley, Welkowitz Joan 1978 A chronography of conversation: in defense of an objective approach. In Siegman Aron W, Feldstein Stanley (eds) *Nonverbal behavior and communication*. Lawrence Erlbaum, New Jersey pp 435–99.

Freed Alice F this volume: Language and gender research in an experimental setting.

Freed Alice F, Greenwood Alice 1996 Women, men and type of talk: what makes the difference? *Language in Society* 25.1: pp 1–26.

Giles Howard, Robinson W Peter (eds) 1990 *Handbook of language and social psychology*. John Wiley & Sons, Chichester.

Greenwood Alice 1989 *Discourse variation and social comfort: a study of topic initiation and interruption patterns in the dinner conversation of preadolescent children*. Unpublished PhD dissertation. City University of New York, New York.

Greenwood Alice forthcoming: Accommodating friends: niceness, meanness, and discourse norms. In Hoyle Susan, Adger Carolyn Temple (eds)

Language practices of older children. Oxford University Press, New York.

Gumperz John J 1982 *Discourse strategies*. Cambridge University Press, Cambridge.

James Deborah, Clarke Sandra 1992 Interruptions, gender, and power: a critical review of the literature. In Hall Kira, Bucholtz Mary, Moonwomon Birch *Locating power: proceedings of the second Berkeley Women and Language Conference*. Berkeley Women and Language Group, Berkeley CA pp 286–99.

Lakoff Robin 1975 *Language and woman's place*. Harper & Row, New York.

Maltz Daniel, Borker Ruth 1982 A cultural approach to male–female miscommunication. In Gumperz John J (ed) *Language and social identity*. Cambridge University Press, Cambridge pp 195–216.

Meyerhoff Miriam this volume: Dealing with gender identity as a sociolinguistic variable.

Mulac A T, Lundell L, Bradac J J 1986 Male–female language differences and attributional consequences in a public speaking situation: toward an explanation of the gender-linked language effect. *Communication Monographs* 53: 115–29.

Murray Stephen O 1985 Toward a model of members' methods for recognizing interruptions. *Language in Society* 14: 31–41.

Natale Michael, Entin Elliot, Jaffe Joseph 1979 Vocal interruptions in dyadic communication as a function of speech and social anxiety. *Journal of Personality and Social Psychology* 37: 865–78.

Rhode Deborah L 1990a Theoretical perspectives on sexual difference. In Rhode Deborah L (ed) pp 1–12.

Rhode Deborah L (ed) 1990b *Theoretical perspectives on sexual difference*. Yale University Press, New Haven.

Rim Y 1977 Personality variables and interruptions in small discussions. *European Journal of Social Psychology* 7: 247–51.

Sacks Harvey, Schegloff Emanuel, Jefferson Gail 1974 A simplest systematics for the organization of turn-taking for conversation. *Language* 50: 696–735.

Tannen Deborah 1989 Interpreting interruption in conversation. *Papers from the 25th annual meeting of the Chicago Linguistic Society*. University of Chicago, Chicago pp 266–87.

Tannen Deborah 1990 *You just don't understand: women and men in conversation*. William Morrow, New York.

Thakerar Jitendra, Giles Howard, Cheshire Jenny 1982 Psychological and linguistic parameters of speech accommodation theory. In Fraser Colin, Scherer Klaus (eds) *Advances in the social psychology of language*. Cambridge University Press, Cambridge pp 205–56.

Thorne Barrie 1990 Children and gender: constructions of difference. In Rhode Deborah L (ed) pp 100–13.

Thorne Barrie, Henley Nancy (eds) 1975 *Language and sex: difference and dominance*. Newbury House, Rowley, MA.

Thorne Barrie, Kramarae Cheris, Henley Nancy (eds) 1983 *Language, gender and society*. Newbury House, Rowley, MA.

West Candace 1979 Against our will: male interruptions of females in cross-sex conversations. In Orsanu Judith, Slater Mariam, Adler Leonore Loeb (eds) *Annals of the New York Academy of Science*. New York pp 81–97.

West Candace, Zimmerman Don H 1983 Small insults: a study of interruptions in cross-sex conversations between unacquainted persons. In Thorne Barrie, Kramarae Cheris, Henley Nancy (eds) pp 103–18.

Zimmerman Don H, West Candace 1975 Sex roles, interruptions and silences in conversation. In Thorne Barrie, Henley Nancy (eds) pp 105–29.

5 Women, men and prestige speech forms: a critical review

Deborah James

Introduction

One area of study in sociolinguistics has involved the extent to which one can correlate a person's sex with his or her use of linguistic variables.[1] A finding reported by a large number of studies is that men use linguistic features which are stigmatized or non-standard to a greater extent than women do. However, other studies have found no difference between the sexes in this respect, while still other studies have found the opposite pattern, in which women use stigmatized features to a greater extent than men do. Similar patterns have been found in communities in which more than one language is used and where one language has more prestige than the other. Men often use the less prestigious language to a greater extent than women do; however, the opposite pattern also occurs.

A variety of proposals have been made to account for the differences between women's and men's use of prestige speech. I will here review the major proposals and address the following questions: What is the state of the empirical evidence for each hypothesis? What are the strengths and weaknesses of each hypothesis? Are some factors likely to be relevant only in some communities and not others, and if so, what kinds of communities will these be? If two different factors which would tend to have opposite effects are both relevant in a single community, will one factor tend to outweigh the other, and, if so, which one and why? Further, are there ways of testing the validity of the hypotheses which have not been generally recognized or used by researchers?[2]

It has often been assumed in past variationist research that women and men each form one homogeneous group, sharing one common social agenda and that their speech behaviour can be explained by means of one or two simple generalizations. It will be emphasized in this review that any such assumptions are mistaken. Women's and men's speech choices are determined by the particular social conditions of the community in which they live; these conditions can vary greatly, and, correspondingly, people's motivations for speaking as they do can vary greatly. To understand people's speech choices, it is vital that we take into account the specific cultural settings and discourse contexts in which speech is used.

The proposals which have been made to account for sex differences in the use of prestige speech fall into two main groups. One group focuses on ways in which external economic and social factors can give rise to differences in the use of linguistic variants by women and men; the other group relates speech differences to the fact that women are granted less status and power than men. There are, in addition, various proposals which do not fall into either group. I will begin by looking at the hypotheses for which there is the clearest empirical evidence, that is, those which focus on the effects of external economic and social factors.

Exposure to prestige speech

In a community in which the native speech form is a low-prestige dialect or language, one sex may have more exposure in life than the other sex to standard speech forms or to a more prestigious language. In cases in which men have been found to use more standard speech variants or to use a prestige language more than women do, this has been the explanation most frequently provided. (See, for example, Diebold 1961, Queizán 1977, Nichols 1983 (for one of the two communities she studied), Bortoni-Ricardo 1985, Khan 1991, Knack 1991.) In these cases, women are often described as being more restricted to the private sphere and the immediate community while men regularly have wider social contacts outside the local community. However, in other cases it may be women who have wider social contacts and men who usually interact only with members of their own local speech community. Following the work of Nichols (1983), this factor has been generally accepted as one plausible explanation for why women's speech in working-class communities in the West has very frequently been found to be closer to the standard than men's; the typical jobs performed by working-class women and men differ in that women's jobs are more likely to put them in contact with middle-class people with more standard speech than men's jobs are. This would tend to influence women's speech and put subtle pressure on them to adapt their speech towards the standard. In addition, working-class women's jobs sometimes require a higher level of education than working-class men's jobs. For example, women might work as domestics in a middle-class home, sales clerks, nurses, or school-teachers, while men might work as miners, or as construction or shipyard workers. A classic piece of evidence that such economic factors are important is provided by Nichols (1983), who showed that different patterns of sex-related usage in three groups of speakers in two small South Carolina communities could be explained in terms of differences in the economic options open to women and men in each of the three groups. (I will refer to this hypothesis, after Cameron and Coates (1989), as the 'market forces' hypothesis.)

However, there is evidence that these economic factors can be outweighed in importance by other factors. For example, Holmquist (1985) found that young men in a Spanish village were exposed to standard Spanish more than young women because they often worked outside the community and because of their military service. Despite this, young women's speech was significantly more standard than men's. Also, Brouwer and van Hout (1992), in a study of upper-working-class and lower-middle-class speech in Amsterdam Dutch, examined the relationship between the extent to which an individual's job required or was associated with competence in the standard language and the extent to which that individual used standard variants. They did not find a statistically significant relationship between these, although they did find a non-significant trend in that direction. Clearly, more study is needed to determine how strong a correlation exists here.

Social networks

Another approach to accounting for sex differences in the use of prestige speech which also invokes economic factors is that involving the concept of social networks (originally proposed in Milroy 1980). According to this hypothesis, people who are highly integrated into their community and have all their ties and social relationships within it (and thus belong to 'close-knit' or 'strong' social networks) are more likely to use non-standard local variants. Strong social networks create in their members a strong sense of solidarity and loyalty to that community, and local non-standard speech features function as important symbols of membership in the community. Thus, for example, in working-class communities in the West, it has been argued that men typically belong to closer-knit networks than women do because they are more likely to work in groups with other men from the same community (as miners, construction workers, etc.). Women are more likely either to work at jobs in which they are not with many other people from the same community, or not to work outside the home at all, thus again tending to spend less time with other community members. Therefore, the use of local speech features is more strongly rein-forced for men than for women and this might explain why many studies have found men's speech to contain more non-standard local variants than women's. However, economic conditions and employment opportunities can vary from one community to another, so that in some cases men and women might have equally strong networks, or women might have stronger networks than men; it is predicted that, in the former case, women's and men's speech will not differ with respect to the use of standard variants, and, in the latter case, women will use fewer standard variants than men.

Social network theory is of course related to the market forces hypothesis insofar as both proposals involve the idea that the more time you spend interacting only with people from your own local community, the greater the amount of local, non-standard features you will use in your speech. However, the two proposals do not necessarily simply represent different sides of the same coin. If members of one sex tend to have employment which takes them outside the immediate community (with the result that they have less close-knit social networks than members of the other sex), this does not automatically mean that they will have more exposure to standard speech. The exposure could be to another non-standard dialect. This is a common situation, for example, in Newfoundland (Sandra Clarke, personal communication).

The best-known evidence for the relevance of social networks is provided in the work of Milroy (1980), who shows that sex differ-ences in standardness vary in different parts of Belfast according to the relative degrees of social network strength of women and men, as influenced by economic conditions such as greater amounts of male unemployment in some parts of the city as compared to others. Other studies have also provided support for the social networks hypothesis. For example, Thomas (1989) found that older women in a Welsh village had the strongest social networks and also the highest rate of a local non-standard speech feature. Lanari and Clarke (1993) found that in Burin, Newfoundland, working-class women had stronger social networks than working-class men and correspondingly used one local speech feature significantly more, while exactly the opposite pattern appeared in the case of (younger) middle-class women and men. Cheshire (1982) found that 16-year-old boys in Reading had stronger social networks and correspondingly more non-standard speech than girls. Salami (1991) found that there was no difference between men and women in network strength in Ife-Ife, Nigeria, and correspondingly no difference in amount of speech features which could properly be considered standard. The reliability of the results in this research depends, of course, on how adequate the criteria used for determining network strength are in the particular study. Milroy's original criteria have been criticized (Cameron and Coates 1989, Coates 1993) on the grounds that they are biased towards males. However, in recent research there has been increasing flexibility in defining the criteria used to determine network strength, taking into account what is relevant for the particular social group being studied. In any case, it seems clear that the social networks approach, together with the market forces approach, can provide insights into sex differences in the use of prestige speech.

However, as we noted in the case of market forces, other factors appear able to outweigh the influence of social networks. For example, in the well-known work of Gal (1978, 1979) in a village in Austria, young men and young women of the Hungarian-speaking peasant class did not differ in type of social network, but young women used German, the prestige language, significantly more than young men; and Larson (1982: 404) reports that, in two Norwegian villages, males and females had 'similar social network morphology' but that women's speech nevertheless contained a greater percentage of standard forms. Similarly, V. Edwards (1989) found that women in a black community in Dudley, England, had weaker networks than men but that women's speech did not, as the hypothesis would predict, contain more standard variants. It is evident, then, that the market forces and social networks approaches do not provide a full explanation for sex differences in the use of overtly prestigious versus stigmatized speech. I will now turn, therefore, to other factors which may be important.

Relative power and language loyalty

I will begin with a factor which can be important in working-class and rural peasant communities and which appears able to outweigh the influence of market forces and social networks factors. This phenomenon, first discussed in Gal's work (1978, 1979), can be summarized as follows. Even when women's social networks are just as closely-knit as men's, in some working-class and rural peasant communities, women may have good reason to feel less loyalty to the traditional culture and lifestyle of their community than men do. In the Austrian village studied by Gal, for example, following a traditional lifestyle offered more attractions for men than for women; the reason for this had simply to do with the fact that men had more status and power than women. For example, men, as poor peasant farmers, could feel that they were independent and did not have to take orders from anyone; women had to work extremely hard and for many more hours than their husbands, but without this advantage. The community was in the process of social change, and it was a realistic possibility that women could attain a significantly better way of life by marrying into the German-speaking urban middle class. Thus, young women had less motivation than men to use Hungarian, the community language. By using German in a wider variety of circumstances than men, young women were choosing not to present themselves as peasants and were taking a practical step towards achieving connections with the middle-class German-speaking community. Similarly, Holmquist (1985), as noted earlier, points out that the market forces approach would predict that young men would use more standard speech variants than young women in the Spanish village he studied. However, he found that young women actually used more standard speech and argues that this is as a result of the same type of factor as described by Gal. Similar explanations have been proposed by Swigart (1992) for one group of speakers in Dakar, Senegal; in part by Hill (1987) for a group of Amerindian communities in Mexico; and by Jabeur (1987) for Rades, Tunisia. It has also been argued that the speech behaviour of post-first-generation immigrant women, as compared to men, in the USA and Australia can be explained in similar terms (Buxó Rey 1978, Pauwels 1987). Thus, it seems to be a not uncommon phenomenon for women to adopt prestige speech more than men as part of a shift in cultural loyalty resulting from the fact that women, to a far more marked extent than men, will receive more respect and have a better life in the aimed-at speech community than in their community of origin.

The question then arises: In what kinds of communities will working-class or peasant women be motivated to move away from local speech forms for these reasons? A plausible hypothesis is that this pattern of language use will be most likely to arise when a significant amount of social change is in progress, and when women believe that there is a realistic chance that they will be able to better their lot in life by moving out of their own immediate community.

It is also important to note that this same type of factor may sometimes have exactly the opposite effect on men's and women's speech; that is, it may cause women to use stigmatized speech forms to a greater extent than men, depending on the community. For example, Herbert (1992) shows that among the Thonga people in South Africa, women are much more respected and have much more power in traditional Thonga culture than in the dominating Zulu culture. Men, however, can improve their status if they speak Zulu and assimilate to Zulu culture; this is particularly important in seeking work in the mines and the cities, since the Thonga as a group have low status. Thus, even though both sexes are thoroughly exposed to Zulu, women use the language much less than men do and, Herbert argues, women deliberately speak Zulu much less well than men do. For Thonga women, using the Thonga language, even though it is more stigmatized than Zulu outside of the community, represents a form of resistance to the loss of power and respect which, for them, is associated with Zulu. A similar example is provided by Aikio (1992). Before World War II, women of the indigenous Sámi people in northern Finland retained the Sámi language and resisted the more prestigious Finnish to a much greater extent than men; Aikio argues that this is related to the fact that Sámi women had a much stronger economic position and much more independence than was the case for Finnish women. This traditional high status for women began to break down and change during (and as a result of) World War II; at that point, women began to accept Finnish to a much greater extent.

It is evident, then, that the degree to which women have power and receive respect and thus have a good life in their own local community, as opposed to another higher status community into which they have the possibility of assimilating, can affect their use of language. This hypothesis helps to account for some cases which are not adequately explained by the market forces or social networks hypotheses. However, we have still not accounted for all the cases in which women's and men's speech differs with respect to the use of overtly prestigious versus stigmatized speech. For one thing, the results of some studies are not readily susceptible to explanation along any of the lines so far discussed. In addition, there is a more general problem: all of these hypotheses primarily explain sex differences in speech for working-class and rural communities. What about the middle classes? The most common finding for the middle classes has also been that men's speech tends to be less standard than women's. But with respect to the market forces approach, middle-class women's and men's jobs do not generally differ, as do working-class women's and men's jobs, with regard to the extent to which they require or cause the jobholder to be exposed to standard language. With respect to the social networks approach (since economic conditions are different), middle-class women and men would not be likely to differ in network strength in the way working-class women and men arguably do. Thus, it seems likely that factors other than these may be involved in accounting for female and male speech differences in the middle classes.

Let us now turn, then, to other explanations which have been proposed for such differences. So far, I have focused on hypotheses involving external economic and social factors; the last hypothesis also emphasized the effects of the fact that women are usually granted less respect and influence than men. We will now look at other hypotheses which attach central importance to the effects of such power differentials.

Securing social status

The most commonly cited explanation in the history of research in this area is that originally put forward by Trudgill (1972). Trudgill suggested that since women's social status is less secure than and subordinate to men's, and because women are more likely than men to be evaluated by their appearance than men (whereas men are more commonly evaluated in terms of their occupational status and earning power), women are more likely to make use of overtly prestigious speech forms as a means of securing and signalling social status. This proposal has been widely criticized in the recent language and gender literature. A major problem with it is that it makes the prediction that in all communities in which these social conditions hold, which means virtually all communities, women will be found to use more prestigious speech forms than men. This is, of course, not the case. It also incorrectly assumes that all women in these communities share the same social goals, and in particular that all women focus their aspirations on appearing to be of a higher socioeconomic class. In these respects it differs from the proposals discussed in the three previous sections, all of which emphasize the importance of studying speech in specific social contexts and all of which recognize that women's (and men's) speech reflects different agendas in different settings.

A further problem for Trudgill's hypothesis involves the following: this hypothesis reflects the underlying assumption common in traditional quantitative sociolinguistic studies that socioeconomic class is a more fundamental variable than sex, and that sex differences in usage can best be explained in terms of class. Assuming this for the moment to be correct (I will come back to this point immediately below), it is important that the assignment of women and men to a particular socioeconomic class be methodologically accurate. Various writers, however (e.g., Cameron 1992, Cameron and Coates 1989), have noted that the assignment of women to social class may often not have been accurate, in particular with respect to the upper working and lower middle class. (As noted in Labov (1991), sex differences in standardness do tend to be greatest in these types of communities; thus, particular attention has often been paid to this group.) In many studies, married women have been automatically assigned to the same socioeconomic class as their husbands; however, if they are assigned to a class on the basis of their own individual characteristics, then for the reasons discussed earlier, the typical occupations and education of women married to (upper) working-class men may often place them in a higher social class than their husbands, namely, in the lower middle class. It has been assumed in many studies, in line with Trudgill's hypothesis, that the common pattern by which women in this social group tend to use a greater number of standard variants than their husbands represents an attempt on women's part to try to sound as if they belonged to a higher social class than they do. However, of course, if the women in question are in fact best analysed as belonging to the lower middle class, then they are simply speaking in the way which is normal for their class. A further objection to the assumptions underlying Trudgill's hypothesis is that the speech of males rather than females in a particular class is taken as the norm for that class.

In addition, a more general objection to this approach to explaining sex differences in standardness lies in the fact that there is now considerable evidence that socioeconomic class is not necessarily a more basic variable than sex or gender (Milroy 1992, Horvath 1985). It is often misguided, and far too limiting, to attempt to explain such differences in usage solely in terms of social class. With respect to the types of community just mentioned (i.e. those Western communities in which, on the basis of occupation and education, women would tend to be classified as lower middle class and men as upper working class), the market forces and social networks hypotheses, as discussed earlier, help to provide far more satisfying explanations for the common pattern that women's speech is closer to the standard than any explanation which tries to account for this pattern purely in terms of social class norms.

A note might also be made at this point about the proposal of Labov (1991). Labov suggests that the reason why sex differences in standardness tend to be greater in this type of community than in those involving other social classes is that women in this type of community are especially likely to be more socially ambitious than men. Here again, he is explaining sex differences in terms of social class. Labov comments: ' ... in the U.S., the forces behind [this phenomenon] are associated with upward mobility' (p. 244). 'Women in this group ... frequently have considerably more political and economic power than working-class or lower-class women. Moreover, they frequently make more money and have more opportunity than their upper-working-class male partners' (p. 226). Considering the fact that many lower-middle-class jobs typically held by women pay significantly less than many unionized blue-collar jobs held by men, this last claim that women in this group frequently make more money than their husbands seems questionable. The suggestion that women in this group tend to be relatively powerful *vis-à-vis* their husbands is, I would argue, also highly questionable. I would suggest, again, that the market forces and social networks hypotheses provide much more satisfactory approaches to explaining sex differences in linguistic usage in these types of community than social class.

It is evident then that there are a number of problems with Trudgill's hypothesis that women, because of their subordinate position, are more likely than men to use prestige speech to signal and secure social status. However, the possibility remains that elements of this hypothesis may be correct at least for some women and men in some communities. Eckert (1989) has proposed an explanation for sex differences in the use of prestige versus stigmatized speech which incorporates some features of Trudgill's hypothesis; I will now turn to this proposal.

Gaining respect and influence through standard or non-standard speech

Eckert (1989) argues that while both women and men want others to respect them and want to be able to influence others, women, because they have less power, cannot as easily attain respect and influence in ways that men can, that is through acquiring goods and status in the public world. As a result women, to a much greater extent than men, are obliged to use symbolic means, including language, as a way of presenting an image of themselves as individuals worthy of respect. One way in which it can be appropriate for women to do this in some settings is by increasing their use of standard language features. Studies show that individuals with standard speech are generally perceived to be more intellectually competent and able than those with non-standard speech (e.g. Bourhis *et al.* 1975, J. Edwards 1982).

However, this is not the only way in which women can use language symbolically to attain respect, and Eckert does not aim to account only for cases in which women use more standard speech than men. Thus, her proposal differs from those of Trudgill and Labov in that for Eckert, women's more frequent tendency to use language for symbolic purposes may manifest itself in different forms in different speech communities and in different contexts, and may have outcomes other than increased use of standard speech; nor does Eckert assume that all women have a common social agenda focusing on improving their standing in the socioeconomic hierarchy. She argues instead that gaining respect and influence involves asserting one's membership in all the social groups to which one belongs. Since non-standard features can be symbols of group identity, this can also lead to greater use of non-standard speech on the part of women as compared to men. Eckert thus predicts that women in two opposed social groups will often differ from each other in their use of linguistic variants to a more extreme extent than men, and she provides some evidence for this from her work among adolescents in a Detroit high school. She shows that with respect to the use of two variables involved in the process of sound change, girls belonging to the 'Burnout' category (a primarily working-class group who rebel against the authority represented by the school) differed in their speech from girls belonging to the 'Jock' category (a primarily middle-class group who embrace the school as the locus of their social activities and identities) to a significantly greater extent than was the case with

Burnout and Jock boys. Of particular relevance here is the fact that this entailed greater use of non-standard variants on the part of Burnout girls than would otherwise be predicted.

I am not familiar with any other data which would help test the validity of the hypothesis that social category differences will tend to be greater among females than among males; this remains a task for future research. It is also not entirely clear what other predictions are implied by the proposal that women are obliged to use symbolic means more than men to assert their membership in all the social groups to which they belong. For example, would this mean that having a strong sense of identity with one's local community, through having close-knit social networks, should tend to have a stronger effect on women's speech than on men's, so that women would produce more non-standard speech than men with equally close-knit networks? I know of no evidence that this is the case.

Here I will address further scrutiny to just one aspect of Eckert's hypothesis, namely the proposal that women may sometimes use standard speech features as a strategy to present themselves as individuals worthy of 'respect and authority. Although additional empirical evidence providing clear support for this proposal is difficult to find, no other plausible explanation appears available for one aspect of a study of two villages in Norway by Larson (1982). Larson's methodology is striking in that she took into account how language is used in discourse, something very rarely done in variationist studies. Recording natural conversation, she found that women's speech contained on the average a larger number of standard variants than men's speech. What was of particular interest, however, was that women were most likely to use standard speech features in one specific type of discourse context, namely when they were trying to influence someone else's behaviour, e.g. trying to get them to do something or trying to persuade them to believe something so that they would subsequently adopt some particular course of action. Men rarely used standard speech in this way. Larson notes that it is not generally sanctioned in Norway for women to use strongly assertive speech, citing research showing that Norwegian women display a general reluctance to give commands. A message delivered in standard Norwegian, however, implies that the speaker is conveying general information as a public representative rather than as an individual, making one's statements sound more authoritative. It is difficult to think of a plausible explanation for the behaviour of the women in this community other than that they were using standard speech as an indirect device for making their speech sound more authoritative and thus for increasing their degree of social control over others. Larson's findings provide some genuine support for the hypothesis that women in at least some communities use standard language as a strategy for gaining more respect and influence.

However, the fact that studies of a number of communities have found no difference between women and men in standard speech features, or have found women's speech to be less standard than men's, suggests that women do not use standard language as a strategy to gain respect and influence in all communities, and indeed there is no reason to suppose that they would. This then raises the question: In what kinds of communities would women be likely to use standard language in this way? For example, one might hypothesize that the extent to which women use standard language as a strategy for gaining respect would be inversely related to their level of participation in public life in a community, that is, to their ability to gain respect and influence in more direct ways. Thus, in communities such as those described by Salami (1991) in Nigeria and Escure (1991) in Belize, where women have a high level of participation in public and economic life, one might predict that women would not use standard speech forms as a strategy for gaining respect, and indeed neither of these studies found any significant sex difference in the use of standard speech features.

Clearly, there are various potential avenues for future research here, and it is strongly recommended that future researchers examine the use of language in different discourse contexts, after the model provided by Larson, if we are to attain more accurate insights into why women and men choose to use the speech forms that they do. Larson's work illustrates the crucial importance of examining language as it is used in real situated contexts.

Power and politeness

Another proposal which also views the power differential between women and men as an important underlying causal factor giving rise to differences in the use of standard speech is that of Deuchar (1989). This proposal aims to explain why women's speech would tend to be more standard than men's. Making use of Brown and Levinson's (1978) theory of politeness, Deuchar notes that relatively powerless individuals are expected to pay more attention to the 'face' – i.e. 'the public self-image that every [person] wants to claim for himself' (Brown and Levinson 1978: 61) – of more power-ful addressees (i.e. to be more polite to them) than is the case if speaker and addressee are reversed. Many acts of politeness dam-age the speaker's face (e.g. apologizing involves admitting that one has done something wrong); at the same time, saying or doing things which protect one's own face may involve threatening the addressee's face (examples would be boasting or using very assertive, forceful speech). However, Deuchar argues, 'the use of standard speech, with its connotations of prestige, [is] suitable for protecting the face of a relatively powerless speaker without attack-ing that of the addressee' (p. 31). This is related to Eckert's idea that using standard speech features can provide a way for women to present themselves as people who deserve respect; both accounts suggest that women are obliged to fall back on symbolic means such as standard language use in order to present themselves in a positive light, and both accounts attribute this to women's having less power than men. However, while Eckert focuses on the idea that women cannot attain respect and influence by their achieve-ments, possessions and institutional status as easily as men can, and for this reason must fall back on symbolic means, Deuchar focuses instead on the idea that women are less free than men to use face-threatening verbal strategies such as assertive, forceful speech as a means of gaining respect; this is presented as the reason why they must fall back on symbolic means. (Of course, both fac-tors could be relevant.)

Crucial to Deuchar's proposal is the idea that the use of standard speech features does not threaten the face of the addressee. Indeed, when speaking to someone with relatively more standard speech than one's own, to increase one's use of standard variants would constitute upward convergence (Giles and Powesland 1975), which is a form of positive politeness in that it represents an attempt to appear more similar to the addressee. Trying to appear similar to the addressee is a basic politeness strategy for addressing their 'pos-itive face', that is, their need to be thought well of (Brown and Levinson 1978).[3]

There is, however, one important limitation to this proposal. Deuchar's hypothesis provides a plausible explanation for findings in which women use more standard variants than men when being interviewed by a standard-speaking researcher, which constitutes the most common type of methodology in variationist studies. However, women's speech has also often been found to be more standard than men's when everyday talk with family and friends has been recorded; for example, this was the case in Larson (1982), in which talk was recorded with no researcher present, in Cheshire (1982), in which adolescents were recorded interacting during long-term participant observation, and in Lanari and Clarke (1993), in which a fellow community member who spoke the same dialect conducted the interviews.[4] When the addressee is another community member whose speech is relatively non-standard, the use of more standard speech would constitute divergence rather than convergence (Giles and Powesland 1975); this could be interpreted as an attempt to appear different from and 'better than' the addressee, which would be threatening to the addressee's face. Thus, Deuchar's hypothesis that the use of standard speech does not threaten and may in fact protect the face of the addressee only seems plausible as an explanation for the findings of studies in which the methodology involved interviews conducted by a standard speaker.

However, given this limitation, it is quite plausible that Deuchar's hypothesis might be valid for at least some communities; that is, it is quite possible that women might converge in speech towards a more standard-speaking addressee to a greater extent than men do for reasons having to do with politeness and the status differential between the sexes. The idea that women tend to pay more attention to the addressee's positive face than men receives support from a variety of studies of conversational behaviour in different communities, involving such phenomena as back channel responses, simultaneous talk to show interest and support, facilitative tag questions, etc. (Coates 1993, Holmes 1993, James and Clarke 1993). Thus, it is a plausible prediction that women in these communities might also be more likely than men to use upwards convergence in speech as a form of positive politeness when talking to a standard speaker. Nevertheless, I know of no conclusive empirical evidence that this functions as a factor, and it is not clear what would constitute such evidence. One might initially suppose that a pattern in which women style-shift to a more extreme extent than men do constitutes evidence that Deuchar's hypothesis is valid for a given community, since her hypothesis would certainly predict this pattern. Indeed, this has been a common finding in some studies (e.g. Russell 1982, Eisikovits 1987), although studies of other communities have found no difference, or have even found more style-shifting towards the standard by men (e.g. Khan 1991). However, such a pattern could also plausibly be produced by various other factors discussed in this chapter, so it does not constitute conclusive support for Deuchar's hypothesis.

Also, facts such as those reported by Keenan (1974) for Madagascar reveal that if politeness does function as a factor, it would certainly be a factor only in some communities and not others; in rural Madagascar, it is men rather than women who are the 'experts' at polite communication. Women express anger and criticism more directly than men, and are considered to be too unskilled at talk to master the intricacies of politeness. Further, there have been various studies in which subjects were interviewed by a standard speaker but women's speech was not found to be more standard than men's, e.g. Thomas (1989), Khan (1991), Rickford (1991), Salami (1991). We can conclude that either women in these speech communities did not practice speech convergence more than men, or alternatively, any tendency which might have otherwise existed in this direction was outweighed and nullified by other factors. For example, women had less exposure to the standard than men in Khan's study, and women had stronger social networks than men in Thomas's study; in both cases women's speech was less standard than men's.

Non-standard speech and masculinity

The last three proposals about male and female speech differences posited that women use special linguistic strategies which men do not need to use. Another frequently mentioned hypothesis in the literature, originally suggested in Labov (1966) and Trudgill (1972), claims, by contrast, that men may use language for symbolic purposes in a way which women do not. The claim is that men may choose to favour non-standard speech because this has connotations of flouting authority and showing independence, notions that are central to the traditional gender construction of masculinity. Working-class men, it is suggested, are stereotypically seen as 'tough, rough and break[ing] the rules' (Chambers and Trudgill 1980: 98), and non-standard working-class speech is thus seen as more 'masculine' than standard speech. The traditional gender construction of femininity, by contrast, encourages the acceptance of authority and conforming to rules for 'correct' speech and behaviour.

There is a fair amount of evidence that, in some communities, people do tend to associate non-standard speech with being male and standard speech with being female. This association has shown up in tests of language attitudes in a variety of studies. For example, Brouwer (1989) found that male speakers of non-standard Dutch in Amsterdam were judged from tape-recordings to be more suitable for a masculine role in a film, while the same men speaking standard Dutch were judged to be more suitable for a feminine role. J. Edwards (1979) found that adults in Dublin, when asked to judge the sex of a child based only on a tape-recording of the child's speech, tended to think that boys with standard speech were girls, and that girls with non-standard speech were boys. They also rated non-standard speech higher on a scale of masculinity than standard speech. Similarly, Elyan *et al.* (1978) found that people in Bristol rated tape-recorded women speaking with standard accents as being more feminine than the same women speaking with non-standard accents. There is also evidence from subject attitude tests that in some communities, men have a more positive attitude towards non-standard speech than women do; for example, this has been found by Brouwer (1989) for Amsterdam and by Kalmar *et al.* (1987) for Guangzhou, China, and one can infer it from Trudgill's (1972) findings of male so-called 'under-reporting' in Norwich. However, is the reason for this indeed what has been claimed, i.e. that non-standard speech has specific connotations for males of flouting authority and showing independence? As in the case of Eckert's and Deuchar's hypotheses, it is difficult to find empirical data that would weigh here, and I know of no absolutely conclusive evidence that non-standard speech has such connotations. However, there is one study for which this does seem the most plausible explanation. Eisikovits (1987) compared the speech of working-class adolescents in Sydney, Australia, when talking to a close friend of the same age and when talking to a middle-class adult female interviewer. While the girls' speech converged towards that of the interviewer, containing more standard features than when talking to a peer, the boys' speech did the opposite; of particular interest is the fact that the boys actually used a significantly *greater* number of stigmatized features when they were talking to the interviewer than they did when talking to a peer. It seems clear that the use of strongly non-standard speech symbolized for the boys a display of their refusal to accept the values and authority represented by the interviewer. (This is also the interpretation which would be provided by Giles' and Powesland's theory of interpersonal speech accommodation (1975).) Support for this interpretation is also provided by the fact that the boys' most common theme in talking to the interviewer was stories about their conflict with police, teachers and parents; Eisikovits notes that they typically spoke 'with defiance and bravado' (1987: 56). Similar behaviour on the part of men, but not women, has also been noted in the case of speakers on the island of Ocracoke off North Carolina; men used as many non-standard variants as possible when being interviewed, including forms which were in fact native to adjacent dialects and which they did not use in their normal vernacular speech (Natalie Schilling-Estes, personal communication).

Thus, we have reasonably plausible evidence that, at least in some communities, males tend to associate non-standard speech with flouting authority and expressing independence. In what kinds of communities, then, are males likely to make that association? It is obvious that it is not universally done, since, as we have seen, there are a number of cases in which men's speech has not been found to be more non-standard than women's, and also since not all studies of language attitudes have found men to have a more positive attitude towards non-standard speech than women (e.g. Clarke 1985, for St John's, Newfoundland). Future studies of language attitudes, and research methodology similar to that of Eisikovits (1987), may be helpful in answering this question.

Gender display

It was mentioned above that there is a fair amount of evidence that, in some communities, people tend to associate non-standard speech with being male and standard speech with being female. Another possible explanation for these findings is that attitudes of this kind may well arise as a consequence, rather than a cause, of sex differences in language use. Once a difference has become established in the use of standard vs non-standard variants by women and men, whatever the original reason or reasons for the difference (whether related to market forces or social networks or any other factor), children learning the language are likely to pick up on this difference. Both children and adults are generally very aware of 'gender-appropriate' behaviour, and will try to conform in their behaviour to how they see other members of their own group behaving. Thus, for example, in communities in which men use less-standard speech variants than women, children may simply perceive more non-standard speech as gender-appropriate behaviour for males, and more standard speech as gender-appropriate behaviour for females. These language patterns become part of the social construction of gender, and in this way, existing gender differences become perpetuated and even exaggerated. That this can happen with language behaviour is illustrated by work such as that of Mattingly (1966), who found that the separation between male and female distributions for some vowel formants was much sharper than variation in individual vocal tract size could reasonably explain; he suggests that these differences result from men and women exaggerating the formants in order to speak in a gender-appropriate manner. The development by which speech forms come to be seen as markers of gender identity can also explain why in some cases, the use of one variant rather than another can come to be more strongly associated with sex (or with gender) than with social class or any other social factor (Romaine 1978, Horvath 1985, Milroy 1992). In addition, the fact that it is often important to signal *both* gender identity *and* social class or ethnic group identity through one's speech can help explain why in some cases different variables come to function as crucial symbols of social class or ethnic group identity for each sex (e.g. Cheshire 1982, Schatz 1986, Salami 1991).

Once a particular type of speech has come to be seen as a marker of gender identity, this can be a contributing factor in the development of stereotyped beliefs about the sexes, and particularly about women, since male speech is typically taken as the norm. These beliefs can then serve to further reinforce existing speech patterns. One example is provided by Swigart (1992). In Dakar, Senegal, with the exception of one small group of young women who behave like the women in Gal's (1978) Austrian study, women speak the local language, Wolof, significantly more than men do, and speak it with significantly less influence from the prestige language, French. The original reason for this difference appears to be that, in the past, women were more restricted to the private sphere and had less education than men and less exposure to French. However, the Dakarois now claim that these speech differences simply reflect 'natural' behaviour; women are viewed as the natural transmitters and preservers of traditional culture and as more deeply culturally rooted than men.[5] As a result, there is considerable pressure on women to live up to this role by downplaying their knowledge of French or any other language, and by avoiding the use of French loanwords or codeswitching when speaking Wolof.

The development of stereotypical beliefs about women and men based on the way they speak can have a variety of types of problematic consequences. In the West, for example, the fact that it has been a common pattern for women to use more standard speech forms than men has contributed to the myth that women are naturally conservative and men naturally the innovators (Jespersen

1922), and to the negative stereotype that women are more snob-bish than men and are more concerned with superficial appearances. These beliefs, of course, are based on the assumption that male speech is the norm, and are accompanied by a more positive view of men's speech than of women's.

Other proposed explanations

I have so far discussed proposals which attribute sex differences in the use of prestige speech forms to external social and economic factors, to differences in the power granted to women and men, to the covert prestige which non-standard speech may have for men, and to social expectations that one should display one's gender identity. These do not, however, exhaust the proposals that have been made. For example, Gordon (1994) notes that in New Zealand, working-class speech can carry a suggestion of sexual promiscuity and loose morals in a woman; this may provide a motive for women to favour more standard speech forms in that country. Bing (1995) notes that in interactions between those of unequal power, informal speech is the prerogative of the more powerful individual, while the less powerful person is often expect-ed to use a more formal style. Given that standard speech is associated with formal speech style, the role of this factor in explaining sex differences in standardness deserves further investi-gation.

It has also been suggested, originally by Labov (1972), that women may be more motivated than men to use standard speech forms because they are the primary care-takers of children. This proposal assumes that women see 'good' speech as important for their children's success in life; thus, they would try to use more standard speech themselves so as to provide a good role model. Holmes (1992) suggests that this idea is somewhat implausible since interactions between a mother and her child are normally very relaxed and informal, and it would be surprising to find any-thing other than vernacular speech forms in this context. Researchers have rarely directly studied the effect of parenthood on standard versus non-standard speech. One study which has done so is Brouwer and van Hout (1992); here, it was found that upper-working-class and lower-middle-class women in Amsterdam who had children did use a significantly greater percentage of standard speech forms in interviews than similar women who did not have children. However, it was also found that being a parent had the same effect on men's speech, which would not be predicted under this hypothesis. If this hypothesis is indeed at all valid, it would be a relevant factor only in some communities and some social classes; it presupposes that women who are motivated to use standard speech features for this reason believe not only that it would be desirable that their children 'better themselves', which could, of course, involve a rejection of the traditional lifestyle of the community, but that there is a realistic chance that their children will actually be able to do this.

Finally, Chambers (1992, 1995) has proposed that biology plays a major role in accounting for speech differences between women and men. He notes various types of evidence which have been cited in the past to show that women have better verbal abilities than men, arguing that this difference results from biological differences in brain organization. Given this advantage in verbal ability, he proposes that women are able to command a greater range of speech styles than men; this, he argues, would provide a natural explanation for the fact that so many studies have found women to use a greater amount of standard speech features than men. The major problem with this hypothesis is that the evidence for a female advantage in verbal ability is now very tenuous. Hyde and Linn (1988), in a meta-analysis of 165 studies dealing with sex differences in verbal ability and involving 1,418,899 subjects, conclude that when all these studies are taken into account, 'the magnitude of the gender [sex] difference in verbal ability is ... so small that it can effectively be considered to be zero' (p. 64). Another problem lies in the fact that Chambers' proposal would predict that women's speech should universally contain more prestige forms, provided that no factor is present which might counterbalance this advantage. (He acknowledges that if men have significantly more exposure to standard speech than women do through having wider social contacts, this might act as a nullifying factor.) Various studies have examined communities in which no such potentially nullifying factor is present, and have found no significant sex differences in the use of such forms; e.g. Salami (1991) for Ife-Ife, Nigeria, Hibiya (1988) for Tokyo, and Rickford (1991) for Guyana (with respect to younger speakers). These studies constitute counterexamples to the prediction made by Chambers' proposal. Given that the evidence for a biologically based sex difference in verbal ability is tenuous, and given counterexamples such as those above, I would suggest that this is not a very fruitful source of explanation for the facts in this area.

Conclusion

It is evident that there are a variety of different factors which can give rise to differences between women and men with respect to the use of prestige versus stigmatized speech forms. It has been common in the past for researchers to attempt to explain all such differences by means of just one or two simple generalizations. Moreover, hypotheses have often been put forward as global explanations which assign the same types of behaviour to all men and all women everywhere. It is now clear that there is far too much variation across and within different communities, for any such simple analyses to be viable. Instead, it is important to 'think practically and look locally' (Eckert and McConnell-Ginet 1992) in attempting to account for differences in women's and men's speech. Thus, for example, local economic conditions, employment and educational opportunities that are open to each sex, social conditions giving rise to differences in social network strength, the amount of status and respect accorded to women in particular communities and the extent to which they can participate in public and economic life are all factors which are important in accounting for the choices that women and men make in the speech forms that they use. At the same time, however, the fact that women appear to be universally granted less status and power than men must be recognized as a relevant underlying factor, one which will certainly not cause all women and all men to act alike, given all the other factors just mentioned, but which may, nevertheless, give rise to similar female behaviour or male behaviour in different communities. How, then, can we explain the fact that the most frequent finding of sociolinguistic studies has been that women's speech makes use of more prestige forms than men's? It appears that a number of different factors conspire to produce this effect. Market forces and social networks factors certainly play their part with respect to working-class communities in the West. Also important is women's lower status relative to men, which tends to have the effect that men will choose less overtly prestigious, and women more overtly prestigious, speech forms.

If we are to better understand the roles and interrelationships of different potential factors in explaining when and why women and men differ in their use of prestige speech forms, various issues need to be investigated in more detail by future researchers. In what kinds of communities are particular factors likely to be salient, such as women's choosing to use prestige speech forms as a strategy for presenting themselves as worthy of respect and authority, and in what kinds of communities are they not likely to be salient? What limitations are there on the role of market forces and social networks in explaining speech differences of this sort? What kinds of factors can outweigh and nullify what other kinds of factors, and in what circumstances will they do so? Only more careful and detailed analyses of the social structure of particular communities, including the use of such research strategies as examining the use of language in different types of discourse contexts, together with comparison of the social structures of different communities taking into account the gender-related speech patterns appearing in them, are likely to lead to answers to these questions.

Notes

1. Variationists have examined speech differences between women and men based on the binary category (or variable) of *sex*. This book, by contrast, focuses on the social construction of *gender*. Since this chapter presents a review of literature, the terminology used reflects the intentions of the works being discussed.
2. Within quantitative sociolinguistics, one major focus of interest has been women's versus men's role in the innovation and diffusion of linguistic change. Where there is variation in the use of stigmatized versus prestigious linguistic forms, this may represent either stable variation, a change in progress in the direction of the prestige variant, or a change in progress in the direction of the stigmatized variant; it is not always easy to tell which is involved in any given case. The proposals to be reviewed in this chapter all involve factors which would tend to cause women and men to differ in the extent to which their speech contains prestige forms, irrespective of whether or not this might represent change in progress. (As has been previously noted – Milroy (1980), Eckert (1989), Coates (1993) – it is evident that no simple generalizations can be made as to which sex will take the lead in change towards or away from a prestige variant. For example, although women have often been found to be in the lead in changes towards increased use of prestige variants, men have also sometimes been found to be in the lead in such cases (e.g. Bortoni-Ricardo 1985). Whether either sex takes the lead in such a change is determined by the kinds of social factors discussed in the body of the chapter.) See also Labov (1991) for a discussion of the role of sex in linguistic change, including change in which no value judgment is yet attached to the variants.
3. On the face of it, Deuchar's proposal appears to predict that women should use standard speech features more when talking to men than

when talking to other women, since (all else being equal) there will be a power imbalance in the former situation, but not the latter. I know of no evidence which would support this prediction. However, even if the sex of the addressee does not make a difference, this should not be taken as invalidating Deuchar's proposal. The research on gender differences in language use suggests strongly that women, to a significant extent because of their lower status relative to men (Ridgeway and Johnson 1990, Cameron this volume), are socialized to generally adopt a positive socio-emotional role in interactions with others (which involves greater positive politeness), no matter the sex of the other participant(s); indeed, same-sex interaction may even reinforce gender-related behaviour patterns.

4. It has sometimes been suggested that the common finding that women's speech is more standard than men's may simply be an artefact of some aspect of the interview situation, and may not reflect the true facts of vernacular speech (Graddol and Swann 1989, Holmes 1992). It is important to note, then, that the same pattern has also often shown up in studies which have reliably recorded vernacular speech.

5. Knack (1991) describes a similar stereotype about women in an upper-middle-class Jewish community in Grand Rapids, Michigan; here, women use a particular non-standard speech feature which is recognized by the community as stereotypically Jewish significantly more than men. It is, of course, interesting to contrast this stereotype of women with the assumption often made in the past by sociolinguists studying working-class communities in Europe and North America that it is males rather than females who are the embodiment of vernacular culture.

References

Aikio Marjut 1992 Are women innovators in the shift to a second language?: a case study of Reindeer Sámi women and men. *International Journal of the Sociology of Language* 94: 43–61.

Bing Janet 1995 Friendly deception: status and solidarity. In Bucholtz Mary *et al.* (eds) *Cultural performances: proceedings of the 1994 Berkeley women and language conference.* Berkeley Women and Language Group, Berkeley, CA pp 44–9.

Bortoni-Ricardo Stella Maris 1985 *The urbanization of rural dialect speakers: a sociolinguistic study of Brazil.* Cambridge University Press, Cambridge.

Bourhis Richard, Giles Howard, Lambert Wallace 1975 Social consequences of accommodating one's style of speech: a cross-national investigation. *International Journal of the Sociology of Language* 6: 55–71.

Brouwer Dédé 1989 *Gender variation in Dutch: a sociolinguistic study of Amsterdam speech*. Foris, Dordrecht.

Brouwer Dédé, van Hout Roeland 1992 Gender-related variation in Amsterdam vernacular. *International Journal of the Sociology of Language* 94: 99–122.

Brown Penelope, Levinson Stephen 1978 Universals in language usage. In Goody Esther (ed) *Questions and politeness*. Cambridge University Press, Cambridge pp 56–310.

Buxó Rey María Jesús 1978 Comportamiento lingüístico de la mujer en situaciones de aculturación y cambio social. In Zamalloa Karmela Ataucha *et al.* (eds) *Bilingüismo y biculturalismo*. CEAC, Barcelona pp 173–92.

Cameron Deborah 1992 *Feminism and linguistic theory*. St Martin's Press, New York.

Cameron Deborah this volume: The language–gender interface: challenging co-optation.

Cameron Deborah, Coates Jennifer 1989 Some problems in the sociolinguistic explanation of sex differences. In Coates Jennifer, Cameron Deborah (eds) pp 13–26.

Chambers J K 1992 Linguistic correlates of language and sex. *English World-Wide* 13.2: 173–218.

Chambers J K 1995 *Sociolinguistic Theory*. Basil Blackwell, Oxford and Cambridge.

Chambers J K, Trudgill Peter 1980 *Dialectology*. Cambridge University Press, Cambridge.

Cheshire Jenny 1982 Linguistic variation and social function. In Romaine Suzanne (ed) *Sociolinguistic variation in speech communities*. Edward Arnold, London pp 153–6.

Cheshire Jenny (ed) 1991 *English around the world: sociolinguistic perspectives*. Cambridge University Press, Cambridge.

Clarke Sandra 1985 Sex differences in language usage: Are women really more standard speakers? In Bremner Sue, Caskey Noelle, Moonwomon Birch (eds) *Proceedings of the first Berkeley women and language conference*. Berkeley Women and Language Group, Berkeley pp 16–32.

Coates Jennifer 1993 *Women, men and language*. Longman, London.

Coates Jennifer, Cameron Deborah (eds) 1989 *Women in their speech communities: new perspectives on language and sex*. Longman, London.

Deuchar Margaret 1989 A pragmatic account of women's use of standard speech. In Coates Jennifer, Cameron Deborah (eds) pp 27–32.

Diebold A Richard 1961 Incipient bilingualism. *Language* 37: 97–112. Reprinted in Hymes Dell (ed) 1964 *Language in culture and society*. Harper & Row, New York pp 495–506.

Eckert Penelope 1989 The whole woman: sex and gender differences in variation. *Language Variation and Change* 1: 245–68.

Eckert Penelope, McConnell-Ginet Sally 1992 Think practically and look locally: language and gender as community-based practice. *Annual Review of Anthropology* 21: 461–90.

Edwards John 1979 Social class differences and the identification of sex in children's speech. *Journal of Child Language* 6: 121–7.

Edwards John 1982 Language attitudes and their implications among English speakers. In Ryan Ellen Bouchard, Giles Howard (eds) *Attitudes towards language variation*. Edward Arnold, London pp 20–33.

Edwards Viv 1989 The speech of British Black women in Dudley, West Midlands. In Coates Jennifer, Cameron Deborah (eds) pp 33–50.

Eisikovits Edina 1987 Sex differences in inter-group and intra-group interaction among adolescents. In Pauwels Anne (ed) pp 45–58.

Elyan Olwen, Smith Philip, Giles Howard, Bourhis Richard 1978 RP-accented female speech: The voice of perceived androgyny? In Trudgill Peter (ed) pp 122–31.

Escure Genevieve 1991 Gender roles and linguistic variation in the Belizean Creole community. In Cheshire Jenny (ed) pp 595–606.

Gal Susan 1978 Peasant men can't get wives: Language change and sex roles in a bilingual community. *Language in Society* 7: 1–17.

Gal Susan 1979 *Language shift: social determinants of linguistic change in bilingual Austria*. Academic Press, New York.

Giles Howard, Powesland P 1975 *Speech style and social evaluation*. Academic Press, London.

Gordon Elizabeth 1994 Sex differences in language: another explanation? *American Speech* 69.2: 215–20.

Graddol David, Swann Joan 1989 *Gender voices*. Basil Blackwell, Cambridge.

Herbert Robert 1992 Language, gender and ethnicity: Explaining language shift in Thongaland. Paper presented at the annual meeting of the Linguistic Society of America, Los Angeles, CA.

Hibiya Junko 1988 *A quantitative study of Tokyo Japanese*. University of Pennsylvania PhD dissertation.

Hill Jane 1987 Women's speech in modern Mexicano. In Philips Susan, Steele Susan, Tanz Christine (eds) *Language, gender and sex in comparative perspective*. Cambridge University Press, Cambridge pp 121–62.

Holmes Janet 1992 *An introduction to sociolinguistics*. Longman, London.

Holmes Janet 1993 New Zealand women are good to talk to: an analysis of politeness strategies in interaction. *Journal of Pragmatics* 20: 91–116.

Holmquist Jonathan 1985 Social correlates of a linguistic variable: a study in a Spanish village. *Language in Society* 14: 191–203.

Horvath Barbara 1985 *Variation in Australian English: the sociolects of Sydney*. Cambridge University Press, Cambridge.

Hyde Janet Shibley, Linn Marcia 1988 Gender differences in verbal ability: a meta-analysis. *Psychological Bulletin* 104.1: 53–69.

Jabeur M 1987 *A sociolinguistic study in Tunisia, Rades*. University of Reading Ph.D. dissertation. Cited in Milroy 1992 pp 171–72.

James Deborah, Clarke Sandra 1993 Women, men and interruptions: a critical review. In Tannen Deborah (ed) *Gender and conversational interaction*. Oxford University Press, New York pp 231–80.

Jespersen Otto 1922 *Language: its nature, development and origin*. W W Norton, New York.

Kalmar Ivan, Zhong Yong, Xiao Hong 1987 Language attitudes in Guangzhou, China. *Language in Society* 16: 499–508.

Keenan Elinor 1974 Norm-makers, norm-breakers: uses of speech by men and women in a Malagasy community. In Bauman Richard, Sherzer Joel (eds) *Explorations in the ethnography of speaking*. Cambridge University Press, Cambridge pp 125–43.

Khan Farhat 1991 Final consonant cluster simplification in a variety of Indian English. In Cheshire Jenny (ed) pp 288–98.

Knack Rebecca 1991 Ethnic boundaries in linguistic variation. In Eckert Penelope (ed) *New ways of analyzing sound change*. Academic Press, San Diego pp 251–72.

Labov William 1966 *The social stratification of English in New York City*. Center for Applied Linguistics, Washington.

Labov William 1972 *Sociolinguistic patterns*. University of Pennsylvania Press, Philadelphia.

Labov William 1991 The intersection of sex and social class in the course of linguistic change. *Language Variation and Change* 2: 205 54.

Lanari Catherine, Clarke Sandra 1993 Kinship networks and non-standard dialect maintenance in a rural Canadian context. Paper presented at NWAVE 22, Ottawa.

Larson Karen 1982 Role playing and the real thing: socialization and standard speech in Norway. *Journal of Anthropological Research* 38.4: 401–10.

Mattingly Ignatius 1966 Speaker variation and vocal tract size. Paper presented at Acoustical Society of America. Abstract in *Journal of the Acoustical Society of America* 39 (1966): 1219. Cited in Thorne Barrie, Kramarae Cheris, Henley Nancy (eds) pp 250–1.

Milroy Lesley 1980 *Language and social networks*. Blackwell, Oxford.

Milroy Lesley 1992 New perspectives in the analysis of sex differentiation in language. In Bolton Kingsley, Kwok Helen (eds) *Sociolinguistics today: international perspectives*. Routledge, London and New York pp 163–79.

Nichols Patricia 1983 Linguistic options and choices for Black women in the rural South. In Thorne Barrie, Kramarae Cheris, Henley Nancy (eds) pp 54–68.

Pauwels Anne (ed) 1987 *Women and language in Australian and New Zealand society*. Australian Professional Publications, Sydney.

Queizán María Xosé 1977 *A muller en Galicia*. Edicios do Castro, La Coruña.

Rickford John R 1991 Sociolinguistic variation in Cane Walk: a quantitative case study. In Cheshire Jenny (ed) pp 609–16.

Ridgeway Cecilia, Johnson Cathryn 1990 What is the relationship between socioemotional behavior and status in task groups? *American Journal of Sociology* 95 (March): 1189–1212.

Romaine Suzanne 1978 Postvocalic /r/ in Scottish English: sound change in progress? In Trudgill Peter (ed) pp 144–57.

Russell Joan 1982 Networks and sociolinguistic variation in an African urban setting. In Romaine Suzanne (ed) *Sociolinguistic variation in speech communities*. Edward Arnold, London pp 125–40.

Salami L Oladipo 1991 Diffusion and focusing: phonological variation and social networks in Ife-Ife, Nigeria. *Language in Society* 20: 217–45.

Schatz Henriette 1986 *Plat Amsterdams in its social context*. P J Meertens Institut voor Dialectologie, Volkskunde en Naamkunde, Amsterdam.

Swigart Leigh 1992 Women and language choice in Dakar: a case of unconscious innovation. *Women and Language* XV.1: 11–20.

Thomas Beth 1989 Differences of sex and sects: linguistic variation and social networks in a Welsh mining village. In Coates Jennifer, Cameron Deborah (eds) pp 51–60.

Thorne Barrie, Kramarae Cheris, Henley Nancy (eds) 1983 *Language, gender and society*. Newbury House, Rowley, MA.

Trudgill Peter 1972 Sex, covert prestige, and linguistic change in the urban British English of Norwich. *Language in Society* 1: 179–95.

Trudgill Peter (ed) 1978 *Sociolinguistic patterns in British English*. Edward Arnold, London.

6 Storytellers and gatekeepers in economics

Livia Polanyi and Diana Strassmann

Introduction

This chapter is a collaboration between a feminist economist and a feminist linguist.[1] We work together because as feminists we are interested in the relationship between the rhetoric and practices of economics – not only for the scientific pleasure of investigating how language and social institutions reflect and shape one another, but also, and more fundamentally, because we are interested in the transformation of the practices of academic disciplines through analytic critique of the relationship among language, scientific practice and power. In this chapter, addressed to the community of linguists interested in language and gender issues, we will look at the relationship among stories which are told in economics, the language in which they are told, the communities of practice (Lave and Wenger 1991, Eckert and McConnell-Ginet 1992) which they reflect and the communities of practitioners which they shape.

Throughout this chapter we will maintain that all stories, including the stories economists tell, are inherently connected to the specific social and ideological positioning of the teller, and, furthermore, that the current conversation among economists is positioned by the interests and experiences of the predominant practitioners of the discipline. As feminists, we are committed to changing not merely the stories which economists now tell but also the nature of the community of practitioners for whom today's stories appear so comfortably apolitical.

In the work reported on here, we draw on previous linguistic and conversational analytic work on everyday storytelling to show how apparently simple, straightforward illustrative stories in textbooks can act as gatekeepers in economics. Through careful attention to the language and content of the stories, we will uncover the situated character of these texts. Understanding how the texts reflect the life experiences of the dominant group of economic practitioners will allow us to draw inferences about an important mechanism of disciplinary reproduction which restricts entry into the field to those who most resemble the white middle-class males who currently predominate in the discipline.

In addition, following Harding (1991) and an increasing number of other feminist thinkers, we will argue that feminist studies of language which centre on gender must go beyond considering women as an undifferentiated category and must move to a consideration of difference along a number of dimensions of social marginalization of which gender is only one. Investigating the implications for text production and reception of race, class, ethnicity, sexual orientation and even placement along an urban–rural continuum are important for understanding the performance of gendered subjectivity which Deborah Cameron argues for elsewhere in this volume. We have only to remember Sojourner Truth's 1851 speech 'Ain't I a Woman?' (1985) to understand how dimensions of difference such as race and class must be addressed in seeing another person as a gendered being.

An overview of contemporary economics

Contemporary mainstream economics is dominated to an astonishing degree by one analytic framework which traces its roots to the philosophical work of Adam Smith in the eighteenth century: the neoclassical theory of economic behaviour. Neoclassical theory treats relations among agents in terms of self-interested individualism and contractual exchange.[2] The central character of economic analysis is the autonomous agent who trades with other agents in order to maximize a utility or profit function. The economic agent is a creature with wishes and needs as well as a set of resources which can be deployed to satisfy those desires. Because resources are always limited, the economic agent or *economic man*, as that agent is called, must make choices. Faced with the available array of goods and services, each with an attached price, he [sic] dispassionately considers the various possibilities for satisfaction and carefully weighs their costs against their respective degrees of potential satisfaction. Eventually, he settles on one preferred option which becomes his choice.

Although there is a good deal of diversity represented in economic thought in the USA (i.e. Institutionalist, Marxist, etc.) the mainstream voice predominates at élite universities, in policy circles, at prestigious conferences and symposia, and through the most widely read journals of the discipline. Within the mainstream, there are, of course, substantive disagreements. However, the range of 'acceptable' disagreement is limited; serious challenges to gender and cultural biases in the core conceptual structure of the discipline are ignored as irrelevant. Feminist challenges to the appropriateness of the autonomous self-interested individual for agents who are small children or nursing mothers, for example, are ignored and those feminist economists who mount such challenges are dismissed as 'not doing economics'.[3]

Theoretical economists build models which, by convention, are grounded in the microfoundations of the discipline. Data collection, officially celebrated, is unofficially discouraged. As a result, economists seldom collect their own data but for basic information rely on statistics that others collect, often for reasons which have nothing to do with the question the theoretician is addressing in the model being built. Rhetorically, the style of presentation for economic models rests upon a set of linear equations representing the economist's view of how economic agents arrive at the best choice among the options available to them. This choice, however, has certain constraints such as tastes, natural endowments like wealth, talents and intelligence, or the results of past choices such as human capital investments like education, the social structure and government – in short, the state of the world in all its complexity. Economists take as their task explaining the relations among choices, desires and constraints through models of contractual exchange and constrained optimization. They tend not to consider inquiry into the origin or meaning of these constraints important or productive, leaving such inquiry to sociology which is, for economists, a lesser discipline: economists proudly proclaim their discipline the Queen of the Social Sciences!

When examined critically, optimization emerges as an apology for the status quo as it purports to show how people get what they choose, and reinforces the idea that people get what they deserve (see Strassmann and Polanyi 1995). Oddly, disagreement in economics seldom concerns assumptions. Rather, within the community of economic practitioners, the most valued critiques focus on details of the mathematical machinery used to formalize the construction of economic findings despite the improbable assumptions upon which the models often rest. None of this would matter much, except that economics is an extraordinarily influential discipline. Economic analyses strongly influenced by neoclassical theory, and based on oversimplifications and often ignoring power differentials among the various economic agents, play a role in policy formation in most nations of the world. In North America, economists are everywhere. In academia, they may be found in university-level administrative positions, often serving as university presidents, vice-presidents or provosts, as well as in economics departments, law schools and schools of public policy. In addition, economists often teach and do research in interdisciplinary centres such as regional science and urban planning departments as well as in business schools and schools of public health. In both national and international governmental posts, they are ubiquitous as well. Policy-making UN organizations, such as the World Bank and AID, which greatly impact Third World countries, are largely staffed by economists or those trained in fields where economists dominate. Within the US government, economists are heavily represented on the Federal Reserve Board, in the Office of Management and Budget, and on the staffs of many federal agencies within the Departments of Labor, Treasury and the Interior which determine such key policies as lending rates, types and levels of taxation, amounts of welfare disbursement and unemployment compensation. Outside of government, economists hold key posts in influential non-profit organizations including funding agencies as well as in business and finance. Although, on the whole, economists in the private sector are not as well paid as MBAs or lawyers, the plethora of job possibilities for economists outside of academia drives up faculty salaries in universities where starting assistant professors often earn an initial salary well above that paid to others starting up the academic ladder in schools of liberal arts and in the social and natural sciences.

Due to the influential nature of the discipline in terms of policy formation as well as the high status and generous salaries which practising economists command, women, members of ethnic minorities, or those physically less able may be drawn to study economics upon entering university. Yet the percentages of members of such constituencies who complete undergraduate training in economics, not to speak of graduate work in the field, are very small indeed. Figures from the 1990 census reported in Phillip's (1993) article 'Race, Gender and Economics in the Classroom' in the weekly *Black Issues in Higher Education* reveal that only 22 per cent of economics professors in post secondary institutions are women – and only 4 per cent are full professors, while the total percentage of persons of color teaching economics was just over 12 per cent, of whom very, very few had achieved full professorial rank (p. 18). The point is even more clearly made when one considers that 'the AEA – the largest professional society for economists – has had more than 100 presidents since its inception in 1885. Since that time, only one of its presidents has been an African American. A woman has yet to hold its highest office' (p. 16). (NB: A woman, Anne Krueger, was finally elected in 1995.)

In this chapter, we take our theoretical cue from feminist and other critical interpretive thinkers who argue convincingly that the accounts created by human producers of knowledge are necessarily grounded in the experiences and lives of their producers and reflect their circumstances and interests. For an introduction to this perspective, see Haraway (1988). Related readings include Marcus and Fischer (1986), Harding (1991) and Traweek (1988, 1992). Some of these ideas have also been addressed by institutionalist economists. (See Samuels (1992) for an introduction to this intellectual tradition in economics.) To explore some of the mechanisms which ensure that the field of economics remains the white, middle-class male bastion of influence and position it has always been, we will draw on techniques developed over the past 25 years in linguistics and conversational analysis.

Narrative analysis as a subversive activity

In the next two sections of this chapter we make use of data and analysis presented earlier in Strassmann and Polanyi (1995).[4] We will exploit the sociocultural linguistic narrative analysis methodology developed in Polanyi (1989) to deconstruct disciplinary authority in economics by making explicit the situated nature of mainstream economic texts. We will show how detailed textual analyses may be used to uncover much information about social and intellectual communities, including the positioning of community members along dimensions of race, gender, social status, culture, time and place. In this chapter, we will take as examples selections from a widely disseminated economics textbook, Ehrenberg and Smith's (1991) popular *Modern Labor Economics: Theory and Public Policy*. These economic textbook accounts function as stories, presenting a modelled world in order to make a point relevant both to the storyworld created through language and the socially constructed world in which narrators and recipients live. In the following sections of this chapter we will analyse two examples from this text. We show how the internally coherent portrait of middle-class life which we call the Enjoyable Family is stereotypic and gender biased, while the equally sexist portrait of the financially disadvantaged Other Family, when closely examined, is not even coherent but collapses under a mass of incompatible details. In the final section of the chapter we will use the mechanism of recipient design, introduced originally by the ethnomethodologist Harvey Sacks (1972), to argue that the portrait of the Others may well be received differently by students who have had experience of poverty, illness and discrimination and by those who have not. Furthermore, we will claim that acceptability judgements may themselves play a gatekeeping role. Faced with a majority of students who find nothing disturbing in these tales, students who do find the story of the Enjoyables misogynist or the story of the Others incoherent may conclude that they, themselves, are marginal, excluded by their different sensibilities from the core group of students, teachers and other economists who find the texts unremarkable.

Default assumptions in cognitive processing: filling in the gaps in the storyworld

In order to make our arguments we will consider some dimensions of language used in all storytelling. We begin by arguing that language must be used parsimoniously in building a model of a storyworld. Since it is impossible to express in detail every aspect of the world that is conjured into being through language, a universal assumption underlying storytelling in all world traditions is that, unless the text states otherwise, story recipients assume any storyworld to be very much like the world experienced everyday. Therefore, in order to understand the information which is explicitly given, the recipient is expected to make inferences drawing on aspects of the world which are not explicitly stated or 'default assumptions', as these standard assumptions are termed in Artificial Intelligence.

Members of communities respond to the information explicitly included in texts by making similar default assumptions. Some of these assumptions are based on universal world knowledge – for example, that water is wet – while others reflect more narrowly defined culturally and socially specific beliefs, clichés and stereotypes.

People demonstrate their participation in social institutions in part through making similar assumptions about unspecified portions of story texts. Similar to idiolectal differences, no two people (nor any one person at different times) will make the identical default assumptions. However, as with speakers of the same dialect, the degree to which people are members of the same community will be reflected in the degree to which they respond similarly to specific textual information in the default assumptions they are led to make.[5] For example, in response to learning that a family is eating an evening meal together, recipients will universally fill in a situation in which those eating are breathing in and out and putting objects into their mouths. Exactly where the family members are assembled, what kind of occasion this might be, exactly what categories of individuals are implicated in the term *family*, what sorts of objects are being ingested and in what manner, will vary depending on the cultural and social norms of the story listener and the assumptions the recipient makes about the assumptions of the storyteller. Although clichés and default assumptions are implicated in racist- and gender-based negative stereotyping, we are mistaken in equating the making of default assumptions with negative social practices. The needs to categorize and to make default assumptions are cognitively much more basic and primitive operations than the impulse to draw socially motivated stereotypes; these needs derive ultimately from the necessity of organisms to make predictions about the world on the basis of necessarily incomplete information. Without specific instructions to the contrary, in any situation we expect the familiar.

Default assumptions in the Enjoyable Family

Let us now turn to the first of the two texts we will analyse in detail. We begin our narrative analysis by exploring the default assumptions in the text reproduced below which contains 'an easy example' for students. The authors have included this example, as they explicitly state, in order 'to make several basic points in an easily understood fashion' (p. 228) about the topic of the chapter and the application of the theory of maximal utility to household production.

THE THEORY OF HOUSEHOLD PRODUCTION
Although many adults are unmarried at some points in their lives, most do marry and form family units. The family thus becomes a very

basic decision-making entity in society, and many important decisions concerning both consumption patterns and labor supply are made in a *family* context. Our task in this chapter is to find out in what ways the implications of the individual labor supply theory in Chapter 6 are modified or expanded by consideration of the *family*.

We shall assume that many commodities the family consumes are produced, or can be produced, at home. Food and energy are combined with preparation time to produce the meals from which family enjoyment is derived. A vacuum cleaner and time are combined to contribute to an orderly home. Food, clothing, and supervision time all contribute to the growth of children, whom the parents hope to enjoy. Thus, a marriage partner who stays at home may be engaged more in the production of commodities from which the family derives utility than in the direct consumption of leisure.

A model of household production

Household production models explicitly recognize that both consumption and production take place in the home. The family unit, then, must make two kinds of decisions: *what* to consume and *how to produce* what it consumes. Consider the second decision first by analyzing a family that does not have to worry about what to consume because it consumes only one commodity: meals. ...

Meals that yield equal utility can be produced in several ways. A family can buy prepared foods and simply warm them at home, in which case minimum time is spent in preparation and a maximum of market goods are consumed. The meal could be prepared at home with food bought from a market, or it could be prepared at home with food grown or made at home, which obviously represents a lot of preparation time. Since any combination of goods and household time can produce meals that are equally valuable (in terms of producing utility) to the family, ... [i]f household time is reduced, meal production can be held constant by increasing the purchase of goods. Thus, if a family decides not to grow its own food, it can buy food instead – or if it decides to spend less time cooking food, it could still maintain the same utility from meals by using a microwave oven to heat prepared foods. ... If the family spends a lot of time in meal preparation, it will be easy to replace some of that time with just a few goods (store-bought food easily replaces homegrown food, for example). However, when preparation time is very short to begin with, a further cut in such time may be very difficult to absorb and still keep utility constant. Thus, it will take many goods – a large increase in food quality, for example – to substitute for reduced cooking time.

(Ehrenberg and Smith 1991: 228–9)

In analysing this text, we will not dispute the axioms of neo-classical economics or find fault with the textbook's simplified presentation of the family as a unit which 'consumes only one commodity: meals' (p. 228). And, although this text is not technically a story – not a 'past tense specific narrative which makes a point' (Polanyi 1989) – we will argue that a great deal can be learned about how it functions as a meaningful text within economics using narrative analytic notions and techniques.

To begin, we will show that acculturated American adults know a great deal about this family, a certain imaginary fictional generic American family. Without difficulty, acculturated Americans can build up a model of this family from the default assumptions and stereotypic images which the story evokes. In the tradition of contemporary generative linguistics, we, the authors, will use ourselves as informants. Triggered by the few colourful details presented, we will query our own assumptions about these details, relying upon conventional American ideas to build up a representation of a model world in which normal expectations include pleasant mealtimes, a vacuum cleaner and microwave, a clean and orderly home, and time to spend supervising children whom the parents expect to find enjoyable. Our aim in unpacking these default assumptions is to make explicit how the social positioning of economists along the various dimensions of difference influences how their stories are told and how they are read. When we examine the associations which are evoked by the text, as well as associations evoked by those initial associations, the ideological substrate which supports this simple pedagogical illustration will begin to emerge. By making explicit the influence of social positioning on the tellers of this seemingly apolitical and scientific text, we can begin to glimpse how the texts and language of the discipline of economics work in concert to limit membership in the economics community, in large measure, to middle-class white men. In order to make some of those assumptions clear, we now examine the Enjoyables in some detail. Later on, the world of this story will be contrasted with the world evoked by another, rather different story presented in the same text.

Mealtime at the Enjoyables

The family which is our focus of interest has meals 'from which family enjoyment is derived'. When we read this simple collocation of the words enjoyment and mealtimes a complex representation of what is conventionally believed to be necessary for 'mealtime to be enjoyable' is evoked. Minimally, for the family to 'enjoy' mealtimes, certain elements like tasty, nutritious and abundant food are necessary as well as a pleasant environment in which to eat. One doesn't enjoy a mealtime in which there is no food or in which there is not enough to go around, in which family members are angry, drunk, sick, or otherwise in pain, in which young children are not wearing reasonably clean clothes or babies are not freshly diapered; meals are not enjoyed if taken when it is very cold and there is no heat, or when it is very hot and there is no relief.

'Mealtimes' also conjures up a family which sits down at a table and eats together. 'Grabbing a bite' alone standing up at the kitchen counter does not count as an enjoyable family meal. Taking into account the unmarked workday for American adults, we expect the head of the household to be away from home at midday and any children over the age of 5 to eat lunch at school during most of the year. The pleasant mealtimes the text evokes must therefore refer to the evening meal taken by the family members seated together around a table in the kitchen or dining room. Assuming an evening dinner time allows the inference to be made that, in this family, all the family members are home together in the early evening. Neither parent works nights and misses dinner and neither parent must therefore sleep during the day as family life swirls on silently. The family lives an orderly life and, indeed, the text tells us that the family has a clean and orderly home, functioning appliances, carefully brought-up children who are well nourished, nicely clothed and who are never left at home alone unsupervised. When we read that the parents 'hope to enjoy' their children, we infer that they do not beat or abuse them – psychologically, physically or sexually. Nor, do we imagine, did the grandparents and other older members of the extended family beat or otherwise terrorize the mother and father of these delightful kids. Psychologically and physically, everyone is intact.

Living the enjoyable life

The vacuum cleaner, the microwave, the clean home, the well brought-up children, and the pleasant mealtime communicate a great deal more than merely these few facts: from these facts an entire world is conjured into being. We invite you, the reader, to take a little test along with us, the authors, to see how much we do know about this family and the world in which the story of their lives unfolds. Let's begin by considering the background assumptions we bring to the very first sentence of the chapter in 'Household Production' where we encounter the Enjoyable Family: 'Although many adults are unmarried at some points in their lives, most do marry and form family units' (p. 227).

This introductory remark summons into being an entity, 'the family unit', a 'family' which is being viewed as single economic actor. What comes to mind when the concept 'family' is evoked in a conversation, textbook or newspaper with no further detail about who the family members are, where they live, what they do? What sort of 'family' is the generic family? How many family members are there? Do they live in a house? An apartment building? Do they have a pet? A dog? A llama? What about electricity? Running water? Where do they live? Is there a McDonald's on one side, a factory on the other side? Is there a burned-out building down the street? Do rats walk across the children's faces at night?

Mention 'the family' in a textbook, on television, in the popular press and do not add a modifier such as 'single parent', 'poor', 'African American' (or 'black' or 'Negro') or 'inner-city', 'struggling', 'disadvantaged' or 'homosexual' and the default picture is of a nuclear family composed of two white adults of opposite sexes and more than one but less than five children who live in a single family house, with a pet dog, perhaps a cat or, less likely, a bird or some fish. The family's house has electricity, running water and is surrounded by other houses. The nearest factory is on the other side of town. The nearest McDonald's is about 10 minutes away by car and the family has at least one reasonably new passenger vehicle. They visit the McDonald's from time to time. These stereotypic images do not necessarily match the life experiences of every American reader but, we would argue, they are evoked for every reader who is familiar with American culture from the wealth of texts produced by the dominant disseminators of normative cultural information: the popular broadcast and print media, textbooks, toys and advertisements. These tell a generic tale, over and over. Deviations from the generic exist, but they are marked and do not displace the expected. In the generic family, the family members are basically healthy. Dad is employed. The parents of the children were married when the children were conceived; the family uses credit cards and their car is insured. Since the text provides a vacuum cleaner, default assumptions provide a multi-room dwelling to vacuum; because the family has a microwave, we infer a refrigerator. A refrigerator is a more basic category of appliance for a family than is a microwave: if food cannot be kept without spoiling, it would probably not need to be defrosted or re-warmed, the most common uses of microwaves in contemporary American homemaking practice. Although we have constructed this model out of our own heads, such a complex picture of this family can be generated from a few small details by any cultural initiate who reads the story of this family because each of us has read this story over and over: in textbooks, in the public media and in our own lives – whether we, ourselves, are white, heterosexual, and living in comfortable circumstances or not.

This, then, is the family unit which '… must make two kinds of decisions: *what* to consume and *how to produce* what it consumes' (p. 228), the family evoked into being for the sake of providing an example in which 'to make several basic points in an easily under-stood fashion' (p. 228). A family unit which one encounters as simple, unsituated, generic, but which – when examined in some detail, taking seriously the concepts, ideas and images which are evoked by a few simple details – emerges as heavily laden with the cultural and ideological positioning of the tellers of the tales and their intended recipients.

The tale which we have been considering is, of course, heavily gendered as well. Let us return to the dinner table where the family is enjoying its pleasant repast. Who cooked that meal? Who planned that meal? Who will supervise the clean-up? Who will plan the overwhelming preponderance of future meals this family will enjoy? Who will cook them? Who will supervise that clean-up? Who is considered responsible for the 'clean and orderly home' the family enjoys? Who cleans and orders it? Whose education and professional advancement is viewed as less central to the family's well-being and whose fault is it if one of the delightful kids begins shoplifting when both parents are at work? The answer to these questions – all implicit in the tale of the Enjoyables – is known to us as well: 'Mom', or in the self-consciously non-sexist language of the text, 'the marriage partner who stays at home'. Those who protest that 'Mom' is not necessarily the answer to each of these questions often point to specific examples in which someone who is gendered as a male fulfils traditionally female roles in a given family. 'My brother-in-law is a house husband', they might say, or 'my uncle plans the meals' or 'my mother's work always came first'. With a bit of prompting, however, these same people tell stories detailing how this same family differs from the norm. Following a statement about 'my brother-in-law is a house husband' we often hear a narrative about how the couple's parents think it is really weird that the husband is (temporarily) at home while the wife goes out to work. The default structures of these follow-on stories paint a picture of middle-class American family norms not dissimilar to the portrait we have sketched here.

Social meaning and the language of storytelling

So far we have examined only the content of these texts, picking out specific details and considering the wealth of stereotypic associations which they bring along. Now, to provide an analytic framework in which to examine these texts in more detail, we turn our attention to the language in which the text is written and evoke the notion of evaluation introduced by Labov in two ground-breaking articles, Labov and Waletzky (1967) and Labov (1972), to account for what he perceived as deviations from an expected S–V–O order in elicited narratives.

Labov's work on narrative focuses on the deployment of evaluative devices, rhetorical embellishments and complex syntactic constructions used to encode certain information while other information is communicated in a simpler way. The vital function of evaluation in storytelling, according to Labov, is to allow the storyteller to indicate the intended 'point' of a story being told and to demonstrate its appropriateness to the context in which the story is being recounted. While Labov assumes that information more salient to the point being made will necessarily be encoded in a more complex fashion, Polanyi (1989) argues against the notion that evaluations are necessarily marked by rhetorical embellishment or complexity of encoding. Rather, what marks information as worth attending to is differential encoding: information stands out in a text because it is expressed in a way which differs from how other information is packaged. In other words, information in a text stands out and is assumed to be more relevant to the point the teller is making than is other information by virtue of having been singled out for encoding in a distinctive fashion. Therefore, a simple straightforward statement in a sea of long, convoluted phrases stands out in a text as much as a complex, multi-clause, heavily modified statement will stand out in a text composed of simple active, one-clause sentences.

There are two important general processes of evaluation: evaluation through redundancy and evaluation through exception. Economists, like other storytellers, use both types of evaluation.

Redundancy and exception operate on totally opposing principles. Repetition and redundancy function by impressing some information upon the story recipient by repeating that information more than once. The most redundantly encoded object is remembered merely because it is mentioned most frequently and the recipient assumes that it must be relevant for the storyteller because the teller repeats it more often than other information. Evaluation through exception functions by signalling the importance of a particular situation by treating it in a manner unusual for the portion of a text which calls attention to what is being said. The exceptional object, such as something encountered in an unfamiliar setting, calls attention to itself via the story recipient's own sense of the uncommon: a palm tree mentioned in a story about Hawaii is not unexpected and a recipient will not necessarily accord such an object particular importance. However, that same reader, coming upon a mention of a palm tree in a story set in Helsinki, will store that information away for future reference assuming that such an unexpected object must be relevant for the specific tale being set in that locale. Put most generally, the principles on which evaluation functions are essentially psychological: one remembers the redundantly encoded and the exceptionally encoded. The redundant and the striking emerge from a welter of detail and are foregrounded in relation to other materials which fall together into the background.

In order to apply the concept of evaluation to the story of the Enjoyable Family, let's consider a composite text of the story strung together out of the specific details the textbook presents:

> The family [has meals] from which family enjoyment is derived. [They also have] a vacuum cleaner ... an orderly home. Food, clothing, and supervision time ... [to devote to] children, whom the parents hope to enjoy ... [as well as] ... a microwave oven to heat prepared foods.
>
> (Ehrenberg and Smith 1991: 228)

Here is a list of details about the family's living style which mentions some specific appliances. While such cosy objects, familiar from our everyday lives are unremarkable in many texts, in an economics textbook with its scientific, mathematical tone and rhetoric of 'utility' and 'maximization', such objects pop out at the reader, calling attention to themselves by their novelty. While this is an example of evaluation through the unexpected, we also have examples of evaluation through redundancy. The fact that the lives of family members are 'enjoyable' is underscored several times by the repeated use of the word 'enjoy' both as an adjective and as a verb. This leads the reader to conclude that 'The family enjoys mealtimes with their enjoyable children'. Hence the name, Enjoyable Family, and the reason why we spent so much time earlier exploring the presuppositions lying behind the enjoyability of the family's meals.

Social constraints on conversational storytelling

Linguistic research has revealed two additional features of story-telling which constrain the way stories are told. We will first describe these constraints and then, in the next section, show how they illuminate storytelling in economics. The first requirement is that a story be tailored to a particular audience and reflect in its structure, content, style and level of detail the teller's judgement of the nature of the recipients: who they are, what they are interested in, what they believe to be commonplace, worth mentioning briefly, unusual, or demanding an explanation. Following Sacks (1972), we call this property of stories 'recipient design'. The second requirement is that tellers work to assure that their stories seem to flow naturally out of the topics under discussion and not out of the teller's desire to relate that particular story no matter what other topic is being addressed.

To consider how the constraints on storytelling of recipient design and conversational appropriateness function in economics, we will examine a second story from Ehrenberg and Smith's text. The family in this other story must decide '*what* to consume and *how to produce* what it consumes' (p. 228) just as the Enjoyable Family does. We reproduce below the immediate textual context in which the Others are introduced to the prospective economist-in-training.

THE OTHER FAMILY

The utility-maximizing mode of producing meals depends on the wage rate, nonwage income, and family preferences. In Figure [6].1 the budget constraint of a woman whose husband is disabled and cannot work, who has no nonwage income, and who has a relatively low wage is depicted by XY. The figure suggests that the utility-maximizing mode of meal preparation is to use homegrown food, for the simple reason that when one has a low wage, time-intensive activities are relatively inexpensive. Time spent weeding, tilling, canning, and freezing does not cost a lot, in terms of foregone earnings (goods), in this case. Thus, in the example shown, 9 hours a day

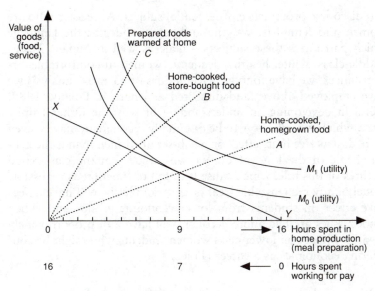

Figure 6.1 The production of family meals

would be spent at home, 7 hours performing work for pay, and meal production on isoquant M_0 represents the highest level of utility that can be attained.

(Ehrenberg and Smith 1991: 229–30)

Unlike the Enjoyable Family, the reader does not meet 'the woman' and 'the disabled husband' in their own paragraph or even in their own sentence. 'The woman' is the object of a prepositional phrase describing an attribute of the subject of the sentence 'the budget constraint', while 'the man' is introduced into the discourse as the possessed object of the 'woman'. Since the decision about consumption and production is the woman's problem – she copes without her husband – and taking into account the effects of having the 'man of the family' (usually defined as co-extensive with the 'family') introduced only as her dependent both in economic and linguistic terms, we surmise that the husband is really quite debilitated and that the weight of the household, psychologically as well as financially, is borne by the woman alone. This, then, by the stereotypes of the contemporary dominant American ethos, is an unnatural family, a family in which the woman is wage earner and financially responsible for the family's well-being even though she is not taken sufficiently seriously as an actor to merit the syntactic and discourse prominence of sentential subject. As readers who are women and feminists, we, the authors, shudder at the language which patronizes these subjects – male as well as female. Yet as middle-class, white, healthy, academic women in comfortable circumstances, we have found the techniques of narrative analysis we have employed above (and discussed at length in Polanyi 1989) useful in developing an understanding of why the Other Family story, which we will show to be essentially incoherent, may be even more destructive in its effect on a sub-set of women than is the gendered tale of the Enjoyables. We will argue that the class-based features of this tale, which cause it to fail to function as a possible model of any recognizable (real or generic) family, will have a negative effect on students from lower economic groups and, when gender issues are taken into account, will have a disproportionately negative impact on lower class women students who might be considering economics as a career choice.

Tilling and weeding, canning and freezing: how texts reveal the situated character of economic knowledge

Unlike the Enjoyable Family, the reader does not learn very much about the details of the Other Family's circumstances. But still we can imagine this couple and their situation, our vision informed by conventional images and stereotypic plots. Unlike the Enjoyables, rested and fit, dressed in their brightly coloured comfortable clothes, the Other couple seem tired and worn; the hues of their portrait are greys, browns, dingy whites. The Other Family is subdued. Perhaps the man sits in a wheelchair, the woman standing beside him as they look out of the window of their spare kitchen. Some may place this family in a rural setting, Appalachia perhaps; while others will set this tableau in a shabby apartment building in a city neighbourhood. It will depend on our own backgrounds and experience where the woman sits as she worries about the bills which need to be paid, the expensive medicine her husband needs, whether there will be presents for the kids at Christmas – all of the clichéd images of poverty which are evoked through the linguistic description of a 'woman whose husband is disabled and cannot work, who has no nonwage income, and who has a relatively low wage'.

Some of the readers of this text may envision the couple in a small but comfortable house on a relatively large lot. Thus the suggestion that 'the utility-maximizing mode of meal preparation is to use homegrown food, for the simple reason that when one has a low wage, time-intensive activities are relatively inexpensive' may initially seem reasonable. We may read on undisturbed, finding compelling the argument that 'time spent weeding, tilling, canning, and freezing does not cost a lot, in terms of foregone earnings (goods), in this case' (p. 229). But what about other readers who place this family in an apartment in a city? What about those of us who have experienced need and want? We may well require specific answers to questions which the text does not provide and which the operation of default assumption does not allow us to infer: Where does the urban family do their 'weeding [and] tilling'? Where did the family get the funds to buy the freezer and the canning equipment and pay the rent on the apartment with the pantry and root cellar evoked by the seductive poetics of 'weeding, tilling, canning and freezing'? The double letters of the spelling of these words attracts the reader's eye as the music of the sounds of the words themselves calls attention to the image of the strong, productive, healthy sunburnt farm woman out in her vegetable garden turning over the soil, planting the seeds, bringing the harvest into her comfortable kitchen to clean, peel, chop, parboil – cheerfully putting up the good foods for the winter. As we read on, the poor urban family conjured up for many of us by the initial description of the woman and her disabled husband is replaced by a relatively prosperous farm family through the juxtaposition of bucolic details and the music and power of language to evoke and to displace one image with another. The poor, worn, worried urban wife and breadwinner morphs into the round-faced farm woman in her sunny garden and steamy kitchen.

Even when captivated by this seemingly pleasant and uncontroversial scene, the reader is puzzled by details. One wonders about this happy farm woman at work outside the home during the '7 hours [she performs] work for pay' as instructed by Figure 6.1 (in addition to the '9 hours a day ... spent at home' (p. 230)). What does she do? Where does she work? Who takes care of her husband when she must be away? We know she has few marketable skills, so she must work either in manufacturing or in the service sector. But out in the country there are no restaurants; in small towns there are very few hospitals or factories. When we take into account that she must be working at night – since tilling and the rest must be done during the day – we can only assume she is employed at one of the very few workplaces in town open at night, and that, in order to keep her job, somehow she manages to get herself to work every night on time despite the facts that keeping a car running reliably is probably an expense beyond her means and there is no public transportation in rural areas. Even more problematic for the coherence of this tale is the nature of the food which this woman is able to produce from all of her 'weeding, tilling, canning, and freezing'. While it may be true that 'store-bought food easily replaces homegrown food, for example' (p. 229), it is not true that homegrown foods easily substitute for store-bought foods. The production of high protein foods, for example, is notoriously difficult, time-consuming, expensive and resource-intensive.[6] While as readers who place the Others in a rural setting we cannot understand where the farm woman works when she is working outside the home, or how she combines external employment with her tilling and weeding activities, from the perspective of a reader who may have resisted the displacement of the urban poor woman by the sturdy farm woman, the tale is hardly less confusing. Is raising homegrown food in an inner-city apartment a viable alternative for anyone?

This simple tale, then – when read with the care a student ought to pay to an illustrative example in an important textbook in a challenging academic discipline – stands revealed as essentially incoherent and dismissive of the very problems which it evokes. Evaluating the effect this story has on different populations of potential young economists is the topic addressed in the remaining sections of this chapter.

The lesson of the Others

While we may appear to criticize this text in a rather heavy-handed way, we do so with serious intent. When we dwell at length on the details of what would be necessary to support the life blithely evoked by the authors of the text, we do so in order to reveal how this simple detail reveals the story's origins in a perspective of privilege unacquainted with, and unsympathetic to, the lives of other people. An alternative account might suggest that this woman spends some of the nine hours a day she works producing food making the rounds of public and private welfare agencies or organizing marches and protests against cuts in social welfare payments. In other words, instead of 'weeding and tilling', Figure 6.1 might suggest that the woman fill her grocery cart by skilfully cultivating the system. The hidden political agenda here at work dictates that poor people accept and work within the status quo, tilling and weeding, rather than taking on more activist forms of optimization. When we examine the implications of the disrespect-ful treatment accorded the Others as representatives of people at the lower end of the economic scale, we can see how this picture is even more pernicious for some women than may be initially obvi-ous to those situated, like the authors, in positions of academic privilege. The fantasy about the lives of the poor presented implic-itly in the Others' story glosses over the pain, hardships, and deprivation their lives would actually entail in favour of an ideal-ized scene of circumstances which appear to the average economist as not really so unfortunate. After all, in the imagination, the home-preserved fruits and vegetables produced by the woman's canning activities compare very favourably with store-bought food served fresh from the microwave. Readers are therefore invited to feel satisfied with the basic analysis as providing a reasonably com-plete story of how even poor families are able to provide for themselves through rational choice based in acceptance of a passive political role.

This account rests on a woman working 16 hours a day, in the home, in food production and outside of the home in paid work. An account of American family economics in which the breadwin-ner were a man would hardly dare to make an assumption that the man worked 16 hours a day. Nor would there be an account of a poor family with a male breadwinner which assumes that, in addi-tion to working a full workday for poor wages, the man spend hours growing food to feed the family and then cooking and pre-serving what he grew. The image evoked of a man in an apron stirring a big pot of peach preserves would be too jarring, too remote from the experience of the envisioned student reader to allow such a text to be a simple, transparent example of con-strained optimization. So this poor family must be headed by a woman and, while any student from a poor background might well experience this story as incoherent and insulting in its incoherence, young women from poor backgrounds would be even harder hit than their male colleagues. Seeing themselves, their mothers, and other adult female relations and friends reflected in this woman – at least in part due to their common class positioning and gender – poor female students might well wonder why a woman should work a 16-hour day when such an expectation would not be blandly made of a man. Thus we can see how class, taken together with gender and, by implication, with other degrees of separation, func-tion to construct us as women and as speakers. After we have considered how the plot of these stories can be linked to the plots of the lives of young student economists, we will return, in the concluding sections of this chapter, to consider how such a tale can function as a mechanism of disciplinary reproduction.

Story plots and recipient design at work in reproducing the community of economic practice

So far we have said nothing about the action in economic stories. It is instructive to consider such stories as stories like any other. Following Prince (1972), we consider that each story begins with a specific situation in the storyworld; an action then transforms the world so that, by the time the story ends, the world has changed. While some change of state is a necessary condition for a successful plot, it is not a sufficient condition for a successful story. To be meaningful to those who listen to a tale, the plot of a story must involve a change of state which is illustrative of events in the world of the storyteller and that change of state must make a sufficiently interesting 'point' about the world inhabited by those listening to the tale.

Returning to the stories of the two families, we must ask how the action in this story is structured so that the intended recipients, other economists and economists-in-training, find it compelling. The plots of the stories are simple and essentially identical:

> The family desires food. The family decides what is the best tradeoff between money and time as a way of obtaining food. The family optimizes its resources. The family obtains food and enjoys its meal.

For an economist, this plot is compelling precisely because it is a version of the generic economic plot in which the economic outcome for an agent is the result of constrained optimization through rational choice – whether the agent is an individual, a family, a commercial enterprise or a nation. Students learn over and over again throughout their career that this is the only plot. Economics, students come to learn, is not so much the study of economies in the common-sense meaning where the term 'economies' implies money and financial transaction, nor a field concerned with explaining a domain of facts about goods and services, but is a field with a much more ambitious view of its domain. Rather than merely dealing with the distribution of money and markets, neoclassical economics is concerned with nothing less than the application to any complex social situation of a theory of rational decision making by individualistic agents out to maximize their own satisfaction (Strassmann, 1993a).[7]

In the plot of making a career as an economist, the role which these two stories play in students' developmental trajectory through the curriculum is very important and formative. In working through these stories, the young economist moves from the state of not knowing how to think like an economist in relation to decision making in the households of ordinary persons to another state, that of thinking like an economist. As we pointed out earlier, the economists' characterization of social phenomena often has important consequences. Students who remain in economics and become economic policy makers use economists' thinking as the basis of the policies which they formulate. These policies, in turn, may have very serious effects on the lives of other people. Admitting into the ranks of economic policy makers individuals who think like economists but who come from backgrounds different from those of the dominant practitioners might result in constrained optimization, suggesting rather different policies than is now typically the case. By telling stories which discourage 'non-standard' students from pursuing economic careers, disciplinary and social control remains firmly in the hands of the 'standard' economists. In the concluding sections of this chapter, we will deal with the mechanics of disciplinary gatekeeping as we examine how these stories, and by implication some of the other stories young economists are exposed to, function to discourage potential economists who may differ from the prevailing disciplinary norm along some dimension of difference. To do so, we will draw upon conversational analytic work which treats talk as collaborative accomplishments of all the parties involved. We will argue that an economist-to-be will be most easily persuaded by a story which takes into account what that student understands about the world, what he or she believes and the inferences that student will make on the basis of information explicitly presented.

Gatekeeping and storytelling in economics

Students who experience the disciplinary texts with which they are presented as reasonably unproblematic are largely unaware of how their easy acceptance of assumptions and arguments reveals them to be appropriate, expected conversational partners in the disciplinary discourse of the field.[8] For those who do experience dissonance with the default assumptions and evaluative signifiers in a story, the situation is different. These people, often women or members of other under-represented groups, will be jarred into the realization that they do not fit the terms of acceptability of the community. Readers of the story of the Other Family, for example, who have experienced urban or rural poverty or poverty re-enforced by handicap or illness, are likely to feel consternation when they read this incoherent account. Their consternation and feeling of isolation can only increase when they look around them and observe that their teachers and those fellow students who most resemble the disciplinary stereotype for an economist apparently feel no dissonance when encountering this tale. The very fact of their own discomfort, taken together with the nonchalance with which others view the same text, allows them – by generalizing rules of recipient design in conversational storytelling – to conclude that they are not among the expected recipients for this story. In other words, given that this story was presented in an elementary textbook for those who are seriously interested in entering the world of the professional economist, students who have problems accepting the premises of a simple example (which arouses no problem in others) will be informed that they are not the type of person for whom the text was meant. They are not potential economists. Furthermore, such readers are not likely to be compelled to try to enter a disciplinary conversation which complacently presents an offensive status quo as normal and acceptable. Even more ominously: should they voice their discomfort, it is entirely likely that other students, as well as the professor leading the class, will also conclude that the malcontents are just not the right sort of people to be economists.

We contend that similar processes of marginalization occurring again and again throughout a student's early training constitute one mechanism through which the community of practitioners reproduces itself. The default assumptions and pattern of evaluation which economists build into their narratives act to select their intended audience. Effectively functioning as a social filter, these stories participate in complex screening processes which eventually remove from the pool of prospective professionals those people whose experiences might lead them to produce alternative stories.

The reproduction of economists

The full story of the reproduction of the community of trained economists remains to be told, but in this chapter we have provided a validation of otherwise anecdotal claims that 'chronic distortions, omissions and stereotypes in the textbooks – and by professors in their lectures – continue to impede the progress of women and minorities in the profession [of economics]', as maintained by Susan Feiner, Chair of the ad hoc Committee of the American Economics Association for Race and Gender Balance in the Economics Curriculum in an article in *Black Issues in Higher Education* (Phillip 1993: 14; see also Feiner and Morgan 1987). We have provided a methodology for refuting the 'reservations about mixing race, gender and economics' of 'Nobel Prize-winning economist Dr. Milton Friedman'[9] who insists in the same article that 'an economics curriculum should have the work of the best people and it should have nothing to do with race and gender. What ought to count is content and quality and not who the persons are that are teaching or who are mentioned in the textbooks.' We have shown that 'the persons who are mentioned in the textbooks', even if they are imaginary persons such as the Enjoyables and the Others, are the content of what is taught. We have demonstrated that race, gender and class are already in the curriculum. By paying more attention to these matters, the gender, class and ethnic makeup of 'the best people' – whose work by virtue of its 'high quality' is included in the curriculum – may change. These people, we maintain, are systematically excluded from the field of economics today in part by the textual techniques we have explored here. This situation has been recognized as pernicious by another Nobel Prize winner, John Kenneth Galbraith, when he says: 'In my own lifetime, I have generally voted for the promotion of people who were most like Galbraith. This is a tendency that must always be watched' (Phillip 1993: 14). Our own purpose in carrying out this analysis is to expose the myths that have kept the gates closed to those potential economists who might tell stories ultimately more reflective of the world in which we actually live than the stories of rational optimization that economists tell today.

Notes

1. Both authors contributed equally to the work in this chapter. In our joint work, we alternate the ordering of our names because academic

administrative accounting practices do not necessarily consider that authorship conventions may differ among the various disciplines.

2. The characterization of neoclassical economic theory given here draws heavily on arguments presented in Strassmann (1993a, 1993b).

3. Such a charge of disciplinary irrelevance recalls similar charges encountered by feminists investigating language and gender within the field of linguistics.

4. In that paper we used our findings to argue that the metaphor of situated knowledge, and not the metaphor of the marketplace of ideas as suggested by McCloskey (1985), provides the superior account of how some arguments in economics prevail over others. The marketplace idea, which implies that prevailing accounts are the best accounts, does not provide an explanation of why the accounts which do prevail by appearing compelling to the majority of practitioners in the discipline reflect their positioning as members of the white, North American, healthy, heterosexual, male, employed élite. Taking into account how knowledge is situated and acknowledging the contextual grounding of scientific accounts, as Harding (1991) suggests, allows us to understand this otherwise strange coincidence and explains why accounts which reflect other positionings are usually judged less self-evidently correct by those in disciplinary control.

5. Those persons who know themselves to be 'different' in some way from the dominant group often understand many of the assumptions of core members and may emulate core responses. This kind of performance requires explicitly thinking through the default assumptions others produce automatically and then planning a response to the information which would be appropriate for the cultural initiate being modelled. Such attempts at passing, whether by members of minorities, by ethnographers or other foreigners or by social isolates, frequently result in feelings of alienation and exhaustion which eventually undermine the effort and lead to the unmasking of the outsider as a fraud.

6. Growing a field of soybeans requires a large plot of land; the rice to eat with it to form a complete vegetable protein requires a flooded paddy. Raising a cow for milk and cheese requires extensive grain production or purchase in addition to storage facilities and processing equipment; even chickens who produce eggs and whose lives can be dispatched by one blow from the woman's handy hatchet require shelter, feed and medical care if they are to provide a steady supply of meal stuff for the family. Even bread is difficult to raise without a large wheat field, access to a mill and all of the other equipment and support needed to harvest the fruit of bread trees.

7. Gary Becker won the 1993 Nobel Prize in Economics for his work applying constrained optimization theory to the household. Becker's work has been characterized by Barbara Bergmann (1995), a prominent

feminist economist, as 'sexist and preposterous' both because it assumes traditional gender roles in the economy and argues for their self-evident correctness.

8. See Smitherman-Donaldson (1988) for a discussion of the differential impact of example sentences in linguistics on African American and European American students.

9. Economists are extraordinarily proud of having a Nobel Prize in their field. No conversation, article or presentation is complete without reference to the Prize. So, in the interest of completeness, we have mentioned it in this chapter. (At least one reviewer of this chapter objected to the 'hyperbole' in our stating that 'No conversation, article or presentation is complete without reference to the Prize'. Oddly enough, taking as data books and articles, conference papers, departmental colloquia, discussions of sponsorship and casual conversation about the field, this generalization appears to be all but literally true.)

References

Bergmann Barbara R 1995 Becker's theory of the family: preposterous conclusions. *Feminist Economics* 1.1: 141–50.

Cameron Deborah this volume: The language-gender interface: challenging co-optation.

Eckert Penelope, McConnell-Ginet Sally 1992 Communities of practice: where language, gender and power all live. In Bucholtz Mary, Hall Kira, Moonwomon Birch (eds) *Locating power: papers from the second Berkeley women and language conference*. Berkeley Women and Language Group, Berkeley, CA pp 89–99.

Ehrenberg Ronald G, Smith Robert S 1991 *Modern labor economics: theory and public policy* (4th edn). Harper Collins, New York.

Feiner Susan F, Morgan Barbara A 1987 Women and minorities in introductory economics textbooks: 1974–1984. *Journal of Economic Education* 18.4: 376–92.

Haraway Donna 1988 Situated knowledges: the science question in feminism and the privilege of the partial perspective. *Feminist Studies* 14.3: 575–99.

Harding Sandra 1991 *Whose science? Whose knowledge?: thinking from women's lives*. Cornell University Press, Ithaca, NY.

Labov William 1972 The transformation of experience in narrative syntax. In *Language in the inner city*. University of Pennsylvania Press, Philadelphia pp 354–95.

Labov William, Waletzky Joshua 1967 Narrative analysis. In Helm June (ed) *Essays on the verbal and visual arts*. University of Washington Press, Seattle pp 12–44.

Lave Jean, Wenger Etienne 1991 *Situated learning: legitimate peripheral participation*. Cambridge University Press, Cambridge.

Marcus George E, Fischer Michael M J 1986 *Anthropology as cultural critique: an experimental moment in the human sciences*. University of Chicago Press, Chicago.

McCloskey Donald 1985 *The rhetoric of economics*. University of Wisconsin Press, Madison.

Phillip Mary-Christine 1993 Race, gender and economics in the classroom. *Black Issues in Higher Education* 10.8 (17 June): 14–18.

Polanyi Livia 1989 *Telling the American story: a structural and cultural analysis of conversational storytelling*. MIT Press, Cambridge, MA.

Prince Gerald 1972 *Narrative analysis*. Mouton, The Hague.

Sacks Harvey 1972 On the analyzability of stories by children. In Gumperz John, Hymes Dell (eds) *Directions in sociolinguistics: the ethnography of communication*. Holt, Rinehart & Winston, New York pp 325–45.

Samuels Warren 1992 Institutional economics. In Greenway David, Bleaney Michael, Stewart Ian (eds) *Economics in perspective*. Routledge, London pp 105–18.

Smitherman-Donaldson Geneva 1988 Discriminatory discourse on Afro-American speech. In Smitherman-Donaldson Geneva, van Dijk Teun A (eds) *Discourse and discrimination*. Wayne State University Press, Detroit, MI pp 144–75.

Strassmann Diana 1993a Not a free market: the rhetoric of disciplinary authority. In Ferber Marianne, Nelson Julie (eds) *Beyond economic man: feminist theory and economics*. University of Chicago Press, Chicago pp 54–68.

Strassmann Diana 1993b The stories of economics and the power of the storyteller. *History of Political Economy* 25.1: 145–63.

Strassmann Diana, Polanyi Livia 1995 The economist as storyteller: what the texts reveal. In Feiner Susan, Kuiper Edith, Ott Notburga, Sap Jolande, Tzannatos Zafiris (eds) *Out of the margin: feminist perspectives on economic theory*. Routledge, London pp 129–50.

Traweek Sharon 1988 *Beamtimes and lifetimes: the world of high energy physics*. Harvard University Press, Cambridge, MA.

Traweek Sharon 1992 Border crossings: narrative strategies in science studies among physicists at Tsukuba Science City, Japan. In Pickering Andrew (ed) *Science as practice and culture*. University of Chicago Press, Chicago pp 429–61.

Truth Sojourner 1985 [1851] Ain't I a woman? Reprinted in Gilbert Sandra M, Gubar Susan (eds) *The Norton anthology of literature by women: the tradition in English*. Norton, New York p 253.

7 *Consensual sex or sexual harassment: negotiating meaning*[1]

Susan Ehrlich and Ruth King

Introduction

Recent work by feminist legal theorists (for example, MacKinnon 1987, 1989, Crenshaw 1992) has exposed the androcentric nature of legal definitions pertaining to rape and sexual harassment and the way that legal adjudication of male sexual aggression tends to protect the interests of men.[2] MacKinnon (1987: 87), for example, shows the crime of rape to be defined 'according to what men think violates women'. First, it is defined around penetration: 'I do think the crime of rape focuses more centrally on what men define as sexuality than on women's experience of our sexual being, hence its violation' (1987: 87).[3] Second, crucial elements of rape, including force or coercion on the part of the man and lack of consent on the part of the woman, are defined from a male perspective (1989: 173):

> Rape cases finding insufficient evidence of force reveal that acceptable sex, in the legal perspective, can entail a lot of force. This is both a result of the way specific facts are perceived and interpreted within the legal system and the way the injury is defined by law. The level of acceptable force is adjudicated starting just above the level set by what is seen as normal male sexual behavior, including the normal level of force, rather than at the victim's, or women's point of violation.

Crenshaw (1992: 437) focuses on legal definitions of consent, making the point that historically the requirement of 'utmost resistance' was a necessary criterion for the crime of rape; that is, if a woman did not resist a man's sexual advances to the 'utmost', then rape did not occur. Estrich (1986: 1122) comments: 'in effect, the "utmost resistance" rule required both that the woman resist to the "utmost" and that such resistance must not have abated during the struggle.' While the criterion of 'utmost resistance' is not currently encoded in criminal definitions of rape, Crenshaw notes that a similar concept is operative in the adjudication of rape and sexual harassment cases. In such inquiries, attention tends to be focused much more on the woman's behaviour and character than on the man's. Thus, whether or not androcentric definitions of sexual harassment or rape are actually encoded in law, the interpretation and characterization of events in such cases are 'overwhelmingly directed toward interrogating and discrediting the woman's character on behalf of maintaining a considerable range of sexual prerogatives for men' (Crenshaw 1992: 409). More generally, the assumptions that structure both the legal definitions of rape and sexual harassment and the adjudication of such cases are informed by ideologically driven notions of male privilege and women's subordination.

In this paper we investigate the way in which sexual harassment and acquaintance rape are constructed in the 'talk' of a sexual harassment tribunal. More specifically, we show how the questions asked in this institutional context do ideological work: they construct the events as consensual sex.[4] By asking certain kinds of questions about the conduct of the female complainants, both the defendant's representative and the tribunal members question whether the women's behaviour meets the criterion of 'utmost resistance', subtly suggesting that the women's lack of 'appropriate' resistance undermines the charges of sexual harassment. Thus, we demonstrate the androcentric assumptions embedded in the linguistic patterns of this adjudication process.

In our previous work (Ehrlich and King 1994), we have investigated the androcentric and sexist (re)definitions that feminist linguistic innovations, terms such as *sexual harassment, sexism, date rape*, take on in the mainstream print media. While feminists have recognized the importance of giving a name to women's experiences, it is not at all clear that as terms such as *feminism, sexism, sexual harassment, date rape*, etc., pervade our culture, that their use is consistent with their intended feminist-influenced meanings. Because linguistic meanings are to a large extent socially constructed and constituted, such terms may get redefined and depoliticized by a speech community that is not predominantly feminist and indeed is often sexist. Just as words such as 'no' (in the context of a woman refusing a man's sexual advances) can undergo a kind of 'semantic reversal',[5] so non-sexist and feminist linguistic innovations may lose their intended meanings as they get integrated into the larger, sexist speech community; in Treichler's (1990) terms, they may be 'cannibalized' by the dominant culture they are intending to subvert. In Ehrlich and King (1994), we identify a number of discursive strategies by which feminist linguistic innovations are systematically redefined and depoliticized in the print media, basing our analysis on texts reflecting both conservative and liberal viewpoints. For example, one strategy of redefinition involves expanding the definition of terms such as sexual harassment and date rape to such extremes (exploiting feminists' attempts to expand the definitions of these phenomena) and then imputing this expanded (unreasonable) definition to feminists. The effect of this kind of expansion strategy is to ridicule and trivialize the phenomenon in question. Taylor (1991: 39) quotes the journalist Stephanie Gutmann of *Reason* magazine who states about date rape:

> The real story about campus date rape is not that there's been any significant increase of rape on college campuses, at least of the acquaintance type, but that the word *rape* is being stretched to encompass **any type of sexual interaction**. (Emphasis added.)

Here Gutmann presumably is referring to feminists' attempts to expand the notion of rape so that it includes more than just penetration and so that mutual consent becomes a crucial criterion in distinguishing rape from non-rape. Gutmann overstates the case significantly by saying that rape now encompasses 'any kind of sexual interaction'. Later in this same article, a feminist revision of the notion of rape attributed to Andrea Parrot that 'any sexual intercourse without mutual desire is a form of rape' is misrepresented when Taylor (1991: 39) incorrectly 'paraphrases' Parrot in the following way: 'by the definition of the radical feminists, all sexual encounters that involve any confusion or ambivalence constitute rape' and then goes on to quote Stephanie Gutmann again: 'Ordinary bungled sex – the kind you regret in the morning or even during – is being classified as rape. ... Bad or confused feelings after sex becomes someone else's fault.'

This same expansion strategy is evident in an article on feminism,

. published in the *National Review* (Minogue 1991: 48), but this time it is sexual abuse that is redefined. Again, the author plays on feminist attempts to broaden notions like sexual abuse, rape and sexual harassment.

> A raised consciousness in this area [feminism] plays with propositions of the form 'X per cent of women have experienced sexual interference before the age of Y,' where X is a very large number, and Y as low as you care to make it, and 'sexual interference' defined so broadly that **it can include hearing an older sibling discuss his/her adolescent sexual experimentation.** (Emphasis added.)

Clearly, women's concern with issues such as date rape and sexual abuse is rendered ludicrous and misguided when date rape refers to 'any kind of sexual interaction' or 'ordinary bungled sex' and when sexual abuse is defined as overhearing a sibling refer to sexual experimentation.

Our previous work, then, shows the way in which words or terms at the heart of political and ideological disputes typically develop diverse meanings and representations within a culture and often become the site of ideological struggle. Similarly, the phenomena of sexual harassment and date rape can themselves be constructed and interpreted in diverse ways, with these diverse meanings being produced, negotiated and challenged in the face-to-face interactions of institutional settings. While the complainants and the tribunal members in the hearing that we describe below characterize the events in different ways, it is the tribunal members' characterizations of events as consensual sex (rather than as sexual harassment or as rape) that dominate the interactions. Those of the complainants are ignored and suppressed due to the structural inequalities that inform the interactional patterns of this kind of institutional setting. Thus, we see how language becomes a site of contestation: sexist and androcentric assumptions about sexual harassment and rape are reflected, challenged and finally reproduced in the linguistic practices of this institutional interaction.

The university disciplinary tribunal

The data we present here come from a York University (Canada) disciplinary tribunal dealing with sexual harassment. York University disciplinary tribunals are university trials that operate outside of the provincial or federal legal system. Members of the university community can be tried for various kinds of misconduct, including unauthorized entry or access, theft or destruction of property, assault or threat of assault and harassment or discrimination that contravenes the provincial Human Rights Code or the Canadian Charter of Rights and Freedoms. Each case is heard by three tribunal members who are drawn from a larger pool consisting of university faculty members and students.[6] Penalties range from public admonition to expulsion from the university. It is normally the case that these tribunals are open to the public. In the case described here, two charges of sexual harassment had been brought against a male student (the defendant) by two female students (the complainants), all undergraduates at York University. The tribunal members hearing the case consisted of a male member of the law faculty (the tribunal's chair), a female faculty member in the faculty of arts and a female graduate student in the faculty of arts. The case against the defendant was presented by the university's legal counsel. According to the regulations of York University, sexual harassment is defined as 'the unwanted attention of a sexually oriented nature made by a person who knows or ought reasonably to know that such attention is unwanted'. The same individual has been charged by the same plaintiffs under the Criminal Code of Canada on two counts of sexual assault. While the defendant's behaviour falls under the category of sexual assault under the Ontario criminal code, York University's rules and regulations do not include sexual assault as a possible offence.

In feminist terms, the defendant has been accused of acquaintance or date rape. Both alleged instances of sexual harassment occurred in the women's residence rooms two nights apart. Each woman had invited the defendant to her room, and in both cases he allegedly persisted in sexual behaviour that was unwanted by the women. In both cases, the women report that they were quite clear and insistent that he stop, but their demands were ignored. In one of the cases, there was another man and woman in the room during the period that the unwanted sexual behaviour took place. This woman served as a witness for the prosecution's case. The two complainants were casual acquaintances prior to the alleged instances of sexual harassment or acquaintance rape. They met coincidentally a short time after the incidents, discovered each other's experience with the defendant, and together lodged a complaint of sexual harassment.

In our analysis of this hearing and our attempt to understand the diverse meanings attached to the events in question, we have focused, first, on the interaction between the defendant's representative[7] and the complainants and their witnesses and, second, on the interaction between members of the disciplinary tribunal and the complainants and their witnesses. During the course of these hearings, cross-examination was allowed once individuals had completed their testimony. In addition, the members of the disciplinary tribunal were at liberty to ask questions of individuals once the individuals had completed their testimony. We have chosen here to focus on two themes evident in the questions asked by both the defendant's representative and the tribunal members – (1) the (so-called) 'inaction' of the complainants and (2) the minimizing of the complainants' fear. It is through an examination of these two kinds of questions that we begin to see how the events in question are interpreted and reconstructed by both the defendant's representative and by two of the tribunal members (the two faculty members) as consensual sex.

Cross-examination by the defendant's representative

It is perhaps not at all surprising that the questions and statements of the defendant's representative[8] attempt to construct the events as consensual sex, rather than sexual harassment or acquaintance rape. The first step in this discursive strategy involves focusing on the complainants' actions (or behaviour), which the defence characterizes as 'inaction'. In (1) below, the representative asserts over a couple of turns that if the complainant, Kelly,[9] had **really** been in trouble or had been in **real** trouble, surely she would have cried out. Notice that many of these utterances with the illocutionary force of assertions are not even in the form of questions. Thus, the complainant's lack of resistance in the form of yelling or screaming is taken to mean that she was not really in trouble, that is, that sexual harassment or sexual assault had not really taken place.[10]

1. Q: Why is it that you made no attempt to scream? Can you explain what you mean by 'I really didn't want anybody to know'? If you were in such difficulty, if you felt threatened, if you felt that an assault was taking place, it strikes me as only natural [to cry out] and that help probably was available as that wall was extremely thin... Could you tell the panel what was in your mind?
   A: I was afraid. I was ashamed that I had lost control of the situation. I was embarrassed and above that, I honestly can't tell you why I didn't scream.

Q: I would submit, though I understand your embarrassment, if your story is correct, the fact is that help overrides embarrassment and if you really were in trouble then the only appropriate way to protect yourself was to yell out. Embarrassment would have been the last thing on your mind at the time if you were in real trouble.

In example (2), we see again that the representative's questions suggest that Kelly's failure to leave the room, her failure to call the police, etc. – that is, her failing to take the type of action that the representative considers appropriate – means that a sexual assault had not taken place.

2. Q: If you were feeling that an assault had taken place why at that point did you simply not leave the room, get dressed, while he was asleep, leave the building and assuming for the moment that you were embarrassed ... uh ... just not go back? Why would you wait for a second assault to take place when he woke up? You had ample opportunity to leave then and call the police. Why did you not call the police?

A: I was in shock. I didn't know what to do. I didn't know what he'd do.

The second step in the construction of these events as consensual sex involves eliminating or minimizing the reasons for the complainant's so-called inaction. That is, if no good justification can be provided for the complainants' lack of loud or public resistance, then this can only be construed as consent to the sexual activity. In response to the numerous questions posed by both the defendant's representative and the tribunal members regarding the complainants' 'inaction', the complainants generally responded by making comments about how frightened they were, how frightening an individual Tom, the defendant, was that night. Here is an example of such a comment from the second complainant, Jenny:

3. I know it was dumb of me to invite ... let Tom stay in my bed but in residence everyone's like your brother and you don't imagine that that could happen. I've definitely learned from this but I didn't yell ... I didn't do anything ... Marg and Bob weren't going to help me. If he hits me they're not going to stop him and the door was locked. He's a scary guy ... I didn't want to get hit. I didn't want to get raped but I didn't want to get hit.

In example (4), what we see is an attempt on the part of the defendant's representative to discredit or minimize Jenny's fear of the defendant, Tom. As stated previously, the second part of constructing these events as consensual sex involves eliminating the justification for the complainant's behaviour.

> 4. Q: You also say here [in your testimony] that I thought I had offended him. And it strikes me that women who feel threatened are not likely to worry about whether or not they offend the person who is in the process of threatening them ... So I guess my question is if you're worried about offending him, were you feeling threatened at that point? Because your testimony implies you were feeling threatened at that point and yet you say that you didn't want to offend him.

In this example, the defendant's representative asserts that a contradiction exists between feeling that you don't want to offend someone and at the same time feeling threatened by that person. He then calls into question the fact that Jenny was feeling threatened, given the apparent contradiction alluded to above. Thus these comments attempt to invalidate the complainant's feelings of fear and, therefore, eradicate the justification for her behaviour. With the justification for the so-called inaction eradicated, the behaviour in question can be construed as not meeting the criterion of 'utmost resistance' and the events can be construed as consensual sex.

Tribunal members' questions of complainants and their witnesses

As stated above, it is perhaps predictable that the defendant's representative would have as his explicit goal the construction of these events as consensual sex, and not sexual harassment or sexual assault. What is perhaps more surprising is that the same themes used by the defence in cross-examination of the complainants are also evident in the questions used by the tribunal members. The tribunal members make up a supposedly neutral body and ultimately are the ones who decide on the guilt or innocence and the penalty of the defendant. Interestingly, one of the tribunal members, the female faculty member, prefaced her questioning of the two complainants and the witness with a lengthy statement asserting the neutrality of her questions. It is our contention, however, that two of the tribunal members (the two professors), like the defendant's representative, also manage to construct and define the events as consensual sex through their questioning.

We see the same two themes in the tribunal members' questions: (1) the so-called inaction of the complainants and the witness and (2) the minimizing of these individuals' fear of the defendant. The behaviour of the complainants and witness was a particular concern of one of the tribunal members, the female faculty member, who asked numerous questions about the women's options. Below is an example from her questioning of Jenny.

5. Q: I realize you were under certain stress but in your story I heard the men left the room twice on two different occasions. And you and Marg were alone in the room. What might have been your **option**? I see an **option**. It may not have occurred to you but I simply want to explore that **option** with you. Uh, did it occur to you that you could lock the room so that they may not return to your room? (Emphasis added.)

A: It did, but it didn't. Now it does. I mean looking back. Everyone was telling me nothing's going on. Don't worry about it. Forget about it. When your friends are telling you nothing's going on, you start to question ... maybe nothing is going on. I just ... I couldn't think.

Q: It didn't occur to you that Marg or you, I mean I understand you were under stress ... was Marg also intimidated by Mr A?

This tribunal member, while producing several interrogative sentences, is not, for the most part, asking information-gathering questions. Rather, her utterances have the illocutionary force of assertions, i.e. *You had other options. You should have locked the door. It should have occurred to you to lock the door.* The illocutionary force of the utterances in (5) is the same as those of the defendant's representative in (1). Both the defendant's representative and the tribunal member are asserting what these women should have or could have done in order to resist the advances of the defendant, although the latter was much bolder about producing assertions in both form and function. In spite of continually questioning the complainants about their 'options', we note that the female faculty member, when questioning the defendant, does not ask questions which focus on the options available to him, for example, to adhere to the women's wishes.

While questioning Marg, the witness for Jenny, the tribunal

member again discusses the options the witness had. This is illustrated in (6) and (7) below.

6. Q: In spite of Jenny telling you that he was trying things that she didn't want, were you ... I don't know how to phrase ... did you feel you had some **options** to do something for Jenny?

   A: Well, I wanted to do something for her but I didn't know what to do. I was afraid that if I said anything to Tom or tried to do anything that he would hurt me or hurt Jenny for trying to stop it. And everything was happening so fast. I didn't even think about knocking on the neighbour's door or anything.

7. Q: I mean ... that evening did you ever feel you knew Bob enough to get him involved because I think you were intimidated?

   A: Yeah. I was close enough with Bob [to]

   Q: [to] tell him 'Get up and do something. I hear some noises.' Or you didn't feel that there was anything really going on. I don't want to put words in your mouth. Tell me how you felt.

   A: Towards Bob?

   Q: What **options** you might have had to tell Bob something?

   A: When I asked Bob to talk to Tom ... was the only thing I could think of ... to get someone to tell Tom to stop it. I thought Bob and Tom are friends. He'll listen to Bob but they didn't get the opportunity. I kind of think that Bob is very much influenced by Tom. ... I think he's scared of Tom. I think Tom is a very intimidating person. He scares a lot of people ... the way he talks.

In example (6), the tribunal member has difficulty phrasing her question as indicated by a couple of false starts and her admission that she doesn't know how to phrase the question, perhaps because what she really wants is not to ask but to assert that the witness should have done something to help Jenny. In example (7), the tribunal member explicitly states what Marg could have/should have said to Bob in order to provoke him into action and then says that she does not want to put words into the witness's mouth. This repeated emphasis on the women's so-called 'options' in examples (5)–(7) functions to highlight their apparent lack of resistance – the fact that they didn't lock the door, the fact that Marg didn't help Jenny, the fact that Marg didn't get Bob to do something. And by focusing on the actions that the women didn't take in spite of 'options', the events begin to get constructed as the result of **choices** the women made. Options after all, and this is the word used consistently by this tribunal member, imply choices. The women are represented as having had options; they simply did not choose the best options. In other words, the women are represented as having exercised some agency in or even having chosen to engage in the sexual activities. In a much more subtle way, then, this tribunal member is also raising the possibility that the women did not adequately resist the sexual aggression of the defendant and, thus, engaged in consensual sex or, in the case of the witness, was a witness to consensual sex.

As stated above, the most frequent response to questions concerning the complainants' apparent 'passive' behaviour in spite of 'options' was fear. We see this in both (6) and (7). After the complainants' and witnesses' expressions of fear (and these occurred numerous times during the testimony and questioning), the tribunal members generally followed with questions attempting to deconstruct the cause or source of the fear. This can be seen in (8) below where the chair of the tribunal, the male law faculty member, is questioning Kelly.

8. Q: In your statement, I think, twice, you mention 'he was sounding very angry' and 'I was scared' and I was wondering if you could elaborate on what you mean by that? What was he saying that you found scary? If you remember anything specific or whether it was an impression.

   A: It was just rough. It was mostly ... he just ... it was demanding. I didn't feel like I had any more choice. And whatever he said was no longer a request. It was a demand.

   Q: So, in your statement when you say he said 'I paid for dinner and you invited me up so what did you expect' ... that was something you perceived as demanding and rough. It wasn't like a joking comment in your mind.

   A: No, it wasn't a joke at all.

   Q: Did he raise his voice? Or was it just very emphatic?

   A: No, he didn't raise his voice but it was very blunt, very ...

   Q: Okay.

Here we see the tribunal member trying to get at the precise causes of Kelly's fear. What was it about Tom that was frightening? Was it his tone of voice?, etc. We also see here a suggestion that some of the defendant's frightening comments might have been jokes. This same tribunal member asks similar questions of Marg, the witness. (This example follows directly after example (7).)

9. Q: Could you explain that? Because we've heard that twice and in your story the only time you mention about being scared of Tom was with the eavesdropping incident ... that he was very scary. He was insisting that you tell him. Were there other things that he did or is it a general demeanour? What do you mean by he's very scary?

    A: He's ... the way he ... it seems to me if his way ... it's either his way or no way. The way he was talking to Bob like even his friend Bob when I asked Bob to come to the bathroom, Tom said 'No, don't go.' And Bob hesitated not to go which sort of led me to believe that Bob was scared of Tom and maybe Bob knows a history of [Tom]

    Q: [Well], let's just stick to what you know. The two times in that evening that you found Tom scary would be the eavesdropping incident and with Bob ... how insistent he was about Bob. You saw a side of him that scared you. Anything else than those two things?

    A: No.

Here we see the questioner again trying to isolate the precise aspects of the defendant or the defendant's behaviour that were frightening to the witness. These attempts to pinpoint so precisely and specifically the causes of the women's fear have the effect of reducing or minimizing the women's fear. (Notice the use of **only** in the first question of example (9).) It seems that it was not sufficient for the women to simply report that the defendant 'was a very scary guy'. Through this tribunal member's questioning and his attempts to break down the women's fear into its component parts, the women's fear begins to be attributed to specific incidents or specific aspects of the defendant's behaviour. In the last part of example (9), we see the tribunal member cutting Marg off and rephrasing her comments about her fear of Tom. What began as a description of how intimidating the witness found the defendant is transformed into the witness feeling frightened only twice over the course of events. We see here how the attempt to deconstruct the witness's fear has the effect of diminishing its impact. And as we have stated previously, by minimizing the complainants' fear, the complainants' justification for their behaviour is eliminated. This is the two-part discursive strategy that functions to construct and define the events in question as consensual sex and not sexual harassment or acquaintance rape: first, the women's apparent lack of resistance is established; second, its justification is minimized and/or eliminated; if no other reason can be provided for the complainants' behaviour, then their apparent lack of resistance means that the sexual activity was consensual. In the case of the defendant's representative, the discursive strategy is quite explicit and conscious; in the case of the tribunal members it operates in a more subtle, less conscious manner perhaps, but the same strategy is operative.

Negotiating meanings

We have argued up to now that the questions asked by the defendant's representative and the tribunal members function to characterize or interpret the events in question in a particular way. This is not to say, however, that the complainants subscribe to this same interpretation of the events. In example (8), for instance, we see the complainant, Kelly, commenting on her perceived lack of choice during the events and the fact that Tom's utterances were demands, not requests. Indeed, throughout the hearing, the complainants and their witness provided an alternative interpretation of the events, i.e. as sexual harassment or acquaintance rape. The question that arises, then, is the extent to which there was a struggle over the meaning or interpretation of these events and, if so, whose meanings prevailed?

Research on both courtroom discourse and doctor–patient discourse (for example, Walker 1987, Fisher 1991) has highlighted the power of the questioners in these settings (i.e. the lawyers or judges, the doctors) to control interactions. Walker (1987: 79), for example, in her research on courtroom discourse, reports on interviews with witnesses who 'report a feeling of frustration at being denied the right to tell their stories their own way and complain of the lack of being in control'. Fisher (1991: 162) compares a doctor–patient interaction to a nurse-practitioner–patient interaction and shows that the doctor, much more than the nurse-practitioner, interrupted the patient and questioned the patient in a way that allowed 'a very limited exchange of information and leaves the way open for his [the doctor's] own assumptions to structure subsequent exchanges'. The nurse-practitioner, on the other hand, used open-ended, probing questions to maximize the patient's voice and to hear how she constructed her life. In example (9) in these data, we have seen how the tribunal member cuts off Marg's speculations about the relationship between Bob and Tom by saying 'Well, let's just stick to what you know'. Through the tribunal member's series of questions, Marg's general comments (about how frightening and intimidating Tom is) become transformed into Marg feeling frightened only twice over the course of the events. It seems, then, that the tribunal member's method of questioning has resulted in his assumptions restructuring the way in which Marg's fear is talked about.

This example is fairly typical of the way that the tribunal members' assumptions and concerns prevail in these interactions because of the questioner's control. Notice that both the defendant's representative and the tribunal members are free to speculate during the course of the proceedings without being interrupted or cut off by a questioner. In example (1), we see the defendant's representative commenting on what he sees as 'natural' behaviour when one is feeling threatened: 'If you were in such difficulty, if you felt threatened, if you felt that an assault was taking place, it strikes me as only natural [to cry out] and that help probably was available as that wall was extremely thin.' Likewise, one of the tribunal members speculates frequently on 'options' the complainants had: 'I see an option. It may not have occurred to you but I simply want to explore that option with you. Uh ... did it occur to you that you could lock the room so that they may not return to your room?' (from example (5)). As Walker (1987: 79) says of lawyers or judges who are legally sanctioned to question witnesses: 'Choice belongs to the examiner, who because of his socially and legally sanctioned role ... has the right to present, characterize, limit and otherwise direct the flow of testimony. It is in the hands of the questioner that the real power lies.'

Outcome of the tribunal

Over a year passed between the time the two complainants laid charges of sexual harassment against the defendant in February 1993 and the tribunal reached a decision in March 1994. The tribunal heard testimony from the complainants, the defendant and their respective witnesses on six occasions over a five-month period. Numerous delays in the proceedings were requested by and accorded to the defendant, ostensibly to allow him sufficient time to prepare his case. Written submissions were then made to the tribunal by the defendant over yet another few months in what is described as a 'piecemeal fashion' in the tribunal's written (40-page) decision document. The tribunal's decision was reached in March 1994. As for the criminal charges (laid within days of the university complaint), in August of 1993 the defendant was ordered in a preliminary hearing to stand trial for sexual assault.

In the university's submission to the tribunal (a 35-page written document presented by the university's legal counsel), the university argues that 'Mr. A. has fallen substantially below the standards of [the university] community in respect to his behaviour towards' the complainants and 'that he be sanctioned accordingly'. In a letter to the tribunal very early in the process, the two women requested that the university apply the harshest penalty possible, that is, expulsion from the university. Indeed, in submissions on sanctions to the panel, the university's legal counsel recommends that the defendant be expelled from the university.

The tribunal's decision acknowledges that

> both partners [i.e. the complainants] were clearly unresponsive to his [the defendant's] sexual advances and this should have been a signal to him that he should desist from further activity until such time as he his [sic] partner clearly expressed interest in engaging in sexual activity.

Further,

> in failing to discharge this duty, Mr A demonstrated an indifference to the wishes of the complainant. His actions were disrespectful and insensitive and as such his actions fell below the standard of conduct we must expect from all members of the University community. (p. 22)

While the Tribunal accepts in its written decision that some unwanted sexual aggression occurred, it also continues to minimize and discredit the complainants' feelings of fear (as two tribunal members did during the trial):

> ... both complainants testified that they were deeply frightened by Mr A; whereas their actions seemed to undercut this claim. For example, both complainants remained in the room with Mr A after the sexual activity had finished and he had fallen asleep. ... It seems somewhat inconsistent to assert fear on the one hand and on the other hand to be comfortable enough to fall asleep alongside the feared individual. In my opinion, this inconsistency (and perhaps overstatement of the level of fear experienced) can be explained by the fact that, prior to the two complainants meeting on Jan. 30, 1993, both complainants felt ashamed that they had allowed the situation with Mr A to progress to a level beyond their control. Both complainants testified that they felt confusion and shame when they individually reflected upon their experiences. It was only during their

coincidental meeting of Jan. 30, 1993 that they were able to recognize the fact that they had been violated, and their indignation in making this discovery might have led to a slight overstatement of their position'. (p. 18)

By discrediting the women's feelings of fear, the tribunal's decision again focuses on the women's behaviour and raises the possibility that the women's 'inaction' or 'lack of resistance' was curious, perhaps unjustified. While deeming Mr A's behaviour to fall 'below the standard of conduct we must expect from all members of the University community' (p. 22), the tribunal did not accept the university legal counsel's recommendation regarding sanctions. Expulsion from the university was judged to be unjustified:

Mr A was clearly insensitive and disrespectful to the complainants and this insensitivity led to harm; however I do believe that Mr A will be far more careful, caring and sensitive in the future. Considering that we do not find that he poses a threat, it is our view that if there is any institution in which Mr A can be sensitized to the need for respecting the sexual autonomy of women, it would be in a university setting. Rustication would be counter-productive to the educational mission which must be part and parcel of the University's disciplinary process. (p. 37)[11]

Thus, the decision was to allow the defendant to continue his studies, but to bar his access to various parts of the university, including its dormitories. We would suggest that such a penalty is lenient for two convictions of sexual harassment or acquaintance rape but, at the same time, is entirely consistent with the interactional patterns of the adjudication process which served to construct the events as consensual sex.[12]

Conclusion

Following Fisher (1991), we assume that the questions asked in these kinds of institutional settings do ideological work. We have shown how the questions asked by the defendant's representative and two of the tribunal members in this university hearing constitute a two-part discursive strategy by which the events in question are reconstructed as consensual sex. By focusing on the 'options' not chosen by the women, one of the tribunal members succeeds in characterizing the women's behaviour as lacking in resistance. We note that this same tribunal member, when questioning the defendant, does not focus on the 'options' available to him, e.g. to adhere to the women's wishes. In both the interaction and the tribunal's written decision, the complainants' feelings of fear are minimized and invalidated, removing the justification for the women's alleged lack of resistance.

By continuing to focus on the women's 'options', the defendant's representative and two of the tribunal members raise the possibility that the 'utmost resistance' standard had not been met, that is, that acquaintance rape had not taken place. This characterization of the women's behaviour as lacking in resistance gives little credence to the fear and confusion that may have paralysed the complainants and their witness. Likewise, in diminishing the complainants' feelings of fear, the defendant's representative and two of the tribunal members fail to acknowledge that women's submission to men's sexual aggression often occurs in a context where physical resistance can escalate the risk of injury and violence. In other words, many of the assumptions informing the questions asked of the complainants in this tribunal were androcentric in nature.

Since the early twentieth century, courts in the USA have found it useful to invoke the notion of 'a reasonable person' in considering whether certain kinds of behaviour should be deemed as harmful or offensive and thus punishable. The 'reasonable person' is supposed to represent community norms; thus, whatever would offend or harm 'a reasonable person' is said to be more generally offensive or harmful. Feminist legal scholars have recently challenged the generalizability of 'a reasonable person's' experiences, arguing that men and women may experience sexual advances or sexual harassment differently. Indeed, some state courts and lower federal courts in the USA have modified the 'reasonable person' standard and introduced 'a reasonable woman' standard for evaluating charges of sexual harassment. One such court (Ellison vs Brady 1991) justifies introducing the 'reasonable woman' standard in the following way: 'a sex-blind reasonable person standard tends to be male-biased and tends to systematically ignore the experiences of women' (cited in Chamallas 1995: 10). Of relevance to the tribunal proceedings under discussion here is the fact that the questions asked by the defendant's representative and two of the tribunal members stem from a profound ignorance of the complainants' experiences. Questions such as 'Why didn't you leave the room?', 'Why didn't you lock the door?' 'Why didn't you talk to Bob?' do not take seriously the complainants' and witness's frequent expressions of fear, paralysis and humiliation in the context of potential sexual violence. That is, most of the tribunal's proceedings are structured by the assumptions of 'a reasonable man'.

In sum, what we see manifested in the interactional patterns of this institutional setting reflects and reproduces the privilege that legal adjudication often bestows upon men. Because, as MacKinnon (1989: 180) claims, 'the crime of rape is defined and adjudicated from the male standpoint', rape trials will often protect the sexual prerogative of a man at the expense of a woman's sexual autonomy.

Notes

1. We thank Vicky Bergvall, Janet Bing, Martha Chamallas, Alice Freed, Sue Levesque and members of the audiences at the COSWL Language and Gender conference (July 1993), at the Linguistic Society of America Symposium 'Linguistic Perspectives on Sexual Harassment' (January 1995) and at the Women's Studies Graduate Programme Colloquium, York University (February 1995) for comments on earlier versions of this chapter. The research reported here was supported, in part, by a Regular Research Grant from the Social Sciences and Humanities Research Council of Canada, Grant # 410–94–1506.
2. The interests of all men are not, of course, protected by the legal system. In a discussion of the under-reporting of rape, MacKinnon (1987: 81) speculates as to the conditions under which women will report rape: 'The rapes that have been reported ... are the kinds of rapes women think will be believed when we report them. They have two qualitites: they are by a stranger, and they are by a Black man.' MacKinnon underscores here the racism inherent in a legal system that demonizes black men.
3. In 1983, the Criminal Code of Canada replaced the offence of 'rape' with that of 'sexual assault' so that acts of sexual aggression that did not include penetration would be punishable.
4. The idea that questions perform ideological work comes from Fisher (1991).
5. We borrow this term from Seidel (1988).
6. The pool of tribunal members consists of three faculty members and three students nominated by the dean of the university's law school, three faculty members nominated by the governing council of the university's residential colleges, three students nominated by the undergraduate student union and three faculty members and three students nominated by the Vice-President, Campus Relations.
7. The defendant chose not to engage a lawyer to represent him at the tribunal, but at various points during the proceedings was represented by both a family member and a family friend.

8. The questions asked by the defendant's representative were asked after the tribunal members' questions of the complainants because initially the defendant represented himself.
9. All names used to designate participants in the tribunal are pseudonyms.
10. Our transcription conventions are as follows:
    .   indicates sentence final falling intonation
    ,   indicates clause-final intonation (more to come)
    ... indicates pause of ½ second or more
    [ ] indicates speech overlap
11. The female faculty member concurred with this judgement while the female graduate student member of the tribunal wrote an addendum to the decision. She said that while she 'substantially' agreed with the contents of the decision document, she disagreed with its characterization of the complainants' fear.
12. The defendant's criminal charges were finally resolved in the spring of 1995. He was found guilty of one of the two charges of sexual assault and sentenced to six months in jail and one year's probation.

References

Chamallas Martha 1995 Comments on papers presented at LSA symposium: linguistic perspectives on sexual harassment. Linguistic Society of America's Annual Meeting, New Orleans.

Crenshaw Kimberle 1992 Whose story is it anyway?: feminist and antiracist appropriations of Anita Hill. In Morrison Toni (ed) *Race-ing justice, en-gendering power*. Pantheon Books, New York pp 402–40.

Ehrlich Susan, King Ruth 1994 Feminist meanings and the (de)politicization of the lexicon. *Language in Society* 23: 59–76.

Estrich Susan 1986 Real rape. *Yale Law Journal* 1087: 1122.

Fisher Sue 1991 A discourse of the social: medical talk/power talk/oppositional talk. *Discourse & Society* 2: 157–82.

MacKinnon Catharine 1987 *Feminism unmodified*. Harvard University Press, Cambridge, MA.

MacKinnon Catharine 1989 *Toward a feminist theory of the state*. Harvard University Press, Cambridge, MA.

Minogue Kenneth 1991 The goddess that failed. *National Review* 18 November: 46–8.

Seidel Gill 1988 The British new right's 'enemy within': the antiracists. In Smitherman-Donaldson Geneva, van Dijk Teun (eds) *Discourse and discrimination*. Wayne State University Press, Detroit, MI pp 131–43.

Taylor John 1991 Are you politically correct? *New York* 21 January: 32–40.

Treichler Paula 1990 Feminism, medicine and the meaning of childbirth. In Jacobus Mary, Keller Evelyn Fox, Shuttleworth Sally (eds) *Body/*

politics: women and the discourse of science. Routledge, London pp 113–38.

Walker Anne Graffam 1987 Linguistic manipulation, power and the legal setting. In Kedar Leah (ed) *Power through discourse.* Ablex, Norwood, NJ pp 57–80.

University publications

In the matter of XXX: reasons and judgement of the university discipline tribunal, York University, 1994.

Sexual assault and harassment on campus. York University Sexual Harassment and Complaint Centre, n.d.

York University discipline tribunal XXX: submissions to the panel on behalf of the university, York University, 1993.

8 Constructing and enacting gender through discourse: negotiating multiple roles as female engineering students[1]

Victoria L. Bergvall

Gender, technology and academic discourse

College is an important setting in which to examine how gender roles are constructed and enacted through discourse. During a student's college years, gender-role differences may be suppressed, since most students, presumably, hope to succeed in their studies and prepare for their chosen careers. However, while the higher educational system rewards the (supposedly gender-neutral) drive for academic success, students' goals are affected by how they accommodate to dichotomized gender roles. Differences in gender roles may be heightened as college students evaluate and choose potential mates from among those of the opposite sex (Holland and Eisenhart 1990), under the force of the heterosexual imperative (Rich 1980, Butler 1993) that drives much of campus social life.[2]

These multiple gender-role demands and conflicts are especially evident in the discourse of women studying at a technological university. Technology has long been considered a masculine domain within which men create and use the tools of science and logic to dominate unruly 'Mother' nature. The male engineer protagonist of Max Frisch's novel *Homo Faber* (1959: 78) proudly claims that 'The profession of technologist, a man who masters matter, is a masculine profession, if not the only masculine profession there is.' Women have successfully made inroads into other traditionally male-dominated fields, such as law, medicine and science, but while

33 per cent of US scientists are now women, the proportion of working engineers is a mere 4 per cent (National Science Foundation 1990).

The engineering profession has deep roots in male-dominated military history, taking its own name from the Latin *ingenium* 'a battering ram', a term generalized first to weapons of war, then to other machinery (Florman 1987, OED 1991: 515). The first engineering schools arose in France, where technical training was fused 'with cultural socialization that stressed hierarchy, discipline, loyalty, and self-control. ... As graduates of these military schools became leaders in civilian society, they shaped organizations and institutions along military and thus patriarchal lines' (Hacker 1989: 61). Engineers today still 'pride themselves on being hard-headed practical **men** concerned only with facts, disdaining mere speculation or opinion' (Layton 1986: 53, emphasis added). Women who are learning to become engineers must either accommodate to or resist the gender roles and discourse of this androcentric profession. Current manifestations of this androcentricity include a traditional hierarchical power structure, competitiveness and assertiveness in and out of the classroom, and the desire to create logical, ordered technology to control illogical, chaotic nature (Keller 1985, Fredrich 1989).

Analysis of the discourse of students in classes and in small-group discussions at a technological university provides evidence that women are caught in the tension between conflicting gender-role demands. In their academic exchanges, women display a variety of linguistic behaviours that defy easy gender stereotypes. At times, these women express their perspectives assertively in ways usually associated with stereotypically 'masculine' speech patterns. Yet they are also facilitative of others' ideas and may be apologetic and hesitant after making some of their most powerful assertions, characteristics associated with stereotypically 'feminine' speech styles (Lakoff 1975, Holmes 1992, Ochs 1992). Thus, they exhibit linguistic behaviours that range from those traditionally considered masculine (competitive, assertive, status seeking) to those traditionally considered feminine (cooperative, affiliative, instrumental) (e.g. Parsons and Bales 1955; see also Bem 1974). By any strict notion of gender as simply a duality of feminine and masculine roles, their behaviours would lead them to be labelled aberrant, not fully subsumable under either category, hence deviant as either females or males. Their behaviour is not easily explained within a two-culture model that assumes a dichotomy of 'women's language styles' and 'men's language styles' (Maltz and Borker 1982, Tannen 1990, Labov 1991). It can be explained, however, within the context of a model that defines gender as a socially situated, on-going performance. This model focuses not on dichotomous differences expected under polarized, categorical roles of feminine and masculine, but on the fluid enactment of gender roles in specific social situations (Butler 1990, 1993; Ochs 1992). Gender identities are constructed through the everyday actions and discourse of participants within a certain social order, influenced by societal expectations. Hence, the task of language and gender researchers is increasingly to examine the 'communities of practice' within which gender is constructed and enacted through discourse (Lave and Wenger 1991, Eckert and McConnell-Ginet 1992a, 1992b; see also Connell 1987, Thorne 1990, 1993, Gal 1992). From this perspective, these engineering students can be seen not as deviant, but as agents symbolically enacting or reacting to situation-specific gender expectations. Their complex linguistic interactions provide, therefore, a critical site for the examination of gender roles, theories of gender, and the role of language in the expression of and challenge to gender.

On the social constructions of gender and education

This study takes as its first premise that gender is a shifting, fluid category, 'an "act", as it were, which is both intentional and performative, where *"performative"* suggests a dramatic and contingent construction of meaning' (Butler 1990: 139). Gender roles are, thus, not predetermined by sex, but constructed and enacted, largely through discourse (Ochs 1992). If gender is a socially constructed act, then we have to look more closely at the context in which a given society engages in such construction. Simply accepting the predefined, dichotomous categories of female and male, as has been done repeatedly in previous linguistic research, may lead to the exclusion of critical variation as noise or aberration, warn Eckert and McConnell-Ginet (1992a: 93) and Bem (1993), rather than an exploration of that variation for its significance in the construction and sanctioning of gender roles. A simple dichotomy also fails to account for resistance and conflict within the production of linguistic forms. Challenges to the gender categories themselves are masked in the normative generalizations based on dual categories of 'female' and 'male', 'feminine' and 'masculine'. (See also Eckert 1989.)

Despite the work of feminist and gender theorists, the assumption of a dichotomy still persists, often strongest among the very participants under study. Most college students would not hesitate to describe themselves as female or male. This can be attributed to the structure and reinforcement of society, where the structures of languages themselves contribute to the perception of a binary opposition of sex or gender categories as opposed to a variability: we frequently use the terms *female* and *male, woman* and *man, feminine* and *masculine,* but rarely use intersex or intergender terms such as *hermaphrodite* and *androgynous* (see Bing and Bergvall, this volume).

Butler (1993: 2) argues that the perception of duality is primarily driven by the 'sedimentation' of social constructions and expectations towards a particular end: to regulate and control the performance of sex and gender, 'to materialize sexual difference in the service of the consolidation of the heterosexual imperative' (see also Rich 1980). Holland and Eisenhart (1990) discuss how women in higher education may participate in the construction of binary, oppositional gender roles by their own responses to social demands of university life as they prioritize issues of romance and attractiveness above their own educational goals. Their study of two university campuses in the southeastern United States explores the social forces that lie behind many women's subordination of their own education and careers in order to follow the men they so actively seek during college. This heterosexual attraction and inter-action reinforces and is reinforced by what Bem (1993) calls 'gender polarization', which she defines as 'the ubiquitous organization of social life around the distinction between male and female.' According to Bem (1993: 80–1),

> Gender polarization operates in two related ways. First, it defines mutually exclusive scripts for being male and female. Second, it defines any person or behavior that deviates from these scripts as problematic – as unnatural or immoral from a religious perspective or as biologically anomalous or psychologically pathological from a scientific perspective.

Although the social atmosphere of educational institutions (the athletic teams, sororities and fraternities, and many dormitories) is organized on a dichotomous assumption of female and male, one might wonder whether this dichotomy extends to the classrooms. Thorne (1993) argues that it does for grade school, at least, pointing to many of the structures of children's schooling that reinforce the separation into two categories, female and male: separate lines for girls and boys, teams of students drawn on female–male lines to compete in class activities, etc. Yet many of these means of dividing the sexes do not seem to occur overtly in classrooms and other academic settings of college campuses.

Nevertheless, Hall and Sandler (1982), Krupnick (1985a, 1985b), Crawford and MacLeod (1990) and Sadker and Sadker (1990) have convincingly documented that college classrooms present a 'chilly climate for women' where women are often either ignored or asked simpler questions, while assertive men receive unequal attention from teachers and learn to command the floor through techniques of quick responses (unmediated by raising hands and waiting politely to be called on by a teacher), patterns learned and reinforced in earlier schooling (Sarah 1980, Spender 1980a, 1980b, 1985, Sadker and Sadker 1985, Swann 1989). This work is supported by previous research indicating that women have unequal access to the conversational floor and are silenced in public contexts (Swacker 1975, 1976, Zimmerman and West 1975, Fishman 1983, West and Zimmerman 1983, Woods 1989, Gal 1989, Houston and Kramarae 1991, Holmes 1992, Lakoff 1992). Belenky *et al.* (1986) and Kramarae and Treichler (1990) argue that the educational system rewards competitive ways of knowing and doing, traditionally regarded as 'masculine', not the traditionally 'feminine' style that prizes mutually constructed ideas above competitive displays of knowledge.

The prevailing model for engineering education includes large competitive courses in mathematics and science prerequisite to the specialized engineering classes. Usually held in huge lecture halls that limit interpersonal connection and foreground a hierarchical, one-way transfer of knowledge from 'master' to 'apprentice', this class format is more conducive to competition and display than to cooperation and interaction. Even in smaller classes where there is more opportunity for interaction, the resulting discourse reflects prevailing cultural values. Science and mathematics themselves are fields that feminists have argued are androcentric in the very structures of their theory, practice and application (Fausto-Sterling 1979, Haraway 1981, 1989, Gornick 1983, Keller 1983, 1985, Harding 1986, Harding and O'Barr 1987). Science may be an androcentric filter for those who wish to enter the even more androcentric domain of engineering. The cultural context in which students learn to become engineers is thus both androcentric and gender-polarized. The dilemma for women who wish to enter this domain is how to respond to the traditionally masculine norms of science and engineering, while simultaneously responding to the conflicting, traditional feminine role expectations arising from the heterosexual social imperative.

Gender theory provides a means of examining this dilemma more closely by exploring gender as a site of resistance and change. This chapter provides a contextualized examination of how gender is enacted in discourse in response to changing social situations. Within this campus culture, the complex constructions of gender that are performed through the linguistic interactions of women and men call into question a simple female–male dichotomy. This study underscores the need for a more complex culturally and linguistically situated theory of gender, a theory of gender as performative and ever-changing rather than fixed.

The social setting of a technological campus

While most gender theorists see gender as non-binary and fluid, it is easy to use the terms *female* and *male* or *women* and *men* to describe two distinct groups at the Midwestern, technological university in this study, Michigan Technological University (MTU). This gender polarization arises from years of strong, dichotomous gender role socialization, starting at birth. College perpetuates this duality, giving only two choices, female or male, when one registers for dormitory room-mates, competes in varsity sports, or chooses the social affiliations of sororities and fraternities. Apart from a small campus lesbian and gay organization, few students seem compelled to overtly question that rigid dichotomy (Remlinger 1995). Traditional linguistic researchers observing this campus and trying to make neat divisions between behaviours of 'men' vs 'women' would be supported by the students' own overt social role assignment. Nevertheless, such divisions overlook the important, socially influenced interplay of roles that are not clearly biologically determinist or essentialist. The women, especially, engage in social interactions that demand a more complex notion of socially constructed and manipulated gender roles.

Many campus activities and expectations revolve around traditional masculine norms and stereotypes, such as competitiveness and independence. The primary campus sports are still men's hockey and football (though the women's basketball and volleyball teams have lately become more competitive on a regional and national level). There is an implicit assumption that students are free to spend many hours, even all night, on labs, group projects, term papers, or computer reports, with no familial or relationship responsibilities to pull them away – and no fears of getting home in the dark at night. The majority of the prerequisite science and math classes in the first two or three years are large lecture classes with bell-curved grading (called 'weeders' for the numbers who flunk out of them), class settings that women report as particularly alienating (Belenky *et al.* 1986, Kramarae and Treichler 1990, Bergvall *et al.* 1994). A significant campus activity is heavy (often competitive) alcohol consumption: the Thursday evening bar runs or fraternity–sorority 'piss calls' feature drinking as the main sport (where women are at a physical disadvantage in capacity). Campus dress tends towards gender-neutral or masculine garb.

In the midst of this androcentricity, women at MTU are widely perceived as (and widely resented for) getting preferential consideration in hiring because they are women, as corporations work under affirmative action to redress the historical shortage of women in the profession. In recent years, with job recruiters limiting campus visits, women in some majors (e.g. chemical engineering) had more interviews on average than men, and they were offered higher initial starting salaries. Women report feeling compelled to downplay their job interview record among their peers, and at least one woman insisted to her prospective employer: 'Don't hire me because I'm a woman; hire me because I'm good' (Aller 1993). The widespread assumption seems to be that women could not be as successful without special treatment. Likewise, the administration's attempts to recruit more women into the engineering and science faculty have been regarded by vocal, conservative opponents on the campus newspaper staff and in the undergraduate student government as inappropriate 'special privileges'; if the women are good enough, the campus editorials claim, they can make it on their own. The prevailing belief among students seems to be that set-asides will only damage the system by attracting the weak and underqualified.

Thus, on the one hand, the campus environment rewards those women who adopt the prevailing norms and accommodate to the system without challenging its essential androcentrism. On the other hand, women are not always valued for acting 'just like the guys'. In a section of the campus newspaper called 'Campus Connect' (1993–4), men placed dating ads looking for 'girls' who would not outdrink or outswear them, and who were thin, sexy, not clingy, and available for uncommitted sexual activity. The common category labels for women reveal the disdain with which many men regard women at the university: women are either *snow-cows* – overweight and unattractive, *bitches* – aloof and career-oriented rather than willing to date them, or *sluts* – too easy or promiscuous (see also Remlinger 1995). These attitudes foster a tension between androgyny and gender polarization, with women acceptable professionally if they blend in quietly and act no different from the men, while acceptable as sexual or social partners only if they are complementary opposites to men. The trick is to know when to behave appropriately.

This social struggle might seem irrelevant to what happens within the classroom, since, once in class, students would seem to share the similar androgynous goals of getting a good education and a good job. However, it is not easy to leave sex and gender behind at the classroom door. Students and their teachers are the products of years of enculturation in a system that does not treat females and males as equals. In class, students still evaluate each other as potential dates, even while competing for the same good grades. Thus, this is a community of practice in which sex and gender are highly salient categories. Nevertheless, when they are asked if their lives in the classroom are affected by whether they are male or female, masculine or feminine, many students deny the significance of gender.

Participants and setting

The conversations reported in this chapter come from a larger, ongoing project on the discourse of college classrooms and other academic settings at Michigan Technological University (MTU).[3] The information has been collected through surveys and through participant-observation. MTU enrolls 7,000 students, about 5,000 of whom are undergraduates; over 90 per cent are engineering, science or technology majors. About 25 per cent of those enrolled are women, while African Americans, Native Americans, and other traditionally under-represented groups account for fewer than 10 per cent of the undergraduates. The students are primarily middle class and from the upper Midwest states.

The first set of examples is drawn from a class of six women and twelve men taking the third quarter of a three-term sequence of composition courses (in which both first-year and upper-class students are enrolled). Capped at twenty-five students to encourage in-class discussion, this class represents a common experience for most of the undergraduates at MTU. The second set of examples come from a small chemical engineering group working on a year-long senior 'capstone' design project. The students, one woman and three men, were enrolled in a fifty-person plant-design course, intended to provide special hands-on, real-world practice for students.[4]

Enacting gender through academic conversation

The composition class

The conversations in classrooms at this university reveal that many women challenge the previous research which has found systematic women's silence in public settings (e.g. Swacker 1975, 1976, Zimmerman and West 1975, Fishman 1983, West and Zimmerman 1983, Woods 1989, Gal 1989, Houston and Kramarae 1991, Holmes 1992, Lakoff 1992): in observations of several different classrooms, the most talkative and assertive people in the class often were women. For example, in a typical meeting of the composition class under analysis here, although outnumbered as students two to one by men in the class (which had a male teacher), the women produced turns at talk (34 per cent) and word counts (42 per cent) roughly proportional to their representation in class numbers (33 per cent). (See Bergvall and Remlinger (forthcoming) for further discussion of this case.) An extended analysis of this same class, however, reveals that not all women and men participated equally. By word count, the two top women take 68 per cent of the turns and the top woman alone takes 58 per cent of the women's turns, with 71 per cent of the women's words. Meanwhile, two of the six women are totally silent. The men's turns are not so radically distributed, though one man does speak 32 per cent of the total words uttered by male students; no man was completely silent.

Thus, at least some of the women are not silent, passive listeners in the class, as the research on classroom discourse sometimes suggests. However, it is also true that not every woman is assertive in the classroom. One problem was that some of the women did not speak loudly enough during discussions for the whole group to hear them. Therefore, though they tried to hold the conversational floor, they did not always command the full attention of other students. When interviewed, these women generally reported feeling like equal participants with men in class, and the transcripts of the class conversation supports this overall impression in measures of words and turns. But Bergvall and Remlinger (forthcoming) demonstrate that merely looking at turn and word counts can obscure what is happening with the content of the turns: we must study the interaction more carefully in order to understand what is really happening. Bergvall and Remlinger observed that, in these class conversations, men did more of the audible, tangential, *task-divergent* talk (e.g. more asides that are audible to the rest of the class). They did not mute their voices as much when making asides to their peers; hence they had a presence in the conversation even when someone else ostensibly held the floor. Meanwhile, the women and some of the men employed more strategies we labelled *task-continuative* – that is, strategies that were supportive of the speakers, strategies that Holmes (1992) would call 'facilitative'.

Some of the conversational strategies used by and towards the most talkative members of the class show other gender-influenced patterns. In the example that follows, taken from a class discussion of Toni Cade Bambara's short story 'Blues Ain't No Mockin Bird', note the use of laughter-within-a-turn by a speaker. In the class transcripts, this occurs almost exclusively within women's turns, with the exception of just two instances by the male teacher. In example (1), a discussion of the use of abstract symbols in the story, this kind of laughter is paired with a self-deprecating remark by Veronica (line 6), a strategy never employed by any of the men in the class, even the two very talkative men, Greg and Don, whom the teacher characterized as struggling with the material (Greg later dropped the class with a failing grade). Although the teacher judged Veronica to be one of the best students in the class, she belittled her own contribution, preceded by her laughter (line 6).[5]

(1)

1	Veronica:	It makes you take the events that she relates
2		and then try to piece things together for yourself,
3		to try and figure out what's exactly going on.
4		But, I don't think it works!
5	Male S:	((laugh))
6	Veronica:	((laugh during first words)) Maybe I'm stupid, bu::t
7	Male S:	((laugh))
8	Male P:	Well, I don't think that [it's stupid,
9		It's just something that didn't work for you,] that's all.
10	Veronica:	[I didn't think it was a very effective style.]

Veronica's laughter takes on its negative connotation by its association with the self-deprecating remark, 'Maybe I'm stupid.' In a later interview, Veronica said that she did not mean to say that she felt stupid, only to offer the disclaimer that she did not know everything.[6] Nevertheless, the words she employs are an overt negative self-assessment to which the teacher feels the need to reply. This may be the attempt of a powerful person trying to mute or mitigate her power, compelled by the class's negative response to her, evident in the next examples.

In another excerpt from this same discussion, Veronica attempts to make a complex analogy between the senseless slaughter of hawks in the story and the slaughter of innocent dolphins caught up in tuna nets (lines 1–10). But she is derailed by derisive asides and the laughter of the class that seems to gain momentum as more students join in (lines 12–13 and 20). The negative assessment by the class is underscored by the students contesting her interpretation and her control of the floor with their asides in lines 13, 14, and particularly in line 19, where the aside is overtly directed against her.

(2)

1	Veronica:	Well, wait a second. All right, this is an example.
2		I'm not trying to make a judgement or anything,
3		but look at the whole debate about, you know,
4		right now, like about tuna.
5		They're talking about the drift nets that kill dolphins and whatever, you know,
6		when they, I mean it's like 'well, do people need those tunas to, you know,
7		produce food, 'n, and all that kind of stuff for people'
8		but, you, but we don't think that it's right for them to,
9		to kill the dolphins along with 'em.
10		So, how is it right to, you know, [to kill the hawks?
11	Marie:	[(Who's killing?)
12	Class:	(extended laugh – 5+ sec., with several bouts of laughter by different people,
13		including Marie. Other asides underneath))
14	Marie:	(inaudible aside)
15	Louis:	All ri:ght
16	Marie:	[(words) ((laugh))]
17	Male P:	[Are these people environmentalists?]
18	Greg:	Not really. I [don't think they [really care.
19	Male S:	[It's good for her [( )
20	Marie:	[((laugh))

After these asides and laughter, Veronica does not pursue or explain her analogy. Usually the most talkative student in the class, she is virtually silent for the next 10 minutes. She has apparently been muted by the class's reactions to her active participation.

Compare Veronica's self-deprecating remark and the class's derailment of her attempt to develop her idea with the situation of Don in (3), as he pursues his analysis of how the characters in Bambara's story should allow outsiders to photograph their house (seeing it as flattery rather than as trespassing). Don is undeterred by class laughter directed at him (lines 20, 26), even by the derisive comment by one of his male peers (line 25) or by Veronica's direct negative responses (lines 14, 21, 38, 40). Despite the challenges and the laughter, Don persists in developing his topic, and the class allows him to do so (as they did not allow Veronica), even overtly supporting his analysis at one point (line 37).

(3)
1	Don:	I mean, like, that goes back to my point, you know.
2		Somebody comes on your property (gradually),
3		without permission and they're taking pictures, um,
4		so right away the parents and grandparents think they're going out
5		and screaming at them. I mean, the grandfather,
6		he would have been going out and kicking them off the lot.
7		I mean, now, if someone had a rich estate or something,
8		uh, maybe, I guess, this is too far to the extreme,
9		but I mean, if you owned a fairly nice house or something,
10		and somebody came up and started taking pictures of it,
11		behind it, and all, wouldn't that make you feel,
12		uh, I mean, decent on the inside,
13		I mean, wouldn't you let them go about their business?
14	Veronica:	[No. ((laugh))
15	Female S:	[((Unclear,
16		about 3 words before overlapped by Don))
17	Don:	[I mean, you might even want, some,
18		somebody in the family might even go out and smile for them,
19		[I mean, especially]
20	Male S:	[((laugh, one or two male students, above male student still talking))

21	Veronica:	[**No because** if I didn't like what they were taking that, I mean,
22		if I didn't like the cause of their reasoning behind wanting pictures of my home,
23		then I wouldn't want to humor their cause by letting them do it.
24	Don:	Well, they're depressed because they're poor then. ((challenging))
25	Shankar:	Bullshit.
26	Male S:	((One or two male students mumble about 3 words, laugh))
27	Veronica:	I didn't say that.
28	Don:	Well, [you're saying that.
29	Male S:	[They didn't even know what they wanted pictures for,
30		originally, she just said, 'yeah, both of those guys get out of here'
31		as soon as she saw them coming.
32	Male S:	Yeah.
33	Ss:	((Three people together laugh softly))
34	Veronica:	You're right. It's her house.
35	Don:	An', then, like I say, that goes back to my, um,
36		if you've got a beautiful house, wouldn't you want it to be known?
37	Male S:	I think you've got a good [point.
38	Veronica:	[I don't think that that's something you can generalize.
39	Don:	To me, some[one else
40	Veronica:	[I can't, I don't think you can say that
41		everybody that has a beautiful house logically wants everybody to know it.

Don persists in the extended development of his topic – a point he had first raised sixty-five turns earlier – despite all the challenges to his position. Apparently, he regards the laughter as a sign of support rather than an attempt to silence him.

By simple count of turns at talk or words, Veronica is the most active speaker in this class. But the class wields effective tools against her with both verbal and non-verbal sanctions in their derogatory asides and laughter. She is a student who engages seriously with the material at hand and is quick to contribute to the conversation with thoughtful opinions about the work. In this sense, she might be considered 'successful'. In terms of gender roles, it appears that she is comfortable enacting the assertive role usually regarded as masculine. However, her success in this class is called into question by the actions of her peers, both men and women. While Don (and other men) are actively supported by class laughter, Veronica is cut off by it.

Thus, the turn and word counts obscure other patterns that may reveal gender biases: men in this class never mitigate or apologize for their comments, via either intra-turn laughter or self-deprecating comments. Derisive asides, paired with laughter, derail a usually powerful woman, while laughter seems to support and encourage at least one less academically adept man (and evidence from the transcripts show this to be the case for other men as well). This analysis is supported by an examination of students' end-of-term, peer-group assessments. Despite Veronica's performance as the most active speaker and her clear and challenging analyses of the texts, her peer group gives her the lowest grade in the class for participation (a B+), a grade equivalent to those another peer group awarded to two men who said virtually nothing in class. Veronica's group also gave its silent female member a higher grade (borderline A−/B+), while Don's group gave him an A−. Hence, Veronica's assertive and active engagement in the class was negatively assessed by her peers in the class, both orally and through written evaluations. Although Veronica fulfils the overtly androgynous goals of excellence in participation, her peers react strongly against this assertive behaviour and (in their peer assessments) criticize her for not facilitating the work of others. When she fails to enact the traditional supportive feminine role, she is negatively sanctioned and is silenced by the gender-normative activities of the class. It appears that, despite their own desire to be successful, some students do not experience the classroom as gender-neutral territory but another ground for the complex performance of resistance to, and enforcement of, gendered roles.

The plant-design working group

Other gender conflicts are expressed in the academic discourse at this institution. The following exchanges detail some of the complex interactions that occur when a project group of four senior engineering students attempts to solve some problems for a plant-design class. Over the course of the year, the students are given design tasks similar to those engineers in industry would encounter. This capstone class is seen as the major curricular event in the engineering student's last year, and its complex demands require sustained group effort.

In the course of several meetings of this small group, the four students attempt to identify and pose solutions to problems within the 'streams' of a engineering plant's flow diagram. Note in these exchanges how the single woman of the group, Olivia, presents herself, as compared to the three men, Sherman, Wayne and Dylan. In example (4), Olivia is discussing with Sherman what they have done since the last time the group met to analyse the plant's flow streams. Compare Sherman's simple questions and responses with the hesitant and mitigated answers that Olivia gives as she describes what she has done.

(4)
1	Olivia:	I wasn't really sure either, so I just ... thought of it,
2		y'know, I just thought'n [did what I thought]
3	Sherman:	[Where'd you get] the numbers for these?
4	Olivia:	Actually, I ... these numbers I just got from ...
5		actually they're ...
6		another thing we'll have to do is, is when somebody gives me stream 14,
7		stream 14 matches up exactly with this one ...
8	Sherman:	Yeah
9	Olivia:	Then, then it's OK, but if it doesn't then I'll have to change these.
10		And all I did was look up these streams [here.]
11	Sherman:	[From the] handout?
12		Yeah, that's what I did.
13	Olivia:	Yeah. Good. That's what I did.
14	Sherman:	(Good) yeah.
15	Olivia:	And that's it. And I just seen what came in and what came out.
16		And that's it.
17		And this one too, and //
18	Sherman:	[Did you work it all out?
19	Olivia:	Umm. [All it did was]
20	Sherman:	[(between)]
21	Olivia:	All I did was compare the streams.
22	Sherman:	Oh, all right.
23	Olivia:	I just, I just, whatever piece of equipment,
24		I just wrote down what came in and what came out,
25		and then with this distillation
26		((pages turning, 10 sec.)

27		( ) just put all these streams together?
28	Sherman:	Yeah, I just took the sections, that we split up?
29	Olivia:	That's a good idea.

Note in this example how Olivia downplays her activities in the research. She has completed the assignments the group divided up at the previous meeting, but as she presents her results, she brackets all her efforts with self-effacing remarks, e.g. 'I wasn't really sure either, so I just … thought of it, y'know' (line 1). The frequent use of the minimizing term 'just' (in lines 1, 2, 4, 15, 23, 24, 27) and the phrase 'all I did' (lines 10, 21) show her self-effacement despite doing the same work that Sherman did, while Sherman sits back and agrees, 'Yeah, that's what I did' without self-deprecation. Olivia, furthermore, praises Sherman for his efforts more than he praises her for hers. Compare her more explicit 'That's a good idea' at the end of the segment to his 'Yeah's' and his almost inaudible 'Good' in line 14.

When the rest of the group joins them, they examine the flow diagram in order to develop a better solution to a problem they find within it. Again, Olivia frequently downplays her own contributions, while overtly encouraging and supporting the rest of the group members, all men. Her facilitative work in the following example has the effect of focusing Wayne's attention on the significance of an observation (line 6) that he was apparently about to dismiss with the words 'Oh well.'

(5)

1	Wayne:	This is just (12) just a heater.
2	Olivia:	( )
3	Wayne:	Just a heater. What's the temperature on twenty?
4		Let's look at what it's heating.
5		((pages turning)) one-fifty-seven::
6		((laughs)) It's only heating from one-fifty-seven to one-sixty-six.
7		((laughs)) Can't imagine a process that would do that. Oh well.
8	Olivia:	Maybe that's one thing that's wrong with this process.
9	Wayne:	Could be. (4)
10		It's pretty darn inefficient to burn fuel to heat something up nine degrees,
11		that's [almost
12	Olivia:	[There y'go, maybe it's somep'n you can put in your fin –

```
13                  somp'n we can put in our final report.
14   Wayne:         Yeah. If you can't find a uh,
15                  y'know, someplace else in the plant where you got
                    some excess heat,
16                  I mean at the same time ...
```

Though Wayne has found an evident problem (lines 3–7), he seems ready to dismiss it and move on to another task, until Olivia points out its potential to him (line 8). She underlines this one turn later with an explicit encouraging remark (lines 12–13). Thus, the discovery task is jointly constructed, but Olivia initially accords Wayne the honour in line 12: 'maybe it's somep'n you can put in your fin(al report)' – which she only then changes to 'we' and 'our'.

Later in the same conversation, when they have determined that this is a crucial problem to solve, Olivia again does critical support work (lines 6, 7 and 10).

```
(6)
1    Olivia:    So what you're saying is uh (2) we could put a heat
                exchanger //
2    Wayne:                 [There's gotta be a way that rather than
3                burning fuel or maintaining a furnace to heat this //
4    Olivia:    [so we'd use the temperature //
5    Wayne:                             [to heat this uh:::
6    Olivia:                            [Yeah that's ridiculous]
7                [yeah, yeah]
8    Wayne:     [that you're wasting enough energy]
                that you could just route that rather from a furnace,
9                route it to a heat exchanger //
10   Olivia:                            [heat exchanger
```

When the whole group assembles, note how Olivia interprets her part in the retelling of the events in examples (5) and (6) as she and Wayne present their discovery to the rest of the group.

```
(7)
1    Wayne:     Sherman, have you –
2                ((to Olivia)) (Do you want to give to Sherman) our
                brainchild?
3    Olivia:    Oh yeah, you got to see this, Sherman.
4                ((Sherman laughs))
5    Olivia:    This is really something. ...
6                Why don't you. ...
7    Wayne:     Go ahead, go ahead. You're much more enthusiastic.
```

8	Olivia:	Well, I think it's pretty good. OK, uh.
9		Wayne figured this out. He said that this is ridiculous,
10		that we have to use this furnace in order to heat
		this temperature up only nine degrees.

Although Wayne had found the flaw, it was primarily Olivia who focused attention on that detail with the result that the two of them pursued Wayne's observation and developed their 'brainchild'. In referring to that discovery (lines 1 and 2 of (7)), however, even though Wayne shares the credit with her, Olivia credits only Wayne (line 9), even attributing to him her previous comment about how 'ridiculous' it was to heat something up only nine degrees. Olivia acts as spokesperson and facilitator for Wayne, but discounts by omission her participation in the discovery. However, she is not always consistently self-effacing.

At a later meeting, Olivia attempts to brings to their attention an article containing critical information that the men have overlooked. Her interruption of Dylan and Wayne's calculations is initially not welcome, but she persists.

(8)

1	Dylan:	That's not bad. We can pump ethyl benzene at five bars.
2	Wayne:	So then you're lookin' at uh five bar, one thousand kelvin –
3		let me make sure that's hot enough. (4)
4	Olivia:	Can I interrupt for just a few minutes.
5	Wayne:	No.
6		((Then in a whispered, growling voice)) No:::
7	Olivia:	Fifteen minutes. Now do you still have that folder,
8		do you still have that folder 'cause that does have that
9		article about capacities that are made in all the
10		companies in the United States. //
11	Dylan:	[Lost that folder you're in trouble
12	Olivia:	Yeah, I'm sorry. I don't mean to give you –
13		brag about it but //
14	Dylan:	[Yes you do!
15	Olivia:	((laughing)) Yeah, I do.
16	Dylan:	Don't be sorry!
17	Wayne:	Number of times …
18		((Dylan laughing))
19	Wayne:	The number of times that you have assured me I didn't
20		mean to be cruel about this **but** I'm gonna be.

21		((papers shuffling. ?Wayne finds folder and gives it to Olivia?))
22	Dylan:	Get it now!
23	Wayne:	((to Dylan)) That's enough?
24	Olivia:	((laughing)) You better have it!
25	Wayne:	That's enough, what'd we have?
26		thirteen oh nine you said you needed?
27	Dylan:	Fifteen oh nine.

In this exchange, Olivia first asserts herself in line 4 by interrupting the two men in order to present the important information she has found, though she prefaces her interruption with a polite request. She persists (lines 7–10), despite Wayne's rejection of her interruption, and explains why the article is crucial. These assertive actions are followed up by a complex act in lines 12–13 that is both an apology and a mitigated boast at having found this information. Dylan acknowledges the boast and chastises her for the apology. Note her in-turn laughter, which accompanies her final assertion in line 24, a strategy that may mark the speaker's sense that she needs to mitigate strong assertions.

The construction and enactment of gender roles in these exchanges is very complex. All of the students collaborate in finding a solution to the engineering problems – traditionally a discourse strategy associated with women – yet they also demonstrate assertive strategies traditionally associated with men. Many of Olivia's strategies are what Holmes (1992) would characterize as 'facilitative' for their encouragement in developing other's ideas, particularly Wayne's. However, Ochs (1992) argues that facilitation, such as that which American mothers engage in with their children, may be culturally devalued. Despite the praise of Holmes, facilitation may be regarded as self-effacing; thus, it is often taken as expected, insignificant, or even invisible within dominant androcentric assumptions. Olivia's frequent self-effacement (despite the times Wayne and Dylan include or support her) suggests that she feels compelled to downplay her exchanges, representing herself not as a valued facilitator, but as a hesitant, self-deprecating participant. Her contributions appear almost to be hedged into insignificance (though in final interviews with the members of this group, the men felt that Olivia might make a fine engineer, if she could only gain some self-confidence).

In these conversations, Olivia displays the conflict between the competing stereotypic gender roles of 'masculine' assertion and 'feminine' facilitation, with the latter predominant. By traditional androcentric norms of engineering, her actions might seem to compromise her success as an engineer, while furthering the men's accomplishments. Thus, we see another instance of gender struggle, as Olivia attempts to balance the demands of the role of assertive engineering-group participant with that of facilitative supporter.

Contesting gender roles in engineering

In the course of examining the linguistic actions of these engineering students, it becomes clear that the women display speech behaviours that transcend easy boundaries: they are assertive, forceful, facilitative, apologetic and hesitant by turns. It appears at times to be a double-bind, no-win situation: when the women are assertive, they are resisted by their peers; when they are facilitative, their work may be taken for granted and not acknowledged. These interactions suggest that these women are subject to the forces of traditional stereotypes, even though, in interviews, they assert that the classroom is gender-neutral territory with equal opportunities for women and men. Their awareness of the problems related to gender seems limited to knowledge of the slang terms for women and men (*snowcows*, *geeks*, etc.) and the effect on dating caused by the 'ratio' of men to women on campus. They are generally unaware of the theoretical and actual battles raging around them that contest the broader issues of gender. Thus, while gender appears to be a crucial issue, it is both salient and suppressed in this community of practice.

Women who have succeeded in engineering have survived a rigorous process that has winnowed out large numbers of other potentially interested women. We might expect that those who survive would be strong and determined. Some might claim that, in order to succeed, women must accommodate to the predominant, androcentric roles, adopting more stereotypically male attributes themselves, becoming assertive and task-driven. By a rigid notion of dichotomous gender, this might indicate that these women would become less feminine, and, thus, aberrant or deviant as women.

Indeed, contrary to data from previous studies on classroom discourse, these women frequently dominate the discussion in some classrooms and lead many small groups. Yet, at other times, these same women remain silent or are silenced in academic discourse, and their work may be seen as facilitative or secretarial rather than substantive or data-oriented; worse, they may be either strongly resisted or altogether disregarded for displaying 'inappropriate' gender behaviours. As these women attempt to accommodate to conflicting and shifting demands, and to find ways to succeed within an androcentric system, they sometimes act in ways associated with traditional masculine stereotypes and at other times in ways associated with traditional feminine stereotypes. Most often, however, they operate outside the limiting norms that would define them on the basis of predetermined, binary, oppositional categories.

These differences are, in fact, not aberrations of gender identity, but arise from challenges to implicitly conflicting gender roles. On the one hand, these women are expected to be actively participating students, assertive in pursuing their scholarly goals. Yet this assertive behaviour comes into conflict with traditional gender expectations of non-competition, especially at this time in their lives when their sexual and social identities may be at their most binary, as they evaluate others and are evaluated in turn as potential heterosexual mates. These traditional gender-role expectations may work to limit these women's success in pursuing an education and a career.

However, most of these women either suppress or fail to perceive gender issues in their academic lives. The very denial of their situation fuels the conflicts they experience, when they are almost forced to apologize for doing well in class and, later, for their success at getting job interviews and jobs. It is these women who most need to be made aware of the nature of the conflicting gender expectations under which they operate and the way those gender conflicts affect their conversations, their intellectual development, and their future success as engineers. The anti-feminist stance of many of the women, reinforced by the conservative campus climate, leads them to be naively apolitical, depriving them of any common ground upon which to work together to contest limiting gender stereotypes. The situation demands radical change, to broaden the conceptions of appropriate gender roles on campus in order to transform an engineering educational system still largely entrenched in top-down, hierarchical, androcentrism.[7]

Gender, challenge and change

Complex struggles over gender identity are enacted when women attempt to enter the historically androcentric domains of engineering and science at a technological university. The resulting destabilization of gender roles arises from a two-fold resistance: first, many women resist the confines imposed by roles traditionally construed as binary and polarized: male/masculine/public vs female/feminine/private. Second, these women in return are resisted by other conversational participants who implicitly support traditional role stereotypes that maintain the status quo (see also Remlinger 1995, Bing and Bergvall this volume, Bergvall and Remlinger forthcoming). Gender on this campus is enacted in response to multiple, shifting social demands and linguistic situations, performed through discourse. To understand this variable behaviour, we need a theory of gender and language that is neither binary nor polarizing, but situated and flexible, grounded in research based not only on the careful examination of discrete linguistic structures, but also on the social settings in which such structures are embedded.

At this technological university, gender is both salient and suppressed. Most students are aware of the ratio of women to men and the strains which that ratio places on social relationships. Nevertheless, they generally believe that the classroom and other academic settings are neutral ground, uninfluenced by gender struggles. But academic discourse is not gender-neutral: evidence from discourse analysis shows that gender roles continue to be reified and challenged through such linguistic means as asides, laughter, support talk, and self-effacing remarks. Because these women lack the critical understanding that may arise from feminist analysis, they are particularly vulnerable to attack when their attempts to enact apparently androgynous behaviours result in retaliatory acts. Their individual challenges to the constraints of an androcentric engineering culture will be ineffectual unless they understand the systemic constraints of that culture.

The blurring of traditional gender roles and the conflicting expectations experienced by these women are symptoms of a system in flux. Helping these women (as well as gender researchers) understand and resolve the complexities raised here requires continuing investigation into the shifting construction and performance of multiple gender roles and open discussion (in classrooms as well as in the pages of academic texts) of the ways in which gender theory can help contest the gender-role stereotypes that limit human potential.

Notes

1. I thank the following people for their comments on previous versions of this chapter: Janet Bing, Jenny Cheshire, Jennifer Coates, Alice Freed, Kate Remlinger, Jerry Savage, Craig Waddell, and an anonymous reviewer.

2. A note on terms: I generally try to adhere to the split usually drawn between sex and gender, where *sex* refers to biological and *gender* to sociologial constructs, because the sources on which I draw for this chapter make this distinction. In her challenge to the foundationalist assumptions that sex is somehow basic and given, Nicholson (1994) argues that both sex and gender are fluid constructions. Because I assume that sex, as well as gender, is socially constructed and reified by action (see Bing and Bergvall this volume) I have sometimes found it difficult to separate where the physical construction ends and the 'social' construction begins. Any fuzziness of reference for terms of sex and gender is a result of our still limited understanding of these concepts.

3. I am especially indebted to Kate Remlinger and Jerry Savage for discussing with me issues of the campus setting, small groups' discussion styles, relevant theory, and the significance of examples used here. Remlinger's dissertation (1995) analyses more thoroughly the replication of and resistance to gender roles (and the backlash of opposition to the resistors), and Savage's dissertation (1994) examines gender as a factor in the collaborative styles of engineering design groups; both are based on detailed ethnographic descriptions of student behaviours, attitudes and language (see also Savage 1991). I am also grateful to Sheryl Sorby, Betsy Aller, Diane Molleson, Nick Schutt, Mabel Cadaret, Rochelle Beckemeyer, Nicole Wertime and other colleagues and students who have worked with me or shared their perspectives on gender and language issues.

4. These examples were collected and transcribed by Jerry Savage as part of his dissertation work (1994); I thank him for providing them and discussing their significance with me. However, as I have extended the analysis on gender beyond our discussions, he is not responsible for any misinterpretations that arise. See Savage (1994) for another view on the gendered interactions of students in this and another chemical engineering design group.

5. The transcription conventions used in this chapter are as follows:

   //   interruption: placed at the end of an utterance when another speaker interjects, or utterance internally where minimal responses occur. Multiple interjections are followed in serial order by the responses.

   [overlap or interruption: marks beginning of overlapping or interrupting speech. An end bracket ( ]) may mark the extent of overlap.

...	short pause: each point indicates about ½ second pause.
(2)	longer pause between utterances; indicates number of seconds
–	self-interruption: placed at point of interruption
.	low intonation fall (at end of sentence)
,	comma or series intonation (where speaker intends to continue)
?	high intonation rise
!	exclamatory utterance
::	lengthened syllable; multiple colons represent prolonged syllable
bold	stressed syllable or word
(( ))	other voice qualities or accompanying non-verbal actions ('stage directions'): e.g. ((laugh)) laughter, ((pages turning))
( )	unclear utterance: words not clear : ( ); approximate number of words: (five words); possible readings are sometimes given: (between)
Male P	Male Professor
S	Student
Female S	Unidentified female student
Male S	Unidentified male student

6. All student names used here are pseudonyms. Veronica began as an electrical engineering major, the major judged by other students at MTU to enrol the brightest students. Over the course of her studies, she became increasingly disillusioned with engineering, switched majors to electrical engineering technology, and finally left the university in her senior year without graduating. During her interview with me, Veronica's comments about the social constraints of being an intelligent woman were revealing. This is one sample:

Q: Is there any kind of stigma against people who are smart?

A: Only in the sense that people who don't feel very smart are jealous of them. I used to be a lot more serious that I am now. I mean, I suffered a lot at the hands of people who didn't feel they were smart, so they hated **me** for being smart, y'know. In that sense, it was a negative thing. But I've never tried to hide my, y'know, I've never tried to hide ... well, that's not necessarily true.

Q: When was it not true?

A: Well, I used to be more, a lot more serious than I am now. At one point, I just decided that I was sick of everybody **perceiving** me as a serious person when I didn't feel that I **was** a serious person. It was like everybody put this, everybody else defined who I **was** and I was supposed to just *do* what they thought I should be doing ((laugh)), and that **bothered** me, and I finally said, '**Look**, I'm not a **brain**!' ... at least, if I'm smart, that's not the only aspect to my personality ... And so, in that sense, I guess, it depends on how you perceive it, ya know. I guess you could say I was covering up my brain in order to be perceived more as a happy-go-lucky person. But to me, I don't think I … I never played stupid. I only played stupid if I really didn't know anything. ((laugh))

7. See Bergvall *et al.* (1994) for recommendations on transforming engineering education in ways that value facilitative, collaborative work, and explicitly acknowledge the insights of feminist researchers. One ironic factor in modern engineering education that might portend change is an increasing demand for engineers who can work well together. Success in addressing complex problems in corporate America is now regarded as highly dependent on group skills, for which cooperativeness and facilitation should be highly valued. The irony is that this new emphasis on collaboration seems to arise not so much out of the years of work of feminist scholars who have politicized the negative effects of the dominance/androcentric/hierarchical model, or those who have celebrated 'difference' and the value of facilitation and cooperation. Instead, most of the credit seems to go to the Japanese, who, in implementing the work of the American, W. Edwards Deming, focused on cooperation between workers and management and quality control through group work (cf. Lumsdaine and Lumsdaine 1993) under the label of Total Quality Management.

References

Aller Betsy 1993 *Denial of difference: self perceptions of women engineering students.* Unpublished Michigan Technological University ms. Houghton, MI.

Belenky Mary Field, Clinchy Blythe McVicker, Goldberger Nancy Rule, Tarule Jill Mattuck 1986 *Women's ways of knowing: the development of self, voice, and mind.* Basic Books, New York.

Bem Sandra L 1974 The measurement of psychological androgyny. *Journal of Consulting and Clinical Psychology* 42.2: 155–62.

Bem Sandra Lipsitz 1993 *The lenses of gender.* Yale University Press, New Haven.

Bergvall Victoria L, Remlinger Kathryn A forthcoming: Reproduction, resistance, and gender in educational discourse: the role of Critical Discourse Analysis. *Discourse & Society* 7.4.

Bergvall Victoria L, Sorby Sheryl A, Worthen James B 1994 Thawing the freezing climate for women in engineering education: views from both sides of the desk. *Journal of Women and Minorities in Science and Engineering* 1.4: 323–46.

Bing Janet, Bergvall Victoria L this volume: The question of questions: beyond binary thinking.

Butler Judith 1990 *Gender trouble: feminism and the subversion of identity.* Routledge, New York.

Butler Judith 1993 *Bodies that matter: on the discursive limits of 'sex'*. Routledge, New York.

Coates Jennifer, Cameron Deborah (eds) 1989 *Women in their speech communities*. Longman, New York.

Connell Robert W 1987 *Gender and power*. Stanford University Press, Stanford, CA.

Crawford Mary, MacLeod Margo 1990 Gender in the college classroom: an assessment of the 'chilly climate' for women. *Sex Roles* 23.3/4: 101–22.

Eckert Penelope 1989 The whole woman: sex and gender differences in variation. *Language Variation and Change* 1: 245–67.

Eckert Penelope, McConnell-Ginet Sally 1992a Communities of practice: where language, gender and power all live. In Hall Kira, Bucholtz Mary, Moonwomon Birch (eds) pp 89–99.

Eckert Penelope, McConnell-Ginet Sally 1992b Think practially and look locally: language and gender as community-based practice. *Annual Review of Anthropology* 21: 461–90.

Fausto-Sterling Anne 1979 *Myths of gender: biological theories about women and men*. Norton, New York.

Fishman Pamela M 1983 Interaction: the work women do. In Thorne Barrie, Kramarae Cheris, Henley Nancy (eds) pp 89–102.

Florman Samuel 1987 *The civilized engineer*. St Martin's Press, New York.

Fredrich Augustine J (ed) 1989 *Sons of Martha: civil engineering readings in modern literature*. American Society of Civil Engineers, New York.

Frisch Max 1959 *Homo Faber*. Bullock Michael (trans.) Harcourt Brace Jovanovich, San Diego.

Gabriel Susan L, Smithson Isaiah (eds) 1990 *Gender in the classroom: power and pedagogy*. University of Illinois Press, Urbana.

Gal Susan 1989 Between speech and silence: the problematics of research on language and gender. *Papers in Pragmatics* 3.1: 1–38. (Also published in di Leonardo Michelle (ed) 1991 *Gender at the crossroads of knowledge: feminist anthropology in the postmodern era*. University of California Press, Berkeley, CA pp 175–203.)

Gal Susan 1992 Language, gender, and power: an anthropological view. In Hall Kira, Bucholtz Mary, Moonwomon Birch (eds) pp 153–61.

Gornick Vivian 1983 *Women in science: portraits from a world in transition*. Touchstone (Simon & Schuster), New York.

Hacker Sally 1989 *Pleasure, power, and technology: some tales of gender, engineering, and the cooperative workplace*. Unwin Hyman, Boston.

Hall Kira, Bucholtz Mary, Moonwomon Birch (eds) (1992) *Locating power: proceedings of the second Berkeley women and language conference*. Berkeley Women and Language Group, Berkeley, CA.

Hall Roberta, Sandler Bernice R 1982 *The classroom climate: a chilly one for women?* Project on the Status and Education of Women, Association of American Colleges, Washington, DC.

Haraway Donna 1981 In the beginning was the word: the genesis of biological theory. *Signs: Journal of Women in Culture and Society* 6.3: 469–81.

Haraway Donna 1989 *Primate visions*. Routledge, New York.

Harding Sandra 1986 *The science question in feminism*. Cornell University Press, Ithaca, NY.

Harding Sandra, O'Barr Jean F 1987 *Sex and scientific inquiry*. University of Chicago Press, Chicago.

Holland Dorothy C, Eisenhart Margaret A 1990 *Educated in romance: women, achievement, and college culture*. University of Chicago Press, Chicago.

Holmes Janet 1992 Women's talk in public contexts. *Discourse & Society* 3.2: 131–50.

Houston Marcia, Kramarae Cheris 1991 Speaking from silence: methods of silencing and of resistance. *Discourse & Society* 2.4: 387–99.

Keller Evelyn Fox 1983 *A feeling for the organism: the life and work of Barbara McClintock*. Freeman, New York.

Keller Evelyn Fox 1985 *Reflections on gender and science*. Yale University Press, New Haven.

Kramarae Cheris, Treichler Paula 1990 Power relationships in the classroom. In Gabriel Susan L, Smithson Isaiah (eds) pp 41–59.

Krupnick Cathyrn 1985a *Sex differences in college teacher's classroom talk*. Unpublished PhD dissertation. Harvard University, Cambridge, MA.

Krupnick Cathryn 1985b Women and men in the classroom: inequality and its remedies. *On Teaching and Learning* 1: 18–25.

Labov William 1991 The intersection of sex and social class in the course of linguistic change. *Language Variation and Change* 2.2: 205–51.

Lakoff Robin Tolmach 1975 *Language and woman's place*. Harper & Row, New York.

Lakoff Robin Tolmach 1992 The silencing of women. In Hall Kira, Bucholtz Mary, Moonwomon Birch (eds) pp 344–55.

Lave Jean, Wenger Etienne 1991 *Situated learning: legitimate peripheral participation*. Cambridge University Press, Cambridge.

Layton Edwin T Jr 1986 *The revolt of the engineers: social responsibility and the American engineering profession*. Johns Hopkins University Press, Baltimore, MD.

Lumsdaine Edward, Lumsdaine Monica 1993 *Creative problem solving: thinking skills for a changing world* (second edn). McGraw-Hill, New York.

Maltz Daniel N, Borker Ruth A 1982 A cultural approach to male–female miscommunication. In Gumperz John J (ed) *Language and social identity*. Cambridge University Press, Cambridge pp 196–216.

National Science Foundation 1990 *Women and minorities in science and engineering*. NSF Report 90–301, January.

Nicholson Linda 1994 Interpreting *gender*. *Signs: Journal of Women in Culture and Society* 20.1: 79–105.

Ochs Elinor 1992 Indexing gender. In Duranti Alessandro, Goodwin Charles (eds) *Rethinking context: language as an interactive phenomenon*. Cambridge University Press, New York pp 335–58.

The Oxford English dictionary [OED] (second compact edn) 1991 Oxford University Press, Oxford.

Parsons Talcott, Bales Robert F 1955 *Family, socialization, and interaction process*. Free Press, Glencoe, IL.

Remlinger Kathryn 1995 *Production, resistance, and opposition: students linguistically constituting ideologies of gender and sexuality*. Unpublished PhD dissertation. Michigan Technological University, Houghton, MI.

Rich Adrienne 1980 Compulsory heterosexuality and lesbian existence. *Signs: Journal of Women in Culture and Society* 5.4: 631–60.

Sadker Myra, Sadker David 1985 (March) Sexism in the schoolroom of the 80's. *Psychology Today*: 54–7.

Sadker Myra, Sadker David 1990 Confronting sexism in the college classroom. In Gabriel Susan L, Smithson Isaiah (eds) pp 176–87.

Sarah Elizabeth 1980 Teachers and students in the classroom: an examination of classroom interaction. In Spender Dale, Sarah Elizabeth (eds) pp 155–64.

Savage Gerald 1991 *The construction of leadership in two collaborative learning peer groups*. Unpublished master's thesis. Michigan Technological University, Houghton, MI.

Savage Gerald 1994 *Inventing disciplinary knowledge and ethos: conversational argument as heuristic inquiry in collaborative groups of chemical engineering students*. Unpublished PhD dissertation. Michigan Technological University, Houghton, MI.

Spender Dale 1980a Disappearing tricks. In Spender Dale, Sarah Elizabeth (eds) pp 165–73.

Spender Dale 1980b Talking in class. In Spender Dale, Sarah Elizabeth (eds) pp 148–54.

Spender Dale 1985 *Man made language* (second edn). Routledge: Boston.

Spender Dale, Sarah Elizabeth (eds) 1980 *Learning to lose: sexism and education*. The Women's Press, London.

Swacker Marjorie 1975 The sex of the speaker as a sociolinguistic variable. In Thorne Barry, Henley Nancy (eds) pp 76–83.

Swacker Marjorie 1976 Women's verbal behavior at learned and professional conferences. In Dubois Betty Lou, Crouch Isabelle (eds) *Proceedings of the conference on the sociology of the languages of American women*. Trinity University, San Antonio, TX pp 155–60.

Swann Joan 1989 Talk control: an illustration from the classroom of problems in analyzing male dominance of conversation. In Coates Jennifer, Cameron Deborah (eds) pp 122–40.

Tannen Deborah 1990 *You just don't understand: women and men in conversation*. Morrow, New York.

Thorne Barrie 1990 Children and gender: constructions of difference. In Rhode Deborah L (ed) *Theoretical perspectives on sexual difference*. Yale University Press, New Haven pp 100–13.

Thorne Barrie 1993 *Gender play: girls and boys in school*. Rutgers University Press, New Brunswick, NJ.

Thorne Barry, Henley Nancy (eds) 1975 *Language and sex: difference and dominance*. Newbury House, Rowley, MA

Thorne Barrie, Kramarae Cheris, Henley Nancy (eds) 1983 *Language, gender, and society*. Newbury House, Rowley, MA.

West Candace H, Zimmerman Don 1983 Small insults: a study of interruptions in cross-sex conversations between unacquainted persons. In Thorne Barry, Kramarae Cheris, Henley Nancy (eds) pp 102–17.

Woods Nicole 1989 Talking shop: sex and status as determinants of floor apportionment in a work setting. In Coates Jennifer, Cameron Deborah (eds) pp 141–57.

Zimmerman Don, West Candace 1975 Sex roles, interruptions and silences in conversation. In Thorne Barry, Henley Nancy (eds) pp 105–29.

9 Dealing with gender identity as a sociolinguistic variable[1]

Miriam Meyerhoff

Introduction

Quantitative approaches to the study of language variation have been strongly influenced by the sociolinguistic methodologies established by Labov's (1982 [1966]) study of the speech community of New York's Lower East Side. The sociolinguistic variables that have been pursued and studied in subsequent work have often used the non-linguistic variables that Labov investigated as their primary focus. This has led to some valuable findings both within and across cultures, and perhaps more importantly provided the field of linguistics with a framework for reaching out and borrowing the methods and existing insights from other fields as a means of enlightening and furthering linguistic praxis. Indeed, much of the essential early work in sociolinguistics research was conducted by extending the frameworks and interests of other fields such as anthropology and sociology.

There has been a recent re-emphasis in sociolinguistics, led by researchers working on the interaction of language and gender, to renew this tradition of reaching out to other fields in order to benefit from what they can tell us about the interpersonal functions of languages and communication. It has been standard practice in sociolinguistic studies to adopt the methodologies of participant observation or network sampling that are drawn from anthropology and sociology. More recently this has been accompanied by interest in the methodologies and theory that underlie much of the last two decades of work in the social psychology of language.

In this chapter, I will try to bring together some of these elements and some previous findings on how language is used as a social marker. In particular, I will use examples that illustrate speakers' use of linguistic markers as markers of group identity, where the in-group/out-group boundary is drawn on the basis of the speaker's sex. I will attempt to show that variationist findings have already shown us the complexity of the notion of sex or gender as a group identity, and that the complexity of this identity for a speaker lies in its own status as a variable. I will take the classic distinctions of social identity theory as my starting point, and assume that communicative events are basically either intergroup encounters or interpersonal encounters. The nature of a single encounter, and the types of group or personal identity that shape communication within it, will depend on which social or personal identity is most salient to the interactants at that time. I will conclude by presenting a proposal for a framework of speaker identity. Some of the more important characteristics of speakers' identities that will be presented are:

1. Speakers possess many different identities, some personal, some group (or social).
2. Identities vary in their salience in different communicative events, but all of a speaker's different identities are always present and are all available to the speaker in every communicative event.
3. Identities vary in salience depending on numerous non-linguistic variables: topic, interlocutor, affective goals of the speaker.
4. A speaker's identification with different identities has the potential to change during the life cycle.

Clearly, the task of determining which identity or identities are most salient to interactants is a sensitive business, and findings from the social psychology research caution us to pay close attention to changes in speakers' perceptions of the situations they are in, and to their perceptions of their interlocutor. I would like to think, however, that it is possible to marry the sensitivity and subjective validity of some of the social psychology findings, with sociolinguistic information on linguistic variation.

I envisage a framework for communication and speaker identity that represents speakers' affective flexibility, both in terms of changes to their cognitive schema, as well as in changes to their linguistic performance. This framework should be able to represent the changes we can observe in individuals across relatively short periods of time (within a single communicative event, and also across related communicative events), but should also be able to reflect the changes we can observe across speakers' lifetimes. The framework is also intended to make clear where and how individual identities fit in with collective identities like gender or class. The framework proposes that the way interlocutors communicate with each other is by means of shared network ties which create sociolinguistically meaningful links between individuals' shared social identities. The framework suggests: (i) a way of determining when and how the salience of one identity rises above any others (see Giles *et al.* 1980: 277), and (ii) a way of indicating the potential overlap of more than one social identity and the influence of multiple societal identities on each other.

Speakers possess many different identities

Within the framework of social identity theory (Tajfel and Turner 1979, 1986, Hogg and Abrams 1988), researchers have commented on the need to deal with gender (or sex) in a more sophisticated way (Giles *et al.* 1980, Hogg 1985, Condor 1986). Hogg and Abrams (1988) believe the main challenge for social psychology is to describe and understand the relationship between the individual and the group. Social identity theory attempts to meet this challenge by focusing on the groups that are proposed to exist *within* the individual (Hogg and Abrams 1988: 3). Social identity theory treats an individual's various group identifications as central to a development of self and as the basis for many kinds of behaviour, not the least of which is linguistic behaviour. Individuals may have a number of identities, some of which are characterized as social (i.e. identities linking an individual to social groups and providing a group basis for interaction with others), some of which are characterized as personal (i.e. identities based on more one-to-one relationships).

Obviously, researchers coming from a social psychology perspective will feel uneasy treating all female respondents as a single group for analysis simply based on their shared biological characteristics. Thus, researchers in the social psychology of language (Giles *et al.* 1980, Hogg 1985, Condor 1986, Hogg and Abrams 1988, Kramarae 1990, Henley and Kramarae 1991) have drawn attention to the need for a theoretical framework that will invoke (i) the salience of gender as an identity in a communicative event, and (ii) the presence and influence of any other identity or identities that may be more salient. Similarly, Eckert and McConnell-Ginet (1992) have encouraged sociolinguistic studies of variation to employ methodologies familiar in anthropology to more appropriately highlight the multiplicity of identities that speakers possess, and have urged that this multiplicity be worked into the analysis of language variation; in doing so they revisit some of the foundation research in sociolinguistics such as Bauman and Scherzer (1974), Hymes (1974), and Sankoff (1980).

Identity as a variable

There are some clear examples of linguistic variation in the literature that indicate speakers do not consistently identify with the same social grouping. We can consider, for example, the way women in Tunis exploit the symbolic value of three different linguistic variables as markers of social identities they relate to or identify with the most, depending on the context.

One variable is the use of the diphthongs /aw/ and /aj/ rather than the monophthongs /u:/ and /i:/ (Trabelsi 1991). The diphthong variants occur only in the speech of Tunis women, and more specifically only in the speech of older Tunis women. According to Trabelsi, they occur categorically in the speech of old women, and variably in the speech of middle-aged women. Younger women have ceased using the diphthongs and now categorically use the monophthongs that characterize the speech of Tunis men. Trabelsi describes the variation in the speech of the middle-aged women as representing a 'phonological identity crisis' (p. 89), where the variation in use of the diphthongs and monophthongs reflects the tug-of-war going on in middle-aged Tunis women between a desire to identify themselves as being locals (the diphthongs traditionally carrying a strong significance as a marker of being a Tunis woman), and a desire to associate themselves with a more educated, modern identity (which they can achieve by using the monophthongs associated with younger women's and men's speech). Trabelsi reports that a middle-aged woman's identification with either one of these groupings (traditional Tunis values versus modernity) is often influenced by her interlocutor. If she is talking to an older woman who clearly identifies with traditional Tunis values in her use of diphthongs, a middle-aged informant is more likely to emphasize her potential identification with these values and likewise to use diphthongs in her speech. If she is talking to a younger woman who habitually uses monophthongs, the same middle-aged woman will emphasize her potential identification with values of modernity by using monophthongs. (These findings have clear theoretical parallels in the principles of communicative accommodation theory outlined by Thakerar *et al.* 1982 and Giles and Coupland 1991.)

Jabeur (1987, cited in L. Milroy 1990) reports, however, that younger women in Tunis do not always align themselves with male norms in their choice of linguistic markers. The situation is rather more complex than an association between youth, modernity and male linguistic markers versus age, tradition and female speech markers. Jabeur found that bilingual speakers in Tunis also display socially significant variation in their pronunciation of the (r) variable in spoken French. The standard French uvular /ʀ/ varies with a characteristically Tunis variant that is articulated as an alveolar trill, /r/. Men virtually never use the uvular variant, while women demonstrate greater variation between the two forms. Jabeur interprets this as Tunis men's favouring a marker with strong significance as an ingroup marker of a Tunis identity, while women are torn more between a desire to identify locally as a Tunis speaker and a desire to establish their identification with the French values of education and greater social freedom for women. Trabelsi also reports that young Tunis women use French borrowings (she discusses lexical borrowings) as a way of getting around some of the linguistic taboos that exist in Arabic. It seems, therefore, that the association between French and freedom from Arab society's restraints on women, reported by Jabeur, is fairly robust.

To summarize, then, part of a Tunis woman's communicative competence lies in managing a number of social identities. Because different identities may be of primary salience in a particular communicative event, her communicative competence lies in choosing the linguistic variables that express these identities. A Tunis woman may identify as a woman, as a Tunis local, as an emancipated person, and/or as an educated person. Depending on which identity is most salient for her in a particular communicative event, her choice of linguistic variants will vary. There is also the possibility that her identification with any of these separate identities will vary within a single communicative event. Thus, we can imagine a scenario where a middle-aged woman might be using a uvular /ʀ/ and the /i:/ and /u:/ monophthongs. She would thereby be exploiting and invoking the meta-messages of education and non-traditionalness that these variables carry, but she could temper that impression by simultaneously observing traditional linguistic taboos, thereby transmitting the meta-message that she is not distancing herself completely from local, traditional, Tunis values. These different identifications might be signalled across a series of communicative events or they might be signalled within one communicative event.

The framework I will present in this chapter is an attempt to clarify the processes unfolding when linguistic variation provides evidence that speakers' identifications are shifting, within and across communicative events and even across a whole lifetime of communicative events. While sociolinguistic studies of variation have often taken the form of reports that such-and-such a variant is favoured by, or more typically found in the speech of women, educated speakers, or speakers of a certain ethnic group, we should keep in mind what these findings mean in interpersonal terms. What they are really stating is that such-and-such a variant is symbolic of and signals a speaker's identification with the social groups 'women', 'educated speakers', 'Arabs', etc. Although this perspective is implicit in much sociolinguistic research, one purpose of this chapter is to make these sorts of assumptions more explicit.

Gender identity as a situational variable and across the life span

In this section, I will review evidence from social psychology research that supports the need to treat gender identity (and by implication, any other identity) as a construct that varies in social significance for an individual depending on the situation. Not surprisingly, social psychology research indicates that the kinds of variables that influence the salience of gender identity in an interaction are precisely the kinds of variables that sociolinguistics research has recognized as important in accounting for linguistic variation. Research by Hogg (1985) and Doise and Weinberger (1973) shows that the sex of the interlocutor, for instance, can affect how much salience the speaker ascribes to their gender identity. Doise and Weinberger (1973) and Deschamps and Doise (1978) found that the situation or task, and the speaker's affective evaluation of the task and their interlocutor(s) also had an effect on the salience of gender. Hogg (1985) also found that contextual variables affected women's identification with a gender-based identity. Subjective reaction tests indicated that speakers' gender identity was more salient to them in same-sex dyads than it was when they were interacting in groups.

In Doise and Weinberger's (1973) study, the extent to which a group of men associated themselves with traits classified as masculine and feminine across different intergroup situations was tested.

Their results provide good indications that gender identity varies in its salience depending on the social context speakers find themselves in. The men in this study disassociated themselves from any feminine traits when they were in an all-male group, but were readier to associate themselves with them when they were interacting in one-on-one same-sex situations. Their association with traits classified as masculine remained high in and across different intergroup situations and with different tasks, but their association with masculine traits was especially high when they were engaged in competitive, as opposed to cooperative tasks. It is possible to use these findings to supplement those of Cannavale *et al.* (1970). This research found that in situations they called 'de-individuated', any gender identification (i.e. masculine or feminine) was reportedly less salient for men. I would suggest that in conjunction with Doise and Weinberger's results, this finding offers a tentative hierarchy of situational gender salience for men. Doise and Weinberger's findings suggest that, for men, all-male group situations are [+masculine], [−feminine], one-on-one interactions are [+masculine], [+feminine], and the findings of Cannavale *et al.* suggest that for men de-individuated situations are [−masculine], [−feminine]. However, regardless of the validity of this hierarchy, the experimental evidence from self-reports (Doise and Weinberger 1973, Cannavale *et al.* 1970) and subjective reaction tests (Hogg 1975) indicates that gender identity varies in salience for adults depending on the composition of the group and the nature of the task.

These studies suggest that, from an early age, gender is a more salient group identity for males than it is for females; it also seems that gender may be salient to women in a more restricted range of interactional settings than it is for men. Therefore, we might ask whether a research agenda and methods of inquiry that assume gender differentiation to be a highly significant form of social categorization might not be reifying a masculine view of the salience of gender identity.

We might also ask at what age gender becomes salient, and at what age people acquire the skill of allowing their gender identity to vary across situations. Deschamps and Doise (1978) found that gender identity has a different significance for female and male primary/elementary school children. In their study, gender identity was a more positively valued and a more salient marker of group distinctiveness for boys than for girls. The boys in this study made greater distinctions between the two genders than girls did, especially when they anticipated some kind of competition between themselves and the girls (cf. Doise and Weinberger's findings about the significance of men's competitive or cooperative orientation on the salience of their masculine identity, mentioned above). In fact, gender identities may fluctuate during a person's lifetime.

Doise and Weinberger (1973) and Deschamps and Doise (1978) show that gender is a salient identity for younger children, even though its salience is potentially mediated by other factors. This seems to be true at least for young boys about whom these studies provide the most evidence. But although gender seems to be a salient identity for younger members of the speech community (primary/elementary school-age speakers), and although it may be a salient identity among adults,[2] there are several studies that provide evidence that during adolescence gender becomes a less salient marker of group identity than other social dimensions.

Eckert (1988, 1991) has shown that, among Detroit adolescents, the degree to which speakers are leaders of innovative vowel variants affected by the Northern Cities Shift and the degree to which they use conservative vowel variants is not primarily affected by their gender identity. Adolescent girls do not, for instance, uniformly lead adolescent boys in use of innovative vowels. Rather, group identities defined within the local adolescent culture are more salient to the introduction of innovative vowels and the maintenance of conservative forms. The relevant groups are called 'jocks' and 'burnouts' by the adolescents that Eckert studied. As Figure 9.1 shows, it is identification as a burnout that correlates with high use of innovative forms of the vowels that are newly participating in the Northern Cities Shift, i.e. the backing of /ɛ/ and /ʌ/, and not identification with one gender group or the other.

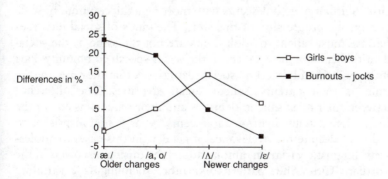

Figure 9.1 Differences in percentage use of innovative forms in the Northern Cities Shift. Contrasts between girls and boys, and between burnouts and jocks (adapted from Eckert 1989: 261–2).

Similarly, in a study of the speech community in Farmer City, Illinois, Habick (1991) found that the progression of various vowel shifts in the speech of adolescents seemed to reflect the adolescents' own social groupings ('burnouts' and 'rednecks' in this community) more than their gender. In Farmer City, fronting of /u/ has progressed throughout most of the community and only four (three boys and one girl) out of the twenty adolescents studied showed less fronted variants of /u/ in their speech. These were all speakers who were part of the redneck group. The most unusual /u/ variant was an innovative form [üʸ], and this form was used in the widest range of phonological environments by two burnout leaders. Thus, the adolescents' own social groupings seem to be better correlates of the fronting of /u/ than gender. However, when the three age groups sampled in the Farmer City study are compared, there is some apparent time evidence that gender may be a more relevant identity affecting /u/ fronting in speakers who are beyond the reach of the social identities and allegiances of adolescence. Data on /u/ fronting in the speech of the parents and grandparents of these adolescents reveal that fronted variants are found in the speech of five out of the six women surveyed, but in the speech of only two out of seven men. This suggests that gender as an identity varies in salience in the Farmer City speech community according to age. Among adolescents, it has less salience, but is more salient for speakers at different stages in their lives even within the same speech community.

A similar argument for the fluctuating sociolinguistic salience of gender as a identity can be made by comparing Eckert's (1988) very specific data on the raising and backing of vowels in the Northern Cities Shift among adolescents with more general, community-wide data on the progression of this shift. The kinds of social identities that are most salient to adolescents are not the same as the social identities that are most salient in the wider speech community. Part of the point of adolescents' social identities is that they are not the same as their parents' salient social identities. The difference between their most salient identities and their parents' is one of the things that defines them as adolescents. So it is not surprising to find that, despite the irrelevance of gender (in this case) to adolescents' linguistic variation, among adults the raising of vowels in the Northern Cities Shift patterns like other sociolinguistic variables and women lead men (Labov *et al.* 1972, Labov 1991, 1994, but see also James this volume).

In other words, Eckert (1988) shows that among adolescents the variables are markers of a speaker's association with an identity that is relevant in adolescent culture. Labov *et al.*(1972) and Labov (1994) show that after adolescence, the same variables are markers of gender identity. What Eckert's and Labov *et al.*'s data suggest is that during adolescence, adolescents reject the socially significant group identities of their parents and the wider speech community in favour of group identities that they have defined for themselves. Adolescents lead the community in the Northern Cities Shift, but they lead it on their own terms; the social identities interacting with linguistic variables are the social identities that are most salient to adolescents. However, as a linguistic change gains a foothold in the wider community, the social groupings that are most salient in the wider speech community assert themselves and become better correlates of the linguistic variables. A speaker's gender identity may become a reliable predictor of the linguistic variant they use.

Greenwood (this volume) also provides evidence that for the adolescents she studied, and their friends, the most salient social grouping is a social identity that unites the speakers in collaborative conversation, stressing shared jokes and the social goal of having a good time together. Speakers who are willing and able to participate in conversational routines that establish themselves as sharing the same goals are accepted as part of one social group. In both Greenwood's and Eckert's data, we find evidence that adolescents use language routines and linguistic behaviour to establish and maintain group identities that distinguish adolescents from the social identities that are most salient to the wider speech community.

Implications of social identity as a variable to the sociolinguistic tradition

Sociolinguists generally work with definitions of the speech community that are predicated on a notion of shared norms for speaking, or shared norms for evaluating different realizations of linguistic variables. The situation in which speakers have many personal and group identities that I have started to outline may require us to sharpen the way in which we conceive of shared norms in a speech community. Members of a speech community may agree that the same kinds of personal or group/social identities normally constitute the basis for interactions in their community but individuals may differ in how relevant or salient they consider one of their several social identities to be.

Horvath's (1985) re-analysis of some of Labov's early work provides evidence that within the same community there are individuals whose linguistic behaviour indicates that they treat one of their group identities as being more salient, while most of their peers treat another group identity as being more salient. Horvath's insightful use of a 'principle components analysis' of the speech community (in which the data are allowed to lead the groupings, rather than vice versa) shows that Nathan B. in Labov's (1982 [1966]) New York City study appears to be a speaker for whom sex is a more salient social identification than social class. This is reflected in his apparently idiosyncratic linguistic behaviour. Horvath points out that if we approach Nathan B.'s performance on its own terms, i.e. if we allow Nathan B. to show through his linguistic behaviour that his identification as a man is more salient for him than his middle-class identity, then his high use of the non-standard /d/ instead of /ð/ is no longer anomalous. Other speakers' performances simply indicate that their class identity is most salient for them, but just as salience of an identity varies within an individual, it varies within a community, and our methodologies and theories should incorporate this.

Community members may also differ in which linguistic markers are used to signal identification with different social groupings. Milroy and Milroy (1985) document the sociolinguistic distribution of variants of /ɛ/ and /a/ in Belfast English. Raising of /ɛ/ and backing of /a/ are both changes occurring in the speech community, but the changes have very different social significance. According to the Milroys, women's use of the innovative, backed forms of /a/ shows a strong correlation with the degree to which they are integrated into the community. They claim that /a/ backing functions as a marker of network strength for women. On the other hand, backing of /a/ is not an important marker of community identity for men. The indicator that appears to function as a signal of men's high levels of integration into the community is, instead, raised /ɛ/. Thus, the Milroys argue, both women and men in Belfast agree that one's identification with and integration into the community is an important social variable that should be marked in speech, but they disagree as to which variants will be used as markers. What the Milroys' data actually show is that the multiple group identifications of an individual speaker are expressed in the selection of one vowel variant.

By using a backed variant of /a/ ([ɑː] or [ɔː]), a young woman from the Clonard area of Belfast may be interpreted by listeners as signalling her strong integration into the community. However, in interpreting the linguistic variant in this way, the listener must already have recognized and processed the salience of her identity as a young Clonard woman. It would be impossible for the listener to correctly interpret the use of [ɑː], for instance, as a marker of network strength, without also working through the computation in terms of the speaker's gender identity. The complexity of some of the Belfast data is graphic support for the complexity and multiplicity of identities that are factored into and used to compute social meaning.

In a similar vein, L. Milroy (1990) reports unpublished work on the glottalization of stops in Tyneside English. These findings suggest that, among men in this community, glottalization of stops has primary significance as a marker of male identity. Women show much greater variation in their glottalization of stops than men, and the variation exhibited by women is linked much more closely to changes in style than is the variation exhibited by men. Thus, glottalization of stops in Tyneside English is a linguistic marker for both men and women but with different symbolic meaning for the two groups. For men, it is a marker of gender; for women, it is a marker of register. This example serves as an important reminder that correlation between speaker sex and use of a linguistic variable does not necessarily indicate that the variable functions primarily as an intergroup marker of gender.

Similarly, as we saw in the discussion of Trabelsi's and Jabeur's reports of sociolinguistic variation in Tunis speech, speakers may sometimes use linguistic variables to signal group identity based on sex, but this identification is not a behavioural constant. We must, therefore, be cautious about overgeneralizing the significance of a group identity based on gender where we do not have other data that specifically supports such a generalization, e.g. similar patterns of linguistic variation in other variables or explicit meta-linguistic comments by speakers.

Furthermore, there is research in social psychology that indicates that we need to be careful to define precisely what it is we intend when we characterize a social identity as being gender-based. Members of a speech community may, for instance, agree upon the labels for some of the group identities that are considered salient, but they may have different perceptions about what the labels mean. Two examples are illustrative: Hunter and Davis (1992) and Condor (1986). Hunter and Davis conducted interviews with thirty-two African American men on what it means to 'be a man'. The interviews generated 108 distinct traits that the respondents felt were important to being a man. Hunter and Davis grouped these into a number of thematic areas, and using the thematic areas identified they concluded that three masculine identities are available to African American men as a basis for constructing their gender identity and for defining the concept of masculinity or manliness. One of these is the dominant notion of manhood that cuts across American society (stressing successfulness and leadership, for example); another is the notion of manhood located within the cooperative, group-survival norms of the African American community; and the third potential influence is a 'hypermasculine' (p. 467) identity associated with sexism and violence. Thus, some of the traits typically associated with masculinity (especially in subjective reaction tests in social psychology): physical strength, competitiveness and aggressiveness, were not necessarily considered central to a manly identity by African American men.

Condor (1986) undertook a similarly subjective inquiry into the nature of sex-role identification among women. She conducted interviews with seventy-seven traditional women, i.e. women who described themselves as supporting 'the existing roles of men and women' (p. 102) and thirty-nine non-traditional women, i.e. women who stated a desire for change in sex role differentiation. Her interviews revealed that not all women share the same meanings for certain terms. This makes it far from simple to compare the beliefs about gender and womanliness of these two groups of women or to establish a common discourse between the two groups in order to discuss sex-role beliefs. The traditional and the non-traditional women agreed to a certain extent: identification as a woman for both groups entails some intergroup comparison between women and men. Generally, both groups of women agree in evaluating men and 'male' characteristics' negatively (p. 106). They also both favour basic levels of equal rights/equal opportunities for women. However, the two groups of women differed markedly in the way in which they conducted the intergroup comparison and these ways were indicative of more fundamental differences in their respective conceptualizations of what it is to be a woman. Traditional women saw their feminine or womanly identity as complementary to men's masculine identity, whereas non-traditional women saw the comparison in more competitive terms. The non-traditional group compared the social prestige and economic security of women and men, and, partly by identifying a disparity, were able to define what it is to be a woman (p. 103). The lesson we can draw from Hunter and Davis's (1992) and Condor's (1986) studies is that research into gender identity and its interaction with variation in language needs to be grounded in a clear and detailed understanding of the speaker's subjective evaluation of the social categories used.

A framework of speaker identity

The framework for speaker identity described in this section is intended to take account of the empirical and theoretical data presented so far. A speaker's gender identity will take its place as one among a number of social and personal identities, varying in salience depending on several factors, including the speaker's ties with his or her interlocutor and the feedback that the speaker gets about the affective nature of the communicative event.

In previous work on the sociolinguistic factors affecting the likelihood of creolization in pidgins (Meyerhoff and Niedzielski 1994), Nancy Niedzielski and I proposed a framework of communicative events which pivoted on a multifaceted conceptualization of speaker identity. We suggest that speaker identity may be a useful way of accounting for the hastening or retarding of some kinds of language change. We present a framework of speaker identity, within a larger framework of communication, which is an attempt to handle the conceptual problem of how theory should represent individuals who are trying to manage multiple identities (some group, some personal). We wanted to capture the fact that the uniqueness of individuals lies in their blend of multiple social and personal identities. We felt that all such identities should be represented in every communicative event, yet we wanted a framework that would reflect the fact that not every one of an individual's identities is equally important in every interaction. Our framework of speaker identity provides the flexibility needed to indicate the way speakers' identities change in salience from one interaction to another (and sometimes within the same interaction), as well as the way speakers' overall identities can change over time. It establishes a more explanatory framework for some of the sociolinguistic and experimental studies reviewed, which show that speakers' linguistic and social behaviour reflects and constitutes numerous social identities.

Speaker identity is pivotal to the proposed framework in the following way: not only does it intentionally shape the linguistic forms of the communicative event and provide speakers with the social and cultural knowledge necessary for making basic sociolinguistic and pragmatic choices (e.g. politeness markers, language in a bilingual setting, conventional implicatures), but the on-going social and personal outcomes of the communicative event feed back into the interlocutor's identities, constantly determining the way speakers will shape subsequent utterances. Thus, speaker identity is both a receiving and a sending post. There are four points that need to be captured in describing how an individual uses social identity to manage this work:

1. In general a speaker interacts with others in terms of one, most salient group or personal identity at a time.
2. That most salient identity is shaped by its relationship to other group or personal identities that the speaker possesses.
3. That identity is also a product of what the speaker's interlocutor perceives to be the speaker's most salient identification.
4. Aspects of an individual's overall identity change over time and across interactions.

In contrast with some existing frameworks, this one does not conceive of speaker identity as an orthogonal relationship between group and personal identifications, nor as a series of distinct selves that are shuffled, like a pack of cards, until one is at the top.[3] Rather, speaker identity is seen as a network of interconnected identifications, operating together as if they were parts of a movable sphere.

Figure 9.2 shows a representation in which an individual's identifications can be described in terms of their relationship to two poles, group and personal, and are positioned relative to each other on a continuous field. The spherical design captures the fact that no identification is wholly independent of the others. Identifications may be complementary to others or they may be in competition with others, but, crucially, the representation entails that no single personal or group identification, even when it is the most salient for a communicative event, exists in isolation.

The framework also integrates two other sociolinguistic and psychological concepts: social networks and ethnolinguistic vitality. A theory of social networks allows us to explain how the on-going feedback in the form of social and personal outcomes in a communicative event is received. Milroy and Milroy (1992) have argued that social networks are crucial to an informed understanding of the social categorization known as 'class', and they suggest that if

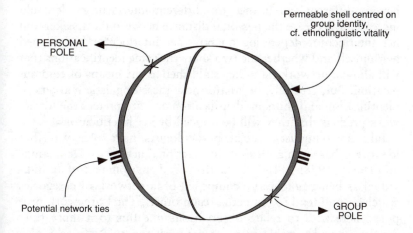

Figure 9.2 Model of speaker identity showing complementarity of personal and social identities, also two possible network ties (one via a more personal identity; one via a more social, or group, identity).

research paid greater attention to the quality and quantity of network ties between interactants, not only would our understanding of the complex sociometric notion of class be improved, but we might also attain a better understanding of the salience of a person's group or personal identifications in an interaction.

These arguments about class as a sociolinguistic variable are similar to the ones about gender that I reviewed earlier. The framework presented here reflects the belief that a communicative event is initiated through the medium of a network tie, and that feedback is received, furthering, maintaining or curtailing the interaction, through the medium of such ties. Thus, network ties are instrumental as *post hoc* explanations of change, as well as being useful predictors of the likely mechanisms of future changes. Figure 9.2 shows a potential network tie with a group identification, and one with a more personal identification. Individuals possess numerous such ties, each associated with different identifications. Consider again the linguistic variables associated with different social identities potentially available to Tunis women (Jabeur 1987, Trabelsi 1991). We noted that a woman might signal different identifications by her choice and combination of these variables, both across and within a communicative event. In terms of the framework proposed here, her unfolding identification with some traditional norms through her choice of linguistic variables will have a different significance for different interlocutors. It could increase or decrease the personal distance between the speaker and her interlocutor depending on how her interlocutor has aligned her/himself and whether the two share the same identifications that will allow a network tie to be established as the means of communication. But, crucially, no matter how these linguistic markers of identification and shifts in identification are interpreted, the framework predicts that they will be noticed by her interlocutor.

Like sociolinguists, social psychologists have observed that identity is based on a series of interactional networks. Deschamps and Doise (1978: 144) describe the social environment of an individual as being potentially composed of 'a network of categories which ... will tend to cut across each other'. The framework proposed here tries to relate observations like this to a more fully developed and testable form of network theory. Networks also allow us to distinguish differences in importance between identities. The fact that all of an individual's identities are present and mutually dependent in this spherical model of speaker identity does not mean that all identities are taken to be equally important (to the individual or to society). Because of its relative permanence and because of the number of network ties a person has connecting with their gender identity, that identity can be more important than some of the other identities an individual possesses (although gender identity can change, see Knight (1992) and Hall and O'Donovan (this volume). The number and nature of the network ties established with a particular iden-tity reflects the extent and frequency with which that identity functions as the basis for communication with others.

If the goal is to establish the mutual influence of networks, speaker identities, and language, how then might this framework be tested? First, the linguistic markers and network ties that are salient to a speaker need to be identified. Second, apparent correlations between the two need to be established. So far, this is standard practice within sociolinguistics. Third, we need to identify key points in discourse at which different identities seem to be most salient for a speaker. At this point, we can check whether the frequency of a linguistic marker that is presumed to index a particular identity increases when that identity is salient or decreases when its salience is reduced. Establishing such a correlation would support the hypothesis that speakers have multiple identities and that they can change easily between them. Fourth, we need to identify episodes in discourse where speaker identifications are clearly being negotiated, e.g. new identifications are being collaboratively constructed or existing identities are being rejected as the medium of communication in a given interaction. Again, we can check whether there are the expected correlations between the frequency of a linguistic marker that is presumed to index such an identity and the emergence or cessation of that identity. I would take such a correlation to support the hypothesis that network ties play an on-going role feeding and bleeding communicative behaviour. Fifth, we would like to establish correlations between the degree of salience of a particular identity in a communicative event and the frequency of a linguistic variable presumed to index this identity. This may require the creative application of measures of correlation. One difficulty will be in deciding whether degrees of salience can or should be quantified in terms any more specific than 'greater or less than'. Some work on steps three and four has been undertaken looking at the behaviour of individuals in these terms (Meyerhoff and Greenwood 1994).

Ethnolinguistic vitality is a measure of the perceived institutional, linguistic and social support of a particular group's language variety and can be compared with that of other groups (Giles *et al.* 1977). It is, therefore, associated with the group identity pole in Figure 9.2. Since perceptions of ethnolinguistic vitality have been shown to be a reliable predictor of linguistic security (Harwood *et al.* in press) and of the likelihood of language shift in multilingual/multidialectal situations (Giles *et al.* 1990), the framework assumes that it functions as a psychological shield, through which the on-going feedback of the communicative event is filtered. This shield, or buffer, is most effective with the group identification(s) that the speaker perceives to have highest vitality. It is assumed that the need for such buffers is implicit in the folk wisdom built into sayings such as 'Don't take it personally'. In other words, something may hurt you if you interpret it through the medium of a personal identity which possesses low ethnolinguistic vitality (e.g. 'That person never returns my calls'), but the same utterance may be easier to accept if you recast the interaction in terms of a group identity (e.g. 'That person never returns calls from students'), since that identity will possess greater ethnolinguistic vitality. For many women, a gender identity is unlikely to have sufficient ethnolinguistic vitality (i.e. sufficient linguistic, social and institutional support) to provide much of a shield at all, and we would expect them to rely on other group identifications with higher ethnolinguistic vitality (e.g. ethnicity, age, expertise, work status, education or class).

The implications of this for the representation of identity are simple. In order for different identifications to become more or less salient and for them to be brought in by the individual as needed protection against communicative assault, the framework of speaker identity must allow identifications to shift. Different identifications (with their associated ethnolinguistic vitality) can move into position as the main point from which communication proceeds and at which feedback is received. Thus, the spherical design is motivated not only by the interrelationship of all identities with each other, but also by the ability speakers have to shift the focus of an interaction from one identity to another, either because it is more salient, or because it provides the best psychological protection.

To summarize, the framework for communication and speaker identity proposed here, and detailed in Meyerhoff and Niedzielski (1994), brings together theoretical tools that can contribute to an understanding of (i) the complex nature of any one of a speaker's numerous identifications, (ii) the complex nature of their overall identity and (iii) how these operate in verbal interactions. It draws on traditions in sociology (network theory), intercultural communication theory (ethnolinguistic vitality) and social psychology (social identity theory).

Application of the framework: gender identity revisited

To the extent that the proposed framework relies on subjective information, there are certain challenges that remain to be met. It does not actually prescribe the way(s) in which researchers in sociolinguistics and the social psychology of language should go about making operational the changes that occur in the salience of different social and personal identities, and I concede that this remains a methodological hurdle. The methods of data analysis used in quantitative studies within a sociolinguistic paradigm, for instance, ideally require that a researcher be able to establish linguistic and non-linguistic variables that are all independent of one another, though the extent to which the social variables used in sociolinguistics have ever been independent of one another is debatable. Be this as it may, by providing a schema in which to frame further methodological and theoretical questions, including some hypotheses that should be testable, I provide some directions for language and gender studies.

For example, consider Condor's (1986) findings in terms of this framework. Condor describes how traditional and non-traditional women understand quite differently what it means to be a woman. Condor's work indicates that traditional and non-traditional women construct an identity of womanliness in different psychological terms, with traditional women seeing their gender identification as being complementary to that of men. Their identity seems to be a composite of several social and/or personal identities, e.g. mother to so-and-so; emotional caregiver rather than material provider; supporter rather than leader.

Condor's study also showed that for traditional and non-traditional women, gender identity is more closely linked to other different identities. Non-traditional women showed links between being a woman, an identity of economic independence, and having high-status/high-prestige identities. The high-prestige identities they linked to their identity of womanliness might include being white, being well-educated, or being affluent in British and American society (i.e. identifications with groups that have high ethnolinguistic vitality). If this is true, it should be testable within the framework proposed here. Imagine the identity of being a woman for a traditional woman, let us call this identity 'Woman-t', and the identity of a non-traditional woman, 'Woman-n'. There may be considerable overlap between Woman-t and Woman-n in terms of behaviour and norms, but suppose they differ crucially in that Woman-t has network ties linking the Woman-t identity with a caretaker identity and a peacemaker-in-the-home identity, whereas the Woman-n identity has network ties linking it to a financial-autonomy identity and a well-educated identity. We would expect that the language associated with the identities Woman-t and Woman-n will differ to the extent that the linguistic markers indexed with the other identities mentioned can be found in the two groups of women's speech. Thus, in addition to finding shared markers of womanly identity (which might contrast with markers indexing male identity in this culture), the speech of women with the Woman-t identity should differ from the speech of women with a Woman-n identity in that the former will include markers consistent with indexing a caretaking identity, and these markers will be absent in the speech of the latter. In addition, we might want to test whether for a woman possessing some of these higher prestige identities, the comparison between the high-prestige identities and their gender identity accentuates a perception that their gender identity is unsatisfactory (cf. Williams and Giles 1978: 436).

Consider also the findings of Hunter and Davis (1992) showing that, for African American men, 'being a man' may actually be a composite of up to three different identities. The framework proposed would allow for an African-American man to potentially possess all three of these identities, and it would allow for the identities to shape each other.

Furthermore, this theoretical framework allows for the possibility of tension between these identifications, and provides an expression of how this tension may be resolved in favour of different salient characteristics, depending on the nature of an interaction. For example, Hunter and Davis mention that they were able to make canonically 'masculine' traits salient by asking about them. Within this framework, this could be expressed in the following way: the traits widely and stereotypically associated with masculinity are available as one of several social identities for these men. When required, they can shift a more canonical notion of masculinity into a position of greatest salience and talk with an experimenter about it, even though, when interacting at home, the overall sphere of their individual identity is spun around so that another more specific African American notion of masculine identity is in a position of salience for interactions with their family. We would predict that different characteristics of manliness would be treated as most salient by a man in his home (where he might be interacting primarily on the basis of his African American male identity), i.e. his individual identity will be spun so that the strong network ties of the family are the primary medium through which communication takes place. This might contrast with the characteristics that might be most salient when the same man is at work, in a law office or the phone company, where dominant American norms of manliness might prevail and this masculine identity would form the basis of network ties which are the medium for interaction and feedback. We would expect that changes in how the man's identity sphere is spun to make the network ties associated with one identity or another the medium for communication will show reflexes in linguistic behaviour in the manner I have already suggested.

In addition, the framework provides for the possibility of a lifestyle change, e.g. from primary identification with the violent hypermasculine identity to an identification with the cooperative African American masculine identification. This framework proposes that an individual spins his or her overall identity so that successful communication takes place through the medium of an identity with a network tie appropriate to the situation and the interlocutors. Thus, the framework would predict that a major change in identification would be the result of either a cessation of interactions via a hypermasculine network tie, or a change in the subjective salience of the hypermasculine and African American identities. If a change in relative salience is involved, this might be motivated by a change in salience of other identities, e.g. as a father versus a child; as head of household versus independent self. These suppositions are not necessarily supported by the data I have reviewed above, but the representation of speaker identity proposed does provide a framework within which some clearly testable hypotheses can be developed.

Above I have considered gender as an identity in people's perceptions of self. We might ask whether other people's perceptions of gender as a component of speaker identity can also be married to this framework. Giles *et al.* (1980) show that other people's perceptions of the salience of gender are just as complicated as individuals' own notions of gender. In a series of studies, Giles *et al.* show that it is a fairly straightforward task to discover the kinds of attributes or traits that people consider 'masculine' or 'feminine', and that it is also fairly straightforward to conduct experiments that reveal which of those traits are associated with an individual's voice when heard on tape. But this does not mean that when people match a female voice with typically feminine adjectives, they are necessarily responding to the presentation of a feminine identity. This is because those adjectives associated with perceived femininity are exactly the same adjectives associated with perceptions of middle-class status, or a generally liberal political outlook.

Conclusion

In this chapter, I have tried to show how the framework for communication, and especially speaker identity that I have proposed, might inform research into gender identity and gender salience. I have used previous work on social psychology to motivate the theory behind the framework, specifically the importance that the framework accords to network ties and the notion of multiple identities managed by the speaker within and across interactions. By linking these theoretical observations with the empirical methodology proposed, I hope that I have suggested useful future directions for language and gender studies. Ultimately, it would be nice if this provided us with some predictive power, perhaps along the lines of what specific effects that changes to intergroup or interpersonal identities might have on speakers' language. At present, this is beyond the theoretical framework outlined here, particularly as the fifth stage in operationalizing the framework remains very much open. Our goal in the short term is, however, no less important a step along the way: a richer understanding of the relationship between variation in language and the core issue of the interaction of gender with other speaker identities.

Notes

1. I would like to extend my thanks to a number of individuals for their helpful comments during the preparation of this chapter. I am particularly indebted to Nancy Niedzielski and Howard Giles who have been willing, incisive and constructive critics. To Nancy, I am further indebted for her encouragement to apply our framework to gender as a sociolinguistic variable. The chapter has also benefited from comments by the editors of this volume; Bill Reynolds and Naomi Nagy; my colleagues in the graduate course on Language and Gender, Department of Education, University of Pennsylvania (Spring 1993), especially Rebecca Freeman; and the audience at the Language-Gender Interface Conference, Columbus, Ohio, 15–18 July 1993.

2. A repeated finding in sociolinguistics research has been that linguistic changes are led by women in the community. Labov (1991) summarizes findings that women are more likely than men to lead phonological change both towards established prestige forms and towards innovative, non-prestigious targets and he concludes that the important generalization to be drawn from this seeming paradox is that, regardless of the direction, women lead phonological change and the real explanatory challenge is to determine why women have this role as innovators. James (this volume) reviews the issue in even wider terms and suggests that we should also ask: What factors can outweigh women's role as innovators? The general point I wish to make is that when we describe a change as being led by women in the speech community, implicit in this statement is the assumption that use of a particular, innovative variant is a marker of speakers' identification as women. This further carries with it the assumption that in the communities reviewed in the sociolinguistic literature, gender is a salient marker of intergroup distinctiveness in adult speech. This assumption may be warranted but it is not always tested and proved for the communities in question.

3. Rebecca Freeman first made clear to me how important it is for any theory that describes individuals in terms of multiple identities to address this issue.

References

Bauman Richard, Scherzer Joel (eds) 1974 *Explorations in the ethnography of speaking.* Cambridge University Press, Cambridge.

Cannavale F J, Scarr H A, Pepitone A 1970 Deindividuation in the small group: further evidence. *Journal of Personality and Social Psychology* 16: 141–47.

Condor Susan 1986 Sex role beliefs and 'traditional' women: feminist and intergroup perspectives. In Wilkinson Sue (ed) *Feminist social psychology: developing theory and practice.* Open University Press, Milton Keynes pp 97–118.

Deschamps Jean-Claude, Doise Willem 1978 Crossed category memberships and intergroup relations. In Tajfel Henri (ed) *Differentiation between social groups.* Academic Press, London pp 141–58.

Doise Willem, Weinberger Monique 1973 Représentations masculines dans différentes situations de rencontres mixtes. *Bulletin de Psychologie* 26: 649–57.

Eckert Penelope 1988 Adolescent structure and the spread of linguistic change. *Language in Society* 17: 183–207.

Eckert Penelope 1989 The whole woman: sex and gender differences in variation. *Language Variation and Change* 1: 245–67.

Eckert Penelope (ed) 1991 *New ways of analyzing sound change.* Academic Press, San Diego.

Eckert Penelope 1991 Social polarization and the choice of linguistic variants. In Eckert Penelope (ed) pp 213–32.

Eckert Penelope, McConnell-Ginet Sally 1992 Communities of practice: where language, gender, and power all live. In Hall Kira, Bucholtz Mary, Moonwomon Birch (eds) pp 89–99.

Giles Howard, Bourhis Richard Y, Taylor D M 1977 Towards a theory of language in ethnic group relations. In Giles Howard (ed) *Language, ethnicity, and intergroup relations.* Academic Press, London pp 307–48.

Giles Howard, Coupland Nikolas 1991 *Language: contexts and consequences.* Brooks-Cole, Pacific Grove, CA.

Giles Howard, Leets Laura, Coupland Nikolas 1990 Minority language group status: a theoretical conspexus. *Journal of Multilingual and Multicultural Development* 11: 1–19.

Giles Howard, Smith Philip M, Ford Barry, Condor Susan, Thakerar Jitendra N 1980 Speech style and the fluctuating salience of sex. *Language Sciences* 2: 260–282.

Greenwood Alice this volume: Floor management and power strategies in adolescent conversation.

Habick Timothy 1991 Burnouts versus rednecks: effects of group membership on the phonemic system. In Eckert Penelope (ed) pp 185–212.

Hall Kira, Bucholtz Mary, Moonwoman Birch (eds) *Locating power: proceedings of the second Berkeley women and language conference.* Berkeley Women and Language Group, Berkeley, CA.

Hall Kira, O'Donovan Veronica this volume Shifting gender positions among Hindi-speaking hijras.

Harwood Jake, Giles Howard, Bourhis Richard Y in press: The genesis of vitality theory: historical patterns and discourse dimensions. *International Journal of the Sociology of Language.*

Henley Nancy, Kramarae Cheris 1991 Gender, power, and miscommunication. In Coupland Nikolas, Giles Howard, Wiemann John M (eds) *'Miscommunication' and problematic talk.* Sage, Newbury Park, CA pp 18–44.

Hogg Michael A 1985 Masculine and feminine speech in dyads and groups: a study of speech style and gender salience. *Journal of Language and Social Psychology* 4.2: 99–112.

Hogg Michael A, Abrams Dominic 1988 *Social identifications: a social psychology of intergroup relations and group processes.* Routledge, London.

Horvath Barbara 1985 *Variation in Australian English: the sociolects of Sydney.* Cambridge University Press, Cambridge.

Hunter Andrea G, Davis James Earl 1992 Constructing gender: an exploration of Afro-American men's conceptualization of manhood. *Gender & Society* 6.3: 464–79.

Hymes Dell 1974 *Foundations in sociolinguistics: an ethnographic approach.* University of Pennsylvania Press, Philadelphia.

Jabeur M 1987 *A sociolinguistic study in Tunisia, Rades.* Unpublished PhD dissertation, University of Reading.

James Deborah this volume: Women, men and prestige speech forms: a critical review.

Knight H Merle 1992 Gender interference in transsexuals' speech. In Hall Kira, Bucholtz Mary, Moonwomon Birch (eds) pp 312–17.

Kramarae Cheris 1990 Changing the complexion of gender in language research. In Giles Howard, Robinson W Peter (eds) *Handbook of language and social psychology.* Wiley & Sons, Chichester, UK pp 345–61.

Labov William 1982 [1966] *The social stratification of English in New York City.* Center for Applied Linguistics, Washington, DC.

Labov William 1991 The intersection of sex and social class in the course of linguistic change. *Language Variation and Change* 2: 205–54.

Labov William 1994 *Principles of linguistic change. Vol. 1: Internal factors.* Blackwell, Oxford.

Labov William, Yaeger Malcah, Steiner Richard 1972 *A quantitative study of sound change in progress.* Report on NSF-GS-3287. University of Pennsylvania, Philadelphia.

Meyerhoff Miriam, Greenwood Alice 1994 Indexing social relationships in the speech of an adolescent. Paper presented at the 3rd Conference on Language and Society, Lincoln University, 22–23 August.

Meyerhoff Miriam, Niedzielski Nancy 1994 Resistance to creolization: an interpersonal and intergroup account of the processes involved. *Language and Communication* 14.4: 313–30.

Milroy Lesley 1990 New perspectives in the analysis of sex differentiation in language. In Bolton Kingsley, Kwok Helen (eds) *Sociolinguistics today: international perspectives*. Routledge, London pp 163–79.

Milroy James, Milroy Lesley 1985 Linguistic change, social network and speaker innovation. *Journal of Linguistics* 21: 339–84.

Milroy Lesley, Milroy James 1992 Social network and social class: toward an integrated sociolinguistic model. *Language in Society* 21: 1–26.

Sankoff Gillian 1980 *The social life of language*. University of Pennsylvania Press, Philadelphia.

Tajfel Henri, Turner John C 1979 An integrative theory of intergroup conflict. In Austin W G, Worchel S (eds) *The social psychology of intergroup relations*. Brooks-Cole, Monterey, CA.

Tajfel Henri, Turner John C 1986 The social identity theory of intergroup behavior. In Worchel S, Austin W G (eds) *Psychology of intergroup relations*. Nelson-Hall, Chicago.

Thakerar Jitendra N, Giles Howard, Cheshire Jenny 1982 Psychological and linguistic parameters of speech accommodation theory. In Fraser Colin, Scherer Klaus R (eds) *Advances in the social psychology of language*. Cambridge University Press, Cambridge.

Trabelsi Chedia 1991 De quelques aspects du langage des femmes de Tunis. *International Journal of the Sociology of Language* 87: 87–98.

Williams J, Giles Howard 1978 The changing status of women in society: an intergroup perspective. In Tajfel Henri (ed) *Differentiation between social groups*. Academic Press, London pp 431–65.

10 *Shifting gender positions among Hindi-speaking hijras*[1]

Kira Hall and Veronica O'Donovan

> I was disowned by the Hindus and shunned by my own wife. I was exploited by the Muslims who disdained my company. Indeed I was like a *hijda* who was neither one thing nor another but could be misused by everyone.
>
> (Singh 1989: 55)

Introduction

The *hijras* occupy a marginalized position in the Indian social matrix, as their ambiguous gender identity provokes conflicting feelings of awe and contempt. Discussed variously in the anthropological literature as 'transvestites', 'eunuchs', 'hermaphrodites', and even 'a third gender',[2] most of India's hijras were raised as boys before taking up residence in one of the many hijra communities which exist in almost every region of India. Since the late 1980s, several European and American cultural theorists (e.g. Nanda 1985, 1990, 1993, 1994, Bullough and Bullough 1993) have pointed to the visibility of the hijra in Indian society in order to suggest the cultural possibility of a more liberating, non-dichotomous organization of gender. Indeed, the hijras' livelihood is contingent upon their inextricable position in the social structure; according to tradition, they are expected to sing and dance at births and weddings, where they are rewarded with gifts of clothes, jewellery, and money.

Yet the life-stories of the Hindi-speaking hijras we interviewed in Banaras during the spring and summer of 1993 reflect a very different reality from that suggested by these theorists – a reality based on familial rejection, cultural isolatio n and societal neglect. When the hijra lifestyle is discussed with respect to this contemporary reality instead of historical or mythical representation,[3] their identification as a uniquely situated third sex becomes much more complicated. In their narratives, the hijras view themselves not simply as 'neither man nor woman', as the title of Nanda's (1990) ethnography on the hijras in a south central Indian city suggests, but also as 'deficiently' masculine and 'incompletely' feminine. Instead of occupying a position outside the female–male binary, the hijras have created an existence within it, one that is constrained by rigidly entrenched cultural constructions of femininity and masculinity. It may be liberating to believe in the possibility of an alternative gender which is not limited by societal expectations, but even the hijra must create self-identity by resisting and subverting a very real and oppressive gender dichotomy – a dichotomy that becomes very apparent in the hijras' own use of feminine- and masculine-marked speech.

Although a number of anthropologists have been interested enough in the hijras' language use to comment on it secondarily in their descriptions of the hijra lifestyle, not one of them, to our knowledge, has attempted to analyse the hijras' speech patterns from any sort of linguistic perspective. Lynton and Rajan remark that the Hindi-speaking hijras they spoke with in Hyderabad 'use "he" and "she", "him" and "her", indiscriminately' (1974: 192) – a misleading statement since gender is marked not on pronouns, but on verbs and adjectives.[4] Similarly, Nanda, in the introduction to her ground-breaking work published almost two decades later, explains somewhat simplistically that 'Indian languages have three kinds of gender pronouns: masculine, feminine, and a formal, gender-neutral form' (1990: xviii). Nanda, an American anthropologist, interviewed hijras from a variety of different linguistic communities, her conversations mediated by translators in Gujarati, Hindi and Panjabi. But in defining all 'Indian languages' as having three kinds of gender pronouns, she makes an inaccurate generalization, especially since India hosts well over 2,000 languages and dialects within its borders, from a variety of language families.

While Nanda does acknowledge that hijras in some parts of India have 'a specialized, feminized language, which consists of the use of feminine expressions and intonations' (1990: 17),[5] she asserts that the hijras in the communities she studied alternate between feminine and masculine forms for no apparent reason:

> Hijras, in their conversations, use these [gender pronouns] randomly and indiscriminately to refer to individual hijras. They insist, however, that people outside their community refer to hijras in the feminine gender. When I am quoting a hijra verbatim, I use the gender pronoun used by that speaker if it is masculine or feminine. If it is the gender-neutral pronoun, I have translated it as a feminine gender pronoun. When I am referring to a hijra, I use the feminine gender pronoun to conform to hijra norms, unless I am referring to the hijra in the past, when he considered himself a male. (1990: xviii)

But Nanda's observation that the hijras 'insist ... that people outside their community refer to hijras in the feminine gender' – a statement completely consistent with the attitudes of the Hindi-speaking hijras we spoke with in Banaras – would suggest that the use of morphological gender is a salient issue in the hijra community, one that comes to symbolize their own acceptance in the society at large. Our reason for criticizing previous synopses of linguistic gender in research on the hijras is not to dismiss such studies as invalid, but rather to illustrate how anthropological fieldwork can be enhanced by an increased awareness of, and attentiveness to, linguistic phenomena. Nanda's work in particular, as one of the first ethnographies to take the hijras' own life-stories as primary, is an essential contribution to anthropological research. Yet her study would have been even more informative had she approached the hijras' life narratives from a linguistic perspective as well as an anthropological one.

Although the four Hindi-speaking communities we spent time with in Banaras are isolated from one another both physically and ideologically, patterns of gesture and speech occur and recur. Constrained by a linguistic system which allows for only two morphological genders, Hindi-speaking hijras, when uttering phrases that are self-referential, must gender themselves as either feminine or masculine. Their use of language reflects a lifestyle that is constantly self-defining as they study, imitate and parody binary constructions of gender in an effort to gender themselves. In contrast to assertions made by previous researchers, we found that the hijras alternate between feminine and masculine reference for identifiable reasons. Because certain verbs, adjectives and postpositions in Hindi are marked for feminine and masculine gender, with verbs showing gender marking on all three persons, the hijras' attempts at alternating constructions of female and male selves become apparent in quite basic choices of feminine and masculine verbal, adjectival and postpositional forms. Critically aware of the cultural meaning attributed to their own use of feminine as opposed to masculine markers, the hijras 'code-switch' between morphological genders in their daily interactions in order to express relations of solidarity and power.

Vocal deviance

Indian and Pakistani sociologists and journalists often make discussions of language central to their exposure of the hijra lifestyle. Naqvi and Mujtaba, for instance, in their article on Urdu-speaking hijras in Pakistan, assert emphatically that 'hijras challenge the very order of language' (1992: 81). Switching arbitrarily between 'he', 'she', 'his', 'her', and 'he/she' when referring to individual hijras, the authors articulate the inability of both Urdu and English to capture the intersexed essence of the hijra:

> In Urdu the entire cosmos is divided into the masculine and feminine genders; the hijras are neither and both. In English, a neuter gender exists, but the use of the adjective 'it' dehumanises the hijra, strips this being of his/her very humanity. And despite the proliferation in English of categorisations related to sexuality – eunuchs, hermaphrodites, transvestites, homosexuals, bisexuals, *et al.* – not one completely defines the hijra. What is the hijra? The masculine and the feminine are two distinct principles, each possessing its distinct mode of being. But the hijra combines traits peculiar to both genders and yet is neither quite one nor the other. (1992: 81–2)

Yet Naqvi and Mujtaba's desire to protect the 'humanity' of the hijras linguistically is not shared by many Indian authors writing in English, who use the masculine gender unyieldingly in reference to the hijras (e.g. Mehta 1945, Mukherjee 1980, Bobb and Patel 1982, Patel 1988) or, at the very best, a qualified 'she' in quotation marks (e.g. Sinha 1967, Sethi 1970, Srinivas 1976), often in order to expose what they perceive to be a deviant or unacceptable lifestyle.[6]

These same authors frequently question the hijras' claims to femininity by remarking on the inappropriateness of their vocal presentations. While a number of researchers have commented on the hijras' 'high-pitched' voice (Rao 1955: 521, Mukherjee 1980:

63, Pimpley and Sharma 1985: 41, Jani and Rosenberg 1990: 103), others have suggested that it is the voice itself that acts as the betrayer of their masculinity. The nature of this betrayal is overtly narrated by Sethi (1970: 40) in his journalistic exposure of the hijras in Bombay, which he opens by recalling his first interaction with a hijra named Kumari:

> Her name was Kumari. She was about 17. She rested her face on the edge of the charpoy on which I sat, a round face with a soft expression, somewhat prematurely sensuous for her age. The eyes held an eloquent appeal. Clean hair, oiled and tied in a knot. 'Must take her photograph,' I thought. 'Would look unusual in the midst of all the squalor.'
>
> I asked if she would pose for one. Kumari nodded assent with delightful eagerness, her eyes suddenly sparkling with anticipation. As she stood in the sun, I asked her to untie her hair.
>
> And then came the shock.
>
> '*Acchaji, khol deti hun!*' – a thick strong male voice.
>
> Yes, 'she' was a *hijra* in a colony of *hijras*. When I went closer to make 'her' stand in a particular manner, I noticed that there wasn't so much girlishness, after all, particularly the flat chest! Yet so authentic was the appearance that I was still ready to believe it was a girl.
>
> Kumari symbolized the tragedy of the hermaphrodite world – treated as subject of bawdy jest and laughter, shunned by most, misunderstood by all.

The 'shock' which Sethi identifies in this passage is the sudden sound of a 'thick strong male voice' projected from a body characterized by roundness, softness, sensuality and eloquence. The author's inability to reconcile this physical contradiction prompts him to qualify all subsequent feminine references to Kumari with quotation marks, ultimately summarizing 'her' interactive performance as symbolic of 'the tragedy of the hermaphrodite world'. Indeed, a photograph of Kumari on a subsequent page sports the caption, 'To look at, Kumari 17, is a girl – until you hear her speak in her thick male voice' (1970: 42).[7]

The same conflict between a feminine physical appearance and a masculine vocality prompts Mondal to argue that even though the hijras he studied in West Bengal wear feminine clothes and jewellery, their 'masculine voice' makes them not only 'objects of ridicule' but also recipients of 'a very painful and pathetic experience from the conventional social environment' (1989: 244).

Similarly, Mohan, in his discussion of recent political moves by the hijras of Uttar Pradesh, claims that 'no one would mistake [the hijras] for women' since 'their faces, their limbs, and their voices have a masculine roughness' (1979: i). And Sharma, in support of his declaration that the hijras, of all those who defy linguistic categorization, are 'the most interesting and outlandish freaks of nature' (1984: 381), focuses on the community's 'ambivalent physical appearance'. Opening his article with the observation that 'certainly every society gives linguistic notice of the differential parts individuals are expected to play', he notes a marked exception in the case of 'individuals who do not belong to either sex' (p. 381). In Sharma's opinion, the fact that the hijras 'shave, smoke, and talk like men but dress and behave in a more feminine way in the society at large' (p. 381) points to their ambiguous status not only in the social structure, but in the linguistic gender system as well.

What is significant about Sethi's narrative, however, is that even though the author is critical of Kumari's masculine-sounding voice, he reports her speech entirely in the first-person feminine. After asking Kumari to let her hair down for a photograph, he quotes her as saying in Hindi, '*Acchaji, khol deti hun!*' – a response which translates into English as, 'Okay sir, I'll untie it.' But by employing the feminine-marked *khol deti* [f] *hũ* instead of the masculine *khol detā*[m] *hũ*,[8] Kumari identifies herself linguistically within the passage as female. Perhaps noticing similar employments of feminine self-reference among hijras in other communities, a number of scholars working with speakers of gendered Indo-Aryan languages have remarked that the hijras 'affect female speech and manners' (e.g. Patel 1983: 121) and 'become adept in feminine speech patterns and gait' (e.g. Mukherjee 1980: 61). The precise meaning of such statements is unclear, yet one thing is certain: the authors remain unconvinced of the hijra's ability to achieve fluency in such patterns. Jani and Rosenberg, displeased with the performances of the Hindi-speakers they interviewed in western India, comment on the hijras' 'largely exaggerated female mannerisms and gesturing' (1990: 103), and Patel, in his work among the hijras in Gujarat, argues that 'in spite of their efforts to look and act like females, their behavior is neither completely masculine nor feminine' (1983: 121).

Such criticism underscores a larger societal refusal to accept the hijras' femininity as genuine, and an accompanying disapproval of what is perceived to be a 'superficially' feminine lifestyle. Mehta, reporting on the *pavaiyās* (a term he uses in reference to 'castrated eunuchs') in Gujarat, sets the stage for future research when he identifies the hijras' verbal femininity as 'bad imitations', 'ghastly mimicry' and 'caricature':

> In the amateur and professional theatrical plays in Gujarat (and probably throughout India), many boys take the part of girls or women and they imitate the gait and gestures of women. As a rule, their attempt is a failure because they overact. Similarly the Pavaiyā's gait and gestures are bad imitations of the feminine gait and gestures. Their features are masculine, their limbs have a masculine shape, their hips are masculine, their voice and shape of the neck (Adam's Apple) are masculine, the chest and the gait are masculine. (1945: 44)

> The speech and manners of Pavaiyās are said to be like those of women. I entirely disagree with this statement. Most of them have a male voice. Their gait is that of a man because of the shape of their pelvis, but Pavaiyās try to imitate the gait of a woman, and I would say that their gait, speech, and mannerisms are a ghastly mimicry or caricature. (1945: 47)

Mehta's equivalence of the hijras' behaviour with a theatrical performance is a revealing simile. While acknowledging the creative nature of the hijra's gait, speech and mannerisms by designating them as a kind of performance, Mehta simultaneously reduces these performances to a prescripted role-playing, thereby denying his social actors any 'essential' femininity. In the folk-dramas mentioned by Mehta, which most likely approximate what is currently referred to in Hindi as *sāng* (travelling dramas predominantly performed in rural areas) or *nautankī* (travelling dramas predominantly performed in urban areas), women's roles are frequently played by young boys, whose higher voices and smaller statures make them more suitable than older men to the performance of female characters.[9]

The connection between linguistic performance and effeminate behaviour is made explicit by Sinha in his psychological analysis of why a child might decide to join the hijra community. Sinha, who notes that over 20 per cent of the hijras he studied had performed *nautankī* in childhood, understands divergent linguistic behaviour to be a precursor to divergent sexuality. Sinha has definitive ideas of what kinds of behaviours constitute femininity and what kinds masculinity, not the least of which are linguistic in nature:

Such boys, due to constant impersonation of women and their habits, adopt quite a good amount of effeminate characteristics in their mannerism and habits ... [O]nce a boy has shown tendencies of girlish habits, effeminacy, and is initiated to homo-sexuality, under suitable circumstances and the 'right' kind of environment, the process of Sexual Inversion begins and there are chances of his ending up as a Hijra. (1967: 175)

Sinha continues this passage by overtly advising parents to keep a strict watch on their child's mannerisms and to correct any noted linguistic oddities: if necessary, parents should send their sons to the 'right type' of school, where they will be forced to interact with other boys, read boys' books, and engage in boys' games. Poorer children, according to Sinha, are particularly susceptible to effeminate behaviours, because their uneducated parents not only fail to realize 'the gravity of the situation' (p. 170), but also lack the money needed to finance corrective procedures.

A comparable opinion is voiced more recently by Patel, who lists 'speech' as one of several areas where a child might deviate from the 'sex-roles, norms, and values' expected of men in Indian society (1988: 73). Like Sinha, Patel lists what he calls 'changing speech' as one of the stepping-stones to girlishness. In his opinion, a young boy who has suffered repeated taunts of *baiylo* ['girlish'] from his peers will ultimately be left with no other choice but to abandon the world of men and women for the hijra community. The notion of vocal deviance, then, although defined rather vaguely in the above articles, is clearly an important concept in the minds of these researchers. The hijra's inability to produce an accurate feminine vocality (as in Sethi's narrative when Kumari speaks in a low, coarse voice), as well as an accurate masculine vocality (as in Sinha's and Patel's discussions of the hijra as an effeminate-sounding boy), symbolizes her own inability to exist in a gendered world.

Gender marking in Hindi

The dissatisfaction articulated by South Asian researchers with respect to the hijras' vocal patterns may have much to do with the fact that many hijras alternate between feminine and masculine self-reference in order to convey certain social meanings. Such gender shifts are particularly evident among the Hindi-speaking hijras we interviewed in Banaras, who have at their disposal a linguistic playground of verbs, adjectives and postpositions awaiting feminine or masculine morphological marking. The alternation between feminine and masculine self-reference in Hindi is quite easy to discern linguistically. The past tense of the verb *honā* ['to be'], for instance (Table 10.1), is realized as *thā* with masculine singular subjects, *the* with masculine plural subjects, *thī* with feminine singular subjects, and *thī̃* with feminine plural subjects:

Table 10.1   Past tense forms of *honā* ['to be']

	Masculine	Feminine	English translation
Sg. 1	*maĩ thā*	*maĩ thī*	I was
Sg. 2	*tū thā*	*tū thī*	you (intimate) were
Sg. 3	*vah thā*	*vah thī*	she/he was
Pl. 1	*ham the*	*ham thī̃*	we were
Pl. 2	*tum the*	*tum thī̃*	you (familiar) were
Pl. 3	*ve the, āp the*	*ve thī̃, āp thī̃*	they were, you (formal) were

The habitual, progressive, and intransitive perfective verb forms in Hindi similarly show gender concord with the subject. These three aspectual tenses are formed by the addition of suffixes and verbal auxiliaries to the verb stem: aspect is indicated through the addition of explicit markers of various kinds to the stem; tense is indicated through the presence of one of the basic forms of *honā* ['to be'] (i.e. present, past, presumptive, subjunctive). Again, the appearance of one of the vowels *-ā*, *-e*, *-ī* or *-ĩ* signals the number (singular vs plural) and gender (feminine vs masculine) of the subject of the verb. Selected examples of Hindi verbal agreement are included in Table 10.2.

Inflecting adjectives also agree with the nouns they modify in gender, number, and case, with *-ā* or *-e* agreeing with masculine nouns and *-ī* with feminine nouns. That is, masculine forms of inflecting adjectives end in *-ā* in the singular direct and *-e* in the singular oblique, plural direct and plural oblique cases; the feminine forms always end in *-ī*, whether singular or plural, direct or oblique. Moreover, inflecting postpositions agree with the gender of the head noun, so that, for example, the postposition translated into English as 'of' will appear as *kā* when modifying a singular masculine noun, *ke* when modifying a plural masculine noun, and *kī* when modifying a singular or plural feminine noun. The hijras' varied use of these forms, as well as their varied use of first-, second- and third-person verbal forms, reflects a unique dual-gender

Table 10.2   Selected examples of first person verbal marking with *jānā* ['to go']

Verb tense	1st person masculine	1st person feminine	English translation
Future	*maĩ jāũgā*	*maĩ jāũgī*	I will go
Past	*maĩ gayā*	*maĩ gayī*	I went
Present Habitual	*maĩ jātā hũ*	*maĩ jātī hũ*	I go
Past Habitual	*maĩ jātā thā*	*maĩ jātī thī*	I used to go
Present Progressive	*maĩ jā rahā hũ*	*maĩ jā rahī hũ*	I am going
Past Progressive	*maĩ jā rahā thā*	*maĩ jā rahī thī*	I was going
Simple Perfective	*maĩ gayā*	*maĩ gayī*	I went
Present Perfective	*maĩ gayā hũ*	*maĩ gayī hũ*	I have gone
Past Perfective	*maĩ gayā thā*	*maĩ gayī thī*	I had gone

position in a society that views them as neither fully feminine nor fully masculine.[10]

'Women's speech' and the notion of *ādat* ['habit']

Most of the hijras we spoke with related tragic stories from their youth, explaining how friends and family ostracized and evicted them from their own households. Whether this ostracism is precipitated by actual anatomical difference or by some sort of effeminate behaviour is unclear from the hijras' narratives, and they apparently feel a political imperative to insist that the designation is entirely physical. Although a number of Indian researchers (e.g. G. Singh 1982, Mitra 1983, Sayani 1986, Sharma 1989, Jani and Rosenberg 1990) have worked to dispel the cultural assumption that hijras are born as hermaphrodites, reporting in-depth about the life-threatening castrations and penectomies that hijras endure, a large portion of Indian society nevertheless believes that all hijras were born with ambiguous sex organs. This belief originates from a rather unyielding cultural connection of gender identity with anatomical appearance, a connection which overtly contradicts Jacobs and Cromwell's assumption that 'in societies that recognize [alternative-sex] variations within their culture, anatomy is *not* destiny in terms of sex, sexuality, and gender' (1992: 57). In fact, hijras have been performing such operations voluntarily within their communities for well over a century (cf. Ebden 1856, Davidson 1884, Faridi 1899), to such an extent that more than 75 per cent of the hijras living in India today have undergone genital surgery – according to the 1990 BBC documentary *Eunuchs: India's Third Gender* (Yorke and Prasad 1990), as well as to one of the more outspoken hijras we interviewed in Banaras.[11]

The hijras have organized their lives in resistance to a social structure that prevents their integration. Their marginalization often begins at a very early age when family members, neighbours, and peers respond negatively to their presence. Sulekha,[12] a 38-year-old hijra who lives with a male partner in a small village outside of Banaras, spoke with great sadness about her childhood, when she was informed because of physical reasons that she was a hijra. The child of a *halvāī*, or 'sweet-maker', Sulekha spoke proudly of her family and regularly alluded to their high social status as Kanya-Kubja Brahmans. Yet when only 7 years old, she was forced to realize that, in the eyes of Indian society, her existence as a gendered being was questionable, if not reprehensible. She recalls a particular moment when she realized that she was different from her peers, for neither boys nor girls would let her into their play-group:

> (1) There were a few boys at my school who I used to study with. When I sat with them, they used to tell me that I was a hijra. Then they started telling other people, 'This is a hijra! This is a hijra! Don't sit near him! Sit separately!' If I sat with the girls, the girls would say, 'This is a hijra! This is a hijra! Don't sit near him! Sit separately!' So I felt very ashamed. I thought, 'How is it that I've become a hijra? The girls don't talk to me; the boys don't talk to me. What terrible thing has happened to me?' I wanted to go and play with them, but nobody wanted to play with me. So life was going like that. Nobody would help me.

When we responded to her description of this incident by asking if there was anyone who had tried to help her, she replied, 'Who would ever help me with a problem like this one?'

Sulekha's realization that she was unsuitable for either boyhood or girlhood hardly made her feel like a mystical third sex; on the contrary, she explains that her family was so disapproving that she ultimately had no other choice but to leave home:

> (2) What could the members of my family think, after all? They didn't think anything. Or they thought, 'Oh! What has he become? He became a hijra! Why doesn't he just die! Oh, why doesn't he just go away! Oh, the name of his father and mother has been

doomed!' It became a house of dishonour. They said, 'How can his life go on? It would have been better if he had just died!' I used to listen to all of that, and finally I just ran away.

The harsh response of Sulekha's parents, as well as her neighbours who taunted her with the designation *nacaniyā* ['little dancer'], reflects a pervasive societal belief that the hijra, by virtue of her own impotence, will prevent family members within the household from marrying. This belief, coupled with a social intolerance for the integration of such figures, has led many parents to ask local hijra communities to take their child away from them.

Because the majority of hijras are raised as boys, they must learn how to perform a new gender identity when they join the hijra community – an identity which distances itself from masculine representations in its appropriation of feminine dress, social roles, gesture and language. Again, the rigidity of this socialization process has not been lost on South Asian scholars. Sharma, for instance, identifies not only how the hijras 'legitimiz[e] the normative order of the home', but also how they teach new recruits their mannerisms. After outlining the hierarchical nature of the hijras' affected kinship systems, Sharma focuses on the 'strictness' of the socialization process:

> The family head's responsibilities consist of socialization of the eunuchs, giving continuity to the home by way of recruitment of new members. The socialization, besides legitimizing the normative order of the home, also consists of teaching dancing, clapping, begging, and passing of sexual overtures. The head of the family passes on strict instructions to the inmates of the home regarding their behaviour pattern. Love and affection are the two major allurement factors which add to the process of proper socialization. ... These tactics, however, do not rule out the use of strictest method, such as beatings etc., on the young eunuchs. (1984: 385)

While the acquirement of feminine speech is not necessarily central to Sharma's discussion, Sinha goes so far as to base his definition of the hijra on this very acquisition. Distinguishing between *jankhas* ['new entrants to the fraternity'] and *hijras* ['full members of the social group or fraternity of a hijra'], he explains that while the former will always wear masculine dress and refer to themselves in the masculine, the latter will always wear feminine dress and refer to themselves in the feminine (1967: 169). If we accept Sharma's and Sinha's observations as valid, we must also entertain the suggestion that the Hindi-speaking hijra, at some point in her socialization process, makes a conscious shift from masculine to feminine self-reference – a shift alluded to by Pimpley and Sharma when they claim that the hijras are 'exhorted to adopt an exaggeratedly feminine mode of attire, gait, speech, gestures, and facial expressions' (1985: 43).

These adoptions often become self-conscious emblems of gender construction in the hijras' narratives. Indeed, Sulekha views gender as something to be put on in the way one would put on a *sāṛī* (a dress traditionally worn by Indian women), an investiture which eventually leads to the acquisition of what she calls calls '*aurat kī bāt*' ['women's speech']:

> (3) Now that I've put on this *sāṛī*, I have to follow through with it. If I went along considering myself a man, what would be the use of wearing a woman's *sāṛī?* Now that I've worn *sāṛīs*, I've worn blouses, I've grown out my hair, and I've pierced my ears, I've become a woman so I have to live like a woman. … When hijras come to the community, when they know all about themselves, they start to dance and sing and everything falls into place. Whoever feels right in his heart becomes a hijra. Whoever doesn't feel right in his heart won't become a hijra. It's not like, 'Oh, when I'm a hijra I've become a woman and when I'm not a hijra I haven't become a woman.' It's not like that. She's put on a *sāṛī*, she's entered the society of the hijras, so her language will become that of a woman's. Finally, she has become a hijra.

In this passage, Sulekha offers her own understanding of the socialization process, one that affirms Sinha's claim that feminine self-reference is a prerequisite to a complete hijra identity. The stepping stones to hijrahood, in Sulekha's opinion, are clearly delineated: first, the initiate wears a sari; second, she joins a hijra comunity; and third, her language changes to the feminine.

Yet her language is not so invariably feminine as the above excerpt might suggest. Sulekha continues her discussion by explaining that when she looks like a woman, she correspondingly walks, laughs and talks like one, employing feminine-marked verb forms like those mentioned in excerpt (4) below, among them *khātī[f] hū̃* ['I eat[f]'] and *jātī[f] hū̃* ['I go[f]']. Alternatively, if she were to wear a *kurtā* or *luṅgī*, a shirt and cloth-wrap traditionally worn by north Indian Muslim men, she would speak as a man, employing masculine-marked verb forms like *khātā[m] hū̃* ['I eat[m]'] and *jātā[m] hū̃* ['I go[m]'][13]:

(4) S:

ādmī kā bāt karnā hogā, to maī sāṛī pahan nahī lūgī^f, (0.5) jab sāṛī pahan lūgī^f, ham mē se to aurat kā bāt hogā, - jab sāṛī *nahī pahan lūgī^f, **tab** mard kā bāt. (0.5) hā. (1.5) jaise maī luṅgī kurtā pahan lūgī^f, - tab 'khātā^m hū̃', 'jatā^m hū̃', hote haī. ... kuch pareśānī nahī hotī hai. - sāṛī pahankar aurat vālā boltī^f hū̃, 'khātī^f hū̃', 'jātī^f hū̃'. - kuch nahī diqqat hotī hai, ... to jo jāntā hai to jāntā hī hai na? - to jāntā hī hai, (1.0) ki hijṛā hai. (1.0) abhī sāṛī pahan liyā abhī luṅgī kurtā pahan liyā to mard kī tarah mardānā ho gayā.

S:

If I have to use men's speech, I won't wear^f a *sāṛī*. When I wear^f a *sāṛī*, I'll of course use women's speech; when I *don't wear^f a *sāṛī*, **then** [I'll use] men's speech. For example, if I wear^f a *luṅgī-kurtā*, then it's like, 'I eat^m', 'I go^m'. ... It's not a problem. When I wear a *sāṛī*, I speak^f like a woman, 'I eat^f', 'I go^f'. It's not difficult at all. ... Whoever knows would surely know, right? He would surely know that [a person talking like this] is a hijra. First I put on a *sāṛī* but then I put on a *luṅgī-kurtā*, so [my conversation] became *mardānā* ['manly'] like a man.

Sulekha's clearly pronounced understanding of 'women's speech' (i.e. *zanānā bolī*) and 'men's speech' (i.e. *mardānā bolī*) as two mutually exclusive styles of dress, worn at non-intersecting times in order to enhance the performance of a gender role, points to a heightened awareness of the social meanings associated with the use of gendered speech. In Sulekha's opinion, a speaker will be identified as a hijra precisely because of this versatility, her alternations of femininity and masculinity signalling to outsiders that she is allied with neither camp.

Even though Sulekha describes feminine speech as a spontaneous activity which merely coincides with the decision to wear a *sāṛī*, she also details the difficulty involved in acquiring it. In particular, she describes a kind of second-language acquisition process that initiates must undergo after entering the community, a process guided and inspired by the behaviour of older community members:

(5) S:

uskā eksan badlā rahtā hai. (0.5) jo pahle pahle āyegā^m na? - to uskā ādmī kā svabhāv rahegā, (1.0) is tarah bāt ho jāyegā, (1.0) kabhī admī kā bāt ho jāyegā, (2.5) tab hijṛe mē jab ā jāyegā^m to rahegā^m, - to dekhegā^m, ki 'are maī- sab baṛī^f ādmī^m hai,' (1.5) ((whispering)) is tarah baiṭhī^f hai to tarah baiṭhegā^m- is tarah khātī^f hai to is tarah khāyegā^m.

S:

His/her actions remain changed. When someone first comes^m here, you know, his/her nature will remain like that of a man's, so that's how his/her conversation will be. Sometimes it will be just like a man's conversation. But when he joins^m the hijras and lives^m among them, he'll see^m [how they act], 'Hey! I- look at me. They're all senior^f people^m.' ((whispering)) She sits^f like this, so he'll sit^m in the same way. She eats^f like this, so he'll eat^m in the same way.

Like Sinha, Sulekha makes a linguistic distinction between newly joined hijras, referring to them throughout the passage in the masculine singular, and the more experienced hijra veterans, identifying them as feminine. This distinction becomes particularly clear when she reports the initiate's surprise at discovering that the older community members behave somewhat differently, and illuminates this disparity by referring to the initiate in the masculine but to his superiors in the feminine: 'She sits[f] like this, so he'll sit[m] in the same way. She eats[f] like this, so he'll eat[m] in the same way.'

Central to the hijras' discussions of feminine-language acquisition is the notion of *ādat*, or 'habit'. The hijras' repeated use of this term invites an interesting extension of Bourdieu's (1977) notion of *habitus*, since speakers develop strategies for expression at an accelerated pace in this alternatively defined linguistic marketplace. The use of feminine speech in the hijra community is in many ways synonymous with the projection of a non-masculine identity, and there is a high value placed on its production. Through an intensive immersion in what Bourdieu would call 'positive and negative reinforcements' (1977: 654), the hijras quickly 'acquire durable dispositions' towards those behaviours deemed appropriate by community members, building them into their own linguistic repertoire. In the following excerpt, Sulekha explains how initiates are reprimanded for the use of masculine speech, physically as well as verbally:

(6) S:

sikhāyā nahĩ jātā hai. - anubhav ho jātā hai. - dekhkar ke, - koĩ baccā to nahĩ hai, usko sikhlāyā jāyegā. ... kaise kar rahe haĩ, - 'is tarah hamko bhī karnā cāhiye. - nahĩ karēge to hijṛā log hamko hansegā.' - to kahegā ki 'are baṛi[f] kuḍhaṅgā[m] hai, baṛi[f] battamīz hai.' ((laughs)) hã. 'apne man se kah rahā[m] hai bhosṛī vālā[m]' ((laughs)) sab mārne uṭh jātā hai cappal se. ((3.0)) hã. (5.0) dekhte dekhte ādat paṛ jātā hai, - tab vaisā svabhāv ho jātā hai.

S:

It's not taught. It's experienced, by watching. After all, he's not a child who needs to be taught. ... [The new hijra will say,] 'I should also act just like they're acting. If I don't, hijra people will laugh at me.' [The hijra people] will say, 'Oh, he's very[f] ill-mannered[m]! He's very[f] ill-behaved.' ((laughs)) Yes! 'He's just saying[m] whatever comes to mind, the *bhosṛī vālā*[m] ['vagina-owner']!' ((laughs)) Then everybody will get up to beat him with their sandals. ((laughs)) Really! So gradually, after watching for a long time, it becomes a habit. Then it just becomes his nature.

Her claim that 'gradually, after watching for a long time, it becomes a habit' (*dekhte dekhte ādat paṛ jātā hai*) points to the interactive nature of the learning process; the *kuḍhaṅgā* or *battamīz* initiate (which translate into English as 'ill-mannered' and 'ill-behaved', respectively) is punished for acting without forethought, his behaviour rebuked through the utterance of a *gālī* ['obscenity'] or the slap of a sandal. The older hijras' employment of the masculine curse *bhosṛī vālā*[m] ['vagina-owner'] is particularly telling in this respect, as it reflects their dissatisfaction with the initiate's attempts at discursive femininity. The term *bhosṛī vālā*, when used among non-hijras, is generally used between men and implies that the referent, although male, has somehow been demasculinized.[14] When used among hijras, the insult lies not in the accusation of demasculation, since the very definition of *hijṛā* depends on the notion of impotence, but in the suggestion of maleness.

The acquisition of a feminine persona is not an easy transition for all hijras, nor is the female/male gender construction as clearly delineated for everyone as it is for Sulekha in her narratives. Rupa, a hijra associated with one of the hijra communities in Banaras, wrestles with the symbolic import of feminine and masculine speech in her everyday interactions. Unlike the other hijras we interviewed, Rupa leads a quiet and secluded life away from her group, seeing her fellow hijras only during their daily song and dance performances. In the home she shares with a small family, she dresses and speaks as a man so that her housemates will feel comfortable with her presence, her femininity visible only in her topknot, earrings, nose ring and understated eye make-up. Rupa spent the first 18 years of her life as a boy, yet never felt wholly comfortable with this role; ultimately, she decided to move to Banaras and adopt the hijra lifestyle. Since she spent most of her boyhood adhering to male roles and representations, this transition was not an easy or fluid one. She explains in excerpt (7) that the acquisition of women's speech in particular was a long and laborious process, so much so that it eventually interfered with her status in the hijra community.

(7) R:

ghar mẽ, to - mardānā rahate[m] the[m], to mardānā bolī bolte-bolte[m] haī. jab hijṛe ko jānā paṛtā hai to parivartan karnā paṛtā hai. ... vahī to bolā, na beṭā?[15] - jab ghar se cale[m],- jab ghar se āye[m], to ghar kī bolī mardānā to mẽ, to mardānā bolī bolā[m]. (3.0) bhaīyā[m] ko 'bhaīyā[m]'

R:

They were[m] living[m] in a *mardānā* ['manly'] way at home, so they're always speaking[m] *mardānā* speech. When a hijra has to leave [home], s/he has to make a change. ... That's exactly what I told you, right dear?[15] When I left[m] home- when I came[m] from home, the bol rahe^m haĩ, - cācā^m ko 'cācā^m' bol rahe^m haĩ, - aise bol rahe^m haĩ. (2.0) to usko parivartan karne mẽ to ṭãĩm lagta hĩ hai. (2.0) to usko parivartan karne mẽ ṭãĩm lagta hai. - bolte-bolte bolte-bolte, ādaṭ ho gayĩ (1.5) sat-chah mahĩne mẽ.

in about

speech I used at home was *mardānā* speech, so I of course spoke^m men's speech. [At home] they're all calling^m their *bhaĩyā*^m ['brothers'] '*bhaĩyā*^m'. They're calling^m their *cācā*^m ['paternal uncles'] '*cācā*^m'. They're speaking^m like that. So it does take time to change from that to this. It takes time to make a change. But gradually, after speaking and speaking continously, it became a habit. In about six or seven months.

Rupa's transition from what she refers to as *mardānā* ['manly'] speech to a more feminine variety was a highly conscious process, one that required several months of practice – or in Rupa's own words *bolte-bolte bolte-bolte* ['speaking and speaking continuously'] before it *ādat ho gayĩ* ['became a habit']. Like Sulekha, Rupa is aware of the social meanings attached to her language use, so much so that she hides her feminine speech while at home with her landlord's family. In contrast to Sulekha, who primarily refers to herself in the first-person feminine, Rupa consistently employs the masculine first-person plural when in her home, as in the previous passage when she uses masculine-marked verbs like *cale*^m ['left'] and *āye*^m ['came']. Yet throughout her conversations with us, Rupa also emphasized how necessary it is for hijras to achieve fluency in women's speech, since group members 'always and only speak as women when together'. This necessity, precipitated by a community desire to distance itself from masculine representation, has encouraged a kind of gendered bilingualism among the hijras. When asked how she became so adept at switching back and forth between these linguistic realms, Rupa again attributed her proficiency to *ādat* ['habit']: 'Gradually, after leading this life,' she explains, 'you just get used to it' (*rahate-rahate ādat paṛ jātā hai*).

Feminine solidarity and masculine power

Sulekha almost always spoke in the first-person feminine in her conversations with us, but she insisted that her choice of linguistic gender is variable, and moreover, that this choice is dependent on the context of the interaction. It is when she talks with a man, she elaborates, that she speaks softly and uses polite forms of the imperative. This style of speaking is at odds with the self she presents when she cooks breakfast or dinner in the kitchen, an activity which prompts her to chat casually with other hijras and neighbourhood women in feminine speech, using intimate and familiar forms of the imperative. Sulekha's choice of language, then, is contingent not only upon the social role she is performing at the moment, but also upon the addressee, whose gender calls for an appropriate level of politeness. She is highly aware of the fact that her pragmatics change with the gender of the hearer, explaining in excerpt (8) that when she converses with a woman she speaks as a woman; when she converses with a man she speaks as a man:

(8) S:

mujh ko koī bāt nahī̃ rahatā hai, maĩ aurat jaisī boltī^f hū̃, - ādmī se ādmī jaisā bāt kartī^f hū̃, - jo jaisā miltā hai us se bāt kartī^f hū̃, ... jaise ab ham- hai na? - ab- ab- auratõ mẽ haĩ, (0.5) to - aurat ā gayī to aurat vālā hī bolū̃gī^f, 'dīdī bahan' kahū̃gī. - ādmī ā jātā hai to ((softly)) 'kyā khāte haĩ. (1.0) kyā bāt hai āpko. (1.0) kyā kām hai.'	It's just not a big deal to me. [Normally] I speak^f like a woman, [but] with a man I speak^f like a man. I use^f the same speech as the person I meet. ... For example, take my case, okay? Now- now- if I'm socializing with women and another woman comes by, I'll just speak^f like a woman. I'll say, 'Dīdī! Bahan!' If a man comes by [I'll say] ((softly)), 'What are you eating? What's the matter, sir? What brings you here?'

Towards the end of the passage, however, it becomes clear that when Sulekha claims, 'I use the same speech as the person I meet', she actually means that she makes her speech correspond to the level of familiarity she feels with the addressee. Her insistence that she uses familiar address terminology with women but the respectful *āp* ['you'] and third-person plural verb form with men suggests that she sees 'women's speech' and 'men's speech' as serving two mutually exclusive functions: the former solidarity, the latter distance. According to Sulekha, the distance which characterizes her speech with men is necessary for the pursuit of her own romantic interests: she employs polite verb, adjective and pronominal forms in order to heighten the gender polarity between herself and a potential male partner. By assuming a submissive and coquettish posture, she is able to have what she refers to as *hā hā hī hī* – an interjection which connotes pleasure, laughter and flirtation.[16]

In light of both Rupa's and Sulekha's clearly articulated reflections on their alternating uses of feminine and masculine speech, it is interesting that Megha, a member of another Banaras community, adamantly insists that hijras *never* speak as men in any circumstances. Like Rupa, Megha creates a number of feminine-marked phrases as examples of hijra speech, together with a number of intimate second-person imperatives, such as *tū khā le* 'you [intimate] eat!' and *tū pakā le* 'you [intimate] cook!':

(9) M:

M:
hã hameśā auratõ kī bolī boltī[f] haĩ	Yes, we always speak[f] women's speech.
kabhī bhī ādmī ke jaisā nahī boltī[f] haĩ,	We never ever speak[f] like a man. It's
- jaise, 'maĩ jā rahī[f] hũ jī', 'jā rahī[f]	like, 'I'm going[f] sir/ma'am', 'Sister is
bahan', 'tū khā le', 'tū pakā le', 'maĩ	going[f]', 'You [intimate] eat!' 'You
abhī ā rahī[f] hũ.'	[intimate] cook!' 'I'm coming[f] now.'

Since imperatives in Hindi are not marked for gender, Megha's inclusion of these forms in the above excerpt as examples of feminine speech works to support Sulekha's claim that familiarity is normally associated with women's language. Her conflation of feminine speech with the use of intimate imperatives is indeed not so surprising given the larger system of honorific address in Hindi. Central to the use of this system is the age and social status of the referent compared to that of the speaker. A speaker's senior, for instance, is normally addressed with the third-person plural pronoun *āp* ['you' (3rd person plural)] and referred to with the plural pronoun *ve* ['they' (3rd person plural)] and a plural verb; any declinable adjectives or postpositions used in reference to one's senior will be pluralized. Conversely, close friends, relatives (especially those not senior to the speaker), and those of lower social status (such as servants or rickshaw drivers) are normally addressed with the second-person plural pronoun *tum* ['you' (2nd person plural)] and referred to with the singular pronoun *vah* ['he/she/it' (3rd person singular)] and a singular verb. A third pronoun of address *tu* ['you' (2nd person singular)], which Megha employs twice in excerpt (9), is used for extreme divergences from high honorific reference, whether it be to signal heightened intimacy and informality with the addressee (such as with a deity, a young child, or one's husband or wife), or, alternatively, to express feelings of contempt or disgust. While the hijras' use of this honorific system is consistent with the larger Hindi-speaking community, they additionally indicate many of these same distinctions through the gender system. By superimposing gender distinctions onto honourific distinctions, the hijras have at their disposal a tool of expression unavailable to the more rigidly gendered non-hijra world.

Megha usually makes linguistic claims like those in (9), however, only after issuing a stream of assertions which might be said to constitute the hijra 'party line': namely, that hijras never have castration and penectomy operations, never have relations with men, never take on new feminine names, and never speak as men. Megha, who has a high profile in her district of Banaras, is very aware of how her own self-presentation affects societal opinion, especially in light of the recent increase of anti-hijra violence in northern India; she is more interested than the other hijras in projecting a self that conforms to societal expectations – a self that is determined by both ascetic and anatomical considerations. Megha's insistence that the hijras were not only given feminine names at birth but have also never spoken in the masculine serves to support the claim that the hijras' femininity is innate, affirming a larger cultural belief that the hijra lifestyle is not socially constructed, but rather something that begins at (or even before) birth.

Most of the hijras we interviewed, with the exception of Rupa who became a hijra as an adult, primarily employ feminine-marked verbs when speaking in the first person or when addressing other hijras in the second person. When using the third person to refer to other hijras, however, the hijras are much less consistent, their choice of marking dependent on the relative social status of the referent in question. When the hijras speak in the third person and express distance from the referent, specifically when the referent is perceived to be either a superior or a subordinate, they tend to make greater use of the masculine; in contrast, when the hijras express solidarity or familiarity with a referent of equal status, they tend to make greater use of the feminine. Hijras rely not only upon their own internal systems of law and order, but also upon elaborate familial structures which delegate various feminine roles to different members of the group, among them *dādī* ['paternal grandmother'], *nānī* ['maternal grandmother'], *mā̃* ['mother'], *mausī* ['mother's sister'], *cācī* ['uncle's wife'], *dīdī* ['older sister'] and *bahin* ['younger sister']. Fundamental to this system is the guru-disciple relationship; the initiate pledges life-long devotion to an older, more experienced hijra, who in turn gives her a share of the community's earnings. The affected kinship situation created by the hijras is unique, in that the guru acts symbolically as both *sās* ['mother-in-law'] and *suhāg* ['state of being in a husband's protection']. Having abandoned all worldly ties upon entry into the community, the hijras appear to transfer every auspicious life-relationship to their guru, regardless of the fact that such a transferral, in the eyes of society at least, results in a superficially incestuous system.[17]

The hierarchical nature of the community becomes transparent in the hijras' use of feminine and masculine reference. When Rupa explains the import of the guru–disciple relationship, she frames her discussion in terms of a father–son relationship; in particular, she compares the leader of the group to a father and its members to his sons. 'It's just like the relationship of a *bāp laṛkā* ['father and son'],' she remarks, later using the Sanskrit-derived phrase *pitā putra* ['father and son'] to imbue the relationship with even more prestige. She similarly explains the structure of the hijra lineage by using masculine terms of reference, among them *dādā guru* ['paternal grandfather guru'], *guru bhāī* ['brother disciple'], *baṛe bāp* ['older father'], and *cācā guru bhāī* ['paternal uncle fellow disciple']. She maintains this use of masculine kinship terms, however, only when speaking in the third person about other hijras from the adopted standpoint of an outsider. When Rupa mimics her own interactions with other hijras in the community, using first- and second-person forms to do so, as in excerpt (10), she shifts from the masculine to the feminine:

(10) R:

to apne logõ mẽ 'cācā[m] vagairah nahī̃
kahte[m] haĩ na? ki- jaise 'mausī[f]', (1.5)
'mausī[f]' kahẽge[m] (2.0) 'mausī[f]' kahẽge[m],
(1.5) apne guru[m] ko 'guru[m]' bolẽge[m],
(1.5) musalmān log rahẽge[m] to
bolẽge[m] -'khālā[f]', - 'khālā[f] guru[m]',- aise
ham hī bāt kartī[f] haĩ. (3.0) zyādātar se
strīlĩg calta hai is mẽ. (2.0) strĩlĩg, (2.5)
auratõ kī bātcīt is mẽ caltī hai. ...
abhī ki vo ā jāẽngī[f], - to ham isī kapṛe mẽ
haĩ, - magar bāt vahī̃ hogā, - 'kyõ gayī[f]
nahī̃', 'kahā̃ thī[f]', 'kya kar rahī[f] thī[f]',
'kahā̃ gayī[f] thī[f]', - 'badhāī kyũ
nahī̃ āyī[f]', - 'khānā khāogī[f]'.

R:

But among ourselves we don't say[m] 'cācā[m]' ['paternal uncle'], etc., right? It's like 'mausī[f]' ['maternal aunt'], we'll say[m] 'mausī[f]', we'll say[m] 'mausī[f]'. We'll call[m] our guru[m] 'guru[m]'. If Muslim people are present[m], they'll say[m] 'khālā[f]' ['maternal aunt'], 'khālā[f] guru[m]'. This is the way we talk[f]. Mostly it's in the feminine – in the feminine. It's like women's conversation. ... If someone [a fellow hijra] would come[f] here right now, even if I were in these clothes [*lungī-kurtā*], our conversation would be like this: 'Why didn't you go[f]?' 'Where were[f] you?' 'What were[f] you doing[f]?' 'Where had[f] you gone[f]?' 'Why didn't you come[f] to the *badhāī* ['congratulations ceremony']?' 'Will you eat[f]?'

Significant in Rupa's discussion is the stream of feminine-marked verbs she produces in the final five lines as an example of what might occur in group interaction, a digression which stands in sharp contrast to her usual employments of the masculine singular and plural when referring to herself. And while she refers to herself and other hijras collectively in the first-person masculine plural at the start of this passage, she later constructs herself as feminine when viewing herself as part of the larger community, a community which aggressively identifies itself as non-masculine. When explaining how she and the other hijras in her community curse, for example, she employs feminine first-person plural verb forms, among them *jhagṛā kar lēgī*[f] ['we will fight[f]'], *bolēgī*[f] ['we will speak[f]'], *gālī bhī dēgī*[f] ['we will also give[f] curses'], *kahēgī*[f] ['we will say[f]']. Similarly, what she earlier defined as *cācā*[m] ['paternal uncle'] becomes *mausī*[f] or *khālā*[f] ['maternal aunt'] in this passage, a switch which is consistent with the other hijras' use of *mā̃*[f] ['mother'] when addressing their guru and *dādī*[f] ['paternal grandmother'] when addressing their guru's guru. It is perhaps this same distinction between terms of reference and terms of address which explains why Rupa refers to her guru as *dādā*[m] in the discussion directly preceding this passage, but as *dādī*[f] when reconstructing a group interaction that revolves around her.

A similar sort of shift is enacted by Sulekha in excerpt (11) below, when she explains how the most well-known hijras in Banaras, namely Channu, Idu, and Chanda, came to be so important within the hijra community. When describing how hijras reach positions of power in the hijra network, and how she herself will someday aquire such a position, Sulekha switches back and forth between feminine and masculine reference. Like Rupa, Sulekha describes the development of the hijra lineage in Banaras by using primarily masculine terminology: *dādā*[m] ['paternal grandfather'], *nātī*[m] ['grandson'], *parnātī*[m] ['great grandson'], and *celā*[m] ['male disciple'].

(11) S:

ye log banāras kā[m]- pahle-pahle banāras mē yahī log the[m]. (1.0) ve log thī[f], ve log mā̃gtī[f] thī[f], khātī[f] thī[f] (0.5) to (0.2) uske bād, jab jitnā hijṛā āyā[m], vo celā[m] banātī[f] gayī[f], vo uskā celā[m] vo uskā celā[m] vo uskā celā[m] vo uskā celā[m], tar par tar tar par tar, (0.5) ātā[m] gayā[m]. (1.0) tab nān[ā][m] guru ban gaye[m], dād[ā][m] guru ban gayī[f], (1.0) isī tarah. ham log kā ek koṭhe[18] sā hotā hai. ham log kā bātcīt alag hotā hai. (2.0) hā̃, jaise ((softly)) celā[m]. (0.5) nātī[m] parnātī[m], ((unclear)) kyā bolalā sabhī log kahte[m] haī, ham logõ mē celā[m] hotā hai. dād[ā][m] guru hotā hai, pardād[ā][m] guru hotā hai, (0.5) maīyā[f] hotī haī,

S:

These people [were] inhabitants of[m] Banaras, those people were[m] the first people in Banaras a long, long time ago. Those people were[f] here, they were[f] demanding[f] their due, they were[f] eating[f]. And from then on, they kept[f] making[f] any other hijras who came[m] [to Banaras] their own *celā*[m] ['disciple']. That one had her *celā*[m], that one had her *celā*[m], that one had her *celā*[m], that one had her *celā*[m], one right after the other, they kept[m] coming[m]. Then they became[m] a *nān[a]*[m] ['maternal grandfather'] guru, or they became[f] a *dād[a]*[m] ['paternal grandfather'] guru - like that. We have a sort of household[18] here. We have a

(1.0) is tarah kā hotā hai. jo aksar baṛā^m admī^m rahtā^m hai, isī tarah kahā jātā hai.

different way of talking, yes, like ((softly)) *celā*^m ['disciple'], *nātī*^m ['grandson'], *parnātī*^m ['great grandson'] - ((unclear)) you know, everybody says^m these [words]. Among us it's *celā*^m, it's *dād[ā]*^m guru, it's *pardād[ā]*^m ['paternal great grandfather'] guru, it's *maīyā*^f ['mother'] - it's like that, that's how someone who is^m a senior^m person^m is called.

Although Sulekha frequently employs feminine marking on the verb when referring to Channu, Idu and Chanda, particularly in the second through sixth lines of excerpt (11) when the three of them act as subjects of a particular action, she consistently employs the masculine kinship term *dādā*^m when relating their social status. At the end of her discussion, however, when she imagines herself in the same position of power as these three elders, she refers to her future self with the feminine terms *malkin* ^f ['female boss', 'landlady'] and *dādī* ^f ['paternal grandmother']:

(12) S:
ab maī yahā kām mālkin^f hū, (0.5) ab ham- koī āyegā^m to uskā celā^m to hamārā celā^m ho jāyegā^m, (0.5) ab phir dūsrā^m āyegā^m, to usko uskā celā^m kārā dūgī^f, to maī dādī^f ban jaūgī^f, (2.0) tab merā hī nām na rahegā, purānī^f to maī ho gayī^f, to merā nām usī tarah vahā purānī^f ho gayī^f. to un logō kā nām hai, (0.5) 'mālkin^f hai.'

S:
Now I'm the *mālkin* ^f ['female boss'] of^m this place. Now I- whoever comes^m here will become^m my *celā*^m. Whenever another one^m comes^m, I'll make^f him his *celā*^m and then I'll become^f the *dādī*^f. That way my name will surely continue, because I'll have become^f elderly^f. That's how I'll have a name when I've become^f elderly^f. So they'll have a name too [as part of my lineage]. [They'll say], 'She's the *mālkin*^f!'

Even though Sulekha portrays herself as a superior in the above excerpt, she continues to self-identify as feminine, reserving masculine terms like *dādā* and *mālik* for third-person reference only. Sulekha uses the masculine for hijras she perceives to be superior or subordinate, an employment which is irrelevant to her own self-identification.

The age of the referent is central to the choice of feminine or masculine terminology in the hijra community, as it is to the choice of either an *āp, tum* or *tu* pronoun of address in the larger system of Hindi honourifics. In excerpts (13) and (14) below, both Rupa and Sulekha make a gendered distinction between the younger and older members of their respective communities when speaking about them in the third person, marking younger members as feminine and older members as masculine:

(13) R:
    jo baṛā^m hotā^m hai to ((softly)) guru.
    (2.0) **guru**. jo choṭī^f hotī^f hai, to kā
    bolalā nām se bulāte haĩ.

R:
    We'll call someone who is^m elderly^m
    ((softly)) guru- guru. But we'll call
    someone who is^f younger^f by their name.

(14) S:
    sabse choṭī^f ek to hai hamāre mẽ vah
    sabse kam umra kī^f hai. uskī umra
    lagbhag 18 varṣ hai. aur 20 varṣ kā^m
    hai, 25 varṣ kā^m hai. maĩ 38 varṣ kī^f
    hũ.

S:
    There's one in our group who's the
    youngest^f-she's^f the youngest of all. Her
    age is about 18 or so. Another one is^m
    20 years old, another one is^m 25 years
    old. I'm^f 38 years old.

Rupa, in her opposing uses of the masculine adjective *baṛā^m* ['elderly', 'big'] and the feminine adjective *choṭī^f* ['young', 'small'] makes this distinction especially clear, her gendered choices echoing the use of the honourific *āp* for one's senior relatives and the familiar *tum* for one's junior relatives. Similarly, Sulekha's use of the feminine adjective *choṭī* and feminine postposition *kī* ['of'] in reference to the 'youngest' member of her group in excerpt (14), but the masculine postposition *kā* ['of'] in reference to older members in her group, would indicate that extreme youthfulness in the hijra community is indicated through the feminine.

Contempt and the use of the masculine

The use of feminine address is so expected from fellow hijras as a sign of solidarity that the use of inappropriate masculine reference will often provoke angry retaliation. An antipathy towards masculine linguistic forms is reflected in the hijras' naming system. When a new member enters the hijra community, she is given a woman's name to replace the name of her former, more male self. The hijras are strongly discouraged from referring to each other by these remnants of their previous lives, yet tellingly, they often employ them in disputes. If a hijra is in a fierce argument with another member of her community, one of the most incisive insults she can give is to question her addressee's femininity by using her male name; as Sulekha explains, 'We use them especially when we fight with each other. We'll tell everybody what the person's real name was, "Oh, so and so was such and such a name!" Then we'll call them by that name.' The strategy Sulekha identifies here is elaborated upon by

Rupa in excerpt (15) below, when she explains that the use of masculine address will be met with strong disapproval in Banaras. Rupa notes that because all of the hijras living in Banaras identify as feminine (in contrast to the hijras living in Panjab who, according to Rupa, adopt masculine as well as feminine identities), they expect, indeed demand, the use of feminine address:

(15) R:
banāras mē mardānā janānā koī pasand nahī̃ kartā hai. (5.0) ((laughs)) mardānā kah do to jhagṛā kar lēgī[f]. ... apne logõ mē to bolēgī[f] to aurat jaisā. (3.0) aurat jaisā.

R:
In Banaras, no one likes to be known as *mardānā* ['manly']. ((laughs)) Address someone as *mardānā* and they'll quarrel[f] [with you]! When we're together in our own group, we'll speak[f] like women. Like women.

Rupa goes on to explain that hijras '*gālī bhī dēgī, to aūrat jaisā*' ['even give curses like women'], meaning that they refrain from using those curses that involve insulting sexual reference to the addressee's mother or sister. According to Rupa, the hijras, infamous throughout northern India for their use of sexualized obscenities, attempt to model even their cursing strategies after women; if they were to invoke curses which were derogatory to women, they would, in essence, be cursing against themselves (see Hall 1996).

The negative connotations which Rupa and Sulekha both associate with masculine reference may very well explain Megha's repeated use of the masculine when referring to Sulekha. Sulekha was previously a member of Megha's community in Banaras, but after having a number of serious arguments with the other hijras who lived there, went to live with a male partner in a neighbouring village outside the city. Megha, in a manner consistent with the claims she makes in excerpt (9), almost always uses feminine forms when referring to other hijras; yet when she refers to Sulekha, who apparently insulted her guru's authority as *mālik* ['master'] of the community, Megha uses the masculine. Two examples of this employment are reproduced in excerpt (16):

(16) M:
bacpan se yahī̃ kā[m] hai, - ab jākar [place name] mē rah rahā[m] hai, - merā jajmānī hai, to maī̃ un logõ ko de detī hū̃.

M:
[Sulekha] belonged[m] to this household since childhood, [but] now he left and is living[m] in [place name]. I had *jajmān*s ['clients'] there, but I transferred those people to him/her.

Through the use of masculine-marked postpositions like *kā*^m ['of^m'] and masculine-marked verb forms like *rah rahā*^m *hai* ['he is living^m'], Megha is perhaps signalling that Sulekha is not only estranged from her, but also inferior to her. Her use of the masculine singular, then, approximates in Hindi the use of the pronoun *tu*, which can signal contempt for an inferior as well as heightened intimacy. (Although comparatively infrequent, Megha sometimes refers to her guru affectionately in the masculine singular instead of the more respectful feminine or masculine plural, such as when she at one point turned to us, paused, and emphatically pronounced *merā*^m *Channu* ['my^m Channu'].)

A similar sort of distancing by use of the masculine gender occurs whenever Sulekha refers to Muslim hijras, with whom, as a Hindu, she feels somewhat at odds. Although Muslims and Hindu hijras often live together harmoniously in the same communities – an arrangement rarely found in mainstream Banaras where the tension between Muslims and Hindus is quite pervasive – Sulekha seems to feel threatened by Muslim hijras, since they hold powerful positions within the Banaras hijra network, and indeed, throughout all of northern India. The contempt Sulekha feels towards Muslim hijras is reflected in her employment of third-person masculine-marked verb forms when Muslim hijras act as subjects, as in the short narrative reproduced in (17):

(17) M:

M:
apnā upar hai. (1.0) maĩ hindū hũ (1.0) to apnā hindū kā kām kartī^f hũ, jo musalmān hai vah apnā musalmān kā kām kartā^m hai, (0.5) apnā dharm nibhātā^m hai (0.2) maĩ apnā dharm nibhātī^f hũ, (2.0) ab khāne pīne kā- to āj kal- (0.5) ḍom-camār ke yahã bhī khā letā hai.	It's up to the individual. I'm Hindu so I do^f the work of Hindus, but whoever is Muslim does^m the work of Muslims. He fulfils^m his own *dharm* faithfully. I fulfil^f my own *dharm* faithfully. As far as eating and drinking is concerned, people nowadays even go and eat with *ḍom-camār* ['corpse burners' and 'shoe-makers']!

Sulekha's use the masculine in the impersonal relative–correlative constructions above would not be so remarkable if she did not regularly overcompensate towards the feminine when talking about Hindu hijras. Her use of the third-person masculine in (17), in sharp contrast to her use of the third-person feminine in comparable constructions in which Hindu hijras act as subjects, reflects her own opinion that Muslims are below her on the social hierarchy; this is evidenced in her insistence throughout her conversations with us that Hindu hijras existed long before Muslim hijras, and, what is more, that it is only hijras from low-caste backgrounds who convert to Islam. Moreover, she angrily complained that non-hijra Muslims are much less generous than Hindus when it comes to paying hijras for their song and dance performances: 'Muslims will never give to Hindus. If a hijra goes to their door, then they'll say, "Our door is polluted for forty days!" (i.e. there has been a death in the family).'

Sulekha's distaste for the hijras in Banaras who have converted to Islam is further instantiated by her insistence that such individuals are not true hijras, but 'men'. This proclamation is premised on her belief that the majority of Muslim hijras in Banaras have not undergone castration operations. For Sulekha, it is this event alone that serves as the defining moment of the hijra's entry into femininity – an event which, in her opinion, should be rewarded with a more consistent use of feminine reference. In excerpt (18), she is clearly hesitant to give this consistency to Channu, one of the oldest and most prestigious hijras in Banaras, as well as to the Muslim hijras living under Channu's jurisdiction:

(18) S:

hã, channū hai, (0.5) [place name] mẽ jo channū hai, to vah bhī ādmī^m hai. hijṛā to hai nahī̃. ... vo buzurg hai. vah sab se mālik^m vahī hai. (1.0) sab se mālik^m vahī hai. [place name] kā^m. (0.2) ye vo channū iske sab ādmī^m haĩ, sab āte^m haĩ jāte^m haĩ. kurtā lungī pahan lete^m haĩ, nācne samay sāṛī pahan lete^m haĩ, (0.2) sabhī jānte^m haĩ, (2.0) maĩ hamko kahne se kyā?

V:

lekin vo sab āpreśan karāye hue haĩ̃?

S:

nahī̃

V:

kuch nahī̃ <hai?>

S:

     <nahī̃.>

V:

tabhī aisī <hai?>

S:

     <hã.>

V:

o:::h. (1.0) acchā?

S:

Yes, Channu is – that Channu who lives in [place name] is a man^m. He's not a hijra. ... He's very old – he's the chief master^m over there. He's the chief master^m over there of^m [place name]. All of the ones under Channu are men^m, all of them who come^m and go^m over there. They wear^m kurtās and lungīs, but when they dance they wear^m sāṛīs. Everybody knows^m it, so what's the use of my saying so?

V:

But haven't they all had operations?

S:

No.

V:

Nothing at all?

S:

No.

V:

So they're just that way?

S:

Yes.

V:

O:::h. Really?

S:
usko- unko maī kaise kahū̃? usko
kahū̃gī^f to merā bāt kāṭ ḍēge^m. ... maī
kah dū̃gī^f (0.5) to ((softly)) maī choṭe
mū̃h baṛī bāt, hamko isī mē rahnā hai.
(0.5) sab māregā^m pīṭegā^m bāl kāṭ
degā^m.

S:
How can I say anything about them? If
I'd say^f anything, they'd of course just
contradict^m me anyway. ... If I'd give^f
anything away, then ((softly)) I [would be
like] a small mouth with big talk. I have
to live in this community, after all.
They'd all hit^m me, beat^m me up, cut^m
my hair.

Sulekha's use of the third-person masculine singular to describe the
78-year-old Channu stands in opposition to comparable descriptions by both Rupa and Megha, who, depending on the immediate
context, refer to Channu by using either the respectful third-person
masculine plural or feminine-marked adjectival forms, such as
when they affectionately call her *moṭī*^f *vālī*^f ['big^f one^f'] and
būḍhī^f *vālī*^f ['senior/superior^f one^f']. Since Rupa and Megha are
both related to Channu in the hijra family tree (Rupa as her dis-
ciple and Megha as her grand-disciple), they are perhaps more keen
than Sulekha to show Channu both respect and solidarity, granting
the other Muslims under her jurisdiction feminine reference as well.
Sulekha, on the other hand, displeased with her own 'smallness'
relative to these Muslim hijras, refuses the entire community any
acknowledgement of femininity, whether it be linguistic or anatomical.

Emphatic masculinity

Hijra speakers sometimes refer to themselves in the masculine for
emphatic purposes, such as in Sulekha's use of the term *mālik*
['master', 'landlord'] in examples (19) through (21). Although
Sulekha normally refers to herself as a *mālkin* ['female boss', 'landlady'], as she did earlier in example (12) when she was explaining
the structure of the hijra family lineage, she refers to herself in
examples (19) and (20) as a *mālik*. Proud of the fact that she is a
homeowner – an accomplishment shared by few hijras in India –
Sulekha underscores the import of her position by portraying herself as a landlord instead of a landlady, using the
masculine-marked adjective *akelā*^m ['alone'] instead of its feminine
counterpart *akelī*:

(19) V:
to kyū̃ āp grup mē nahī̃ rahtī haī?
S:
ham log grup mē **haī**

V:
So why aren't you in a group?
S:
But we are in a group!

V:
to grup ke sāth nāctī haĩ, gātī haĩ?

S:
hã, **sab** hai. (1.0) maĩ ab- apnā ghar lekar
akelā[m] rahtī[f] hũ. yahã apnā ghar
apne nām se akelā[m] banvāī[f] hũ. to maĩ
iskā mālik[m] hũ to maĩ is mẽ rahtī[f] hũ,
(1.0) to hamāre yahã 4 ṭho 5 ṭho āyegī[f]
nāckar, (1.0) apnā hisāb lekar calī[f]
jāyegī[f].

V:
So you dance and sing with a group?

S:
Sure, everything! Now I just bought my
own house and live[f] alone[m]. I've regis-
tered[f] my house here in my name alone[m],
so I'm its *mālik*[m] and I live[f] in it. So four
or five people will come[f] to my house,
they'll dance, take their share, and
leave[f].

(20) S:
dūsre mẽ jāũngī[f] gāungī[f] nācũngī[f].
hamko mazdūrī milegā. (1.0) vahã kā
mālik[m] maĩ nahī̃ ban saktī[f]. maĩ
mālik[m] banũgī[f] yahī̃ kā.

V:
keval isī ilāke kā?

S:
hã. ilāke-ilāke kā. (2.0) **thāne** kā.

S:
I'll go[f] and sing[f] and dance[f] in other
places. I'll get wages. I just can't[f]
become the *mālik* [m] there. I can only
become[f] the *mālik* [m] here.

V:
Only in this area?

S:
Only in this area right here. In this police
district.

Sulekha's use of the masculine in the above examples seems to be
influenced by a local understanding of home ownership as a man's
activity. When she refers to herself as a *mālkin* in excerpt (12), she
is talking about herself not as a homeowner, as in these two passages, but as a member of the hijra lineage. The issue of home
ownership becomes especially salient in example (20), when she
explains that even though she can work and collect wages in a district designated as belonging to another hijra community, she can
never buy a house in a district other than her own.

First-person masculine verb forms, which occur much more
rarely in the hijras' conversations than do third-person forms, occasionally surface in highly emphatic moments. Sulekha, when
overtly contradicting claims made by Megha, adds extra weight to
her words by speaking in the masculine first person, as in examples
(21) and (22). Megha had stated in an earlier conversation that
hijras are asexual and lead ascetic lifestyles; Sulekha, wanting to
give us what she perceives to be a more accurate account of the
hijra community, refutes all of Megha's assertions by speaking in
the masculine:

(21) V:
*kaise kah rahī thī 'ham log ko dukh hotā
hai, ham log kā parivār nahī̃ rahtā, ham
log kā sambandh nahī̃ rahtā, ham log*

V:
*Then why was [Megha] saying, 'We have
a lot of sadness. We no longer have a
family. We no longer have relationships.*

bhī sote uṭhte baiṭhte.'
S:
nahī̃. ye galat bāt hai. - galat bāt hai.
maī isko nahī̃ māntā^m. - galat bāt hai.

All we do is sleep, get up, sit around'?
S:
No, that's wrong. That's wrong. I don't
believe^m that. That's wrong.

(22) S:
ādmī ke sāth kartā hai sab. - jaise aurat
*mard sambandh hota hai, – usī tarah
*hijṛe - mard ke sāth sambandh hotā hai.
- kitne *hijṛe- kitne hijṛe rakh lete haĩ
ādmī ko, - kitnā peśāvar hotā hai, (1.0)
peśā kartī, tab (1.0) *sau, pacās, do sau,
cār sau, *sabkā peśā kartī haī̃. - maī
jhūṭh kahtā^m hū̃? nahī̃ kahtā^m hū̃.

S:
They all have relationships with men.
Just like women have relationships with
*men, *hijras have relationships with
men. A lot of *hijras- a lot of hijras
keep men. A lot of them are
professionals. Those who do it as a
profession charge a *hundred, fifty, two
hundred, four hundred rupees, *anything
they can get. Do I tell^m lies? No, I don't
tell^m lies.

The latter example is particularly telling, since Sulekha colours her commentary with a series of flat-handed claps for added emphasis, a gesture so much a part of the hijras' interactional style that we have chosen to represent it in the transcription system with an asterisk. With five claps occurring in seven short sentences, Sulekha's commentary stands in sharp contrast to the other passages quoted in this chapter; the import of her words is further underscored by her use of maculine self-reference in the final two lines: *maī jhūṭh kahtā^m hū̃? nahī̃ kahtā^m hū̃* ['Do I tell^m lies? No, I don't tell^m lies!'].

A final example of first person masculinity comes from an interaction that took place among members of a third community in Banaras. All born into Hindu families who ostracized them, the hijras belonging to this community have adopted the religious practices of the Muslim families they live with – families who in many ways suffer a similar marginalization as residents of a city that is thought of throughout North India as the 'holy Hindu city'. The 80-year-old Shashi is the leader of the group, and after 69 years of speaking like a woman, we rarely heard her use any masculine speech. The third time we visited her, however, Shashi's favourite disciple had fled back to her own village after a serious financial scuffle with another community member. Shashi was feeling intense rage at the cause of this dispute, as well as deep grief for her loss. Wailing *merā beṭā, merā beṭā* ['my son, my son'] and clapping in anger, Shashi screamed about the punishment that the hijra who precipitated the fight would receive, venting her anger entirely through use of the masculine first and third person. It would seem that for the hijras, as both Rupa and Sulekha suggest, anger is an emotion which is best expressed in the masculine. Perhaps rage is a gut-level reaction that recalls the masculine forms that the hijra produced prior to her entry into the community, or perhaps masculine forms are simply a dramatic and forceful tool for venting such rage. Regardless of the reason, the hijra is clearly aware of the social meanings such forms convey.

Conclusion

We would like to suggest that the kind of gendered negotiations discussed in this chapter, while particularly overt in the Hindi-speaking hijra community, are not unique to alternative gender identities; rather, women and men of many communities manipulate linguistic expectations of femininity and masculinity in order to establish varying positions of solidarity and power. That speaking styles recognized culturally as 'women's speech' or 'men's speech' are not determined by the sex of the speaker, but rather constructed collaboratively in social interaction, is a point made salient by linguists working at the intersection of linguistics and queer theory: Barrett (1994, 1996) in his exposition of discursive style-shifting among a community of African American drag queens; Gaudio (1996) in his discussions of the appropriation of feminine speech styles by Hausa-speaking *'yan daudu*; Ogawa and Smith (1996) in their work on appropriations of Japanese 'women's language' by gay men in Tokyo and Osaka; and Livia (1995, 1996) in her articles on the varying uses made of the French linguistic gender system by male-to-female transsexuals, hermaphrodites and gay drag queens. In the interactions described in these articles (which report on four very different linguistic communities on four separate continents), the speech ideologically associated with masculinity and femininity, and indeed sometimes the linguistic gender system itself, is used to express much more than mere gender differentiation. Linguistic gender, in its close association with one of the most basic divisions in social organization, is used as a tool for evoking a wide range of societal discourses on power and solidarity, difference and dominance.

Moreover, the structure of linguistic evocations is not arbitrary, but influenced by societal ideologies of femininity and masculinity. Although Banaras hijras challenge such ideologies in their conflicting employments of masculine and feminine speech, often subverting the gender system in innovative and unexpected ways, their employment of linguistic gender is still constrained by a traditional and dichotomous notion of gender. While the hijra tends to make greater use of the masculine when signalling social distance from the referent, whether it be respect for a superior or contempt for an inferior, she is more likely to employ the feminine when expressing solidarity, particularly when addressing other hijras directly. Occupying an ambiguous position in a society that has marginalized them, hijras are more attentive than their non-hijra peers to the cultural meanings evoked by feminine and masculine markings, enacting and contesting them in their everday projections of self.

Acknowledgements

We conducted this field research jointly after concluding an advanced language programme sponsored by the American Institute of Indian Studies in Banaras, India, during the 1992–1993 academic year. Earlier versions of this chapter, authored independently by Hall (1994, 1995), appear in the *Proceedings of the Twentieth Annual Meeting of the Berkeley Linguistics Society* and in *Hijra/Hijrin: Language and Gender Identity*, respectively. In addition to the editors of the present volume, who offered insightful commentary on the original manuscript, we are grateful to the many people who helped us with this project in both India and America, among them Nancy Chodorow, Penny Eckert, Susan Ervin-Tripp, Linda Hess, Leanne Hinton, Robin Lakoff, Anna Livia, Vinita Sharma, our teachers at the AIIS Hindi Language Institute in Banaras, and above all, the hijras who participated in these discussions. We are especially indebted to Ved Prakash Vatuk, whose knowledge of the folklore and linguistic traditions of northern India were instrumental to the writing of this chapter.

Notes

1. The correct English spelling for the Hindi हिज़ड़ा, according to the transliteration conventions adopted throughout the remainder of this chapter, would be *hijṛā*; we have chosen to use the spelling *hijra*, however, for easier reading.
2. The choice of terminology used to identify the hijras in Indian, European and American scholarship merits a full article in its own right. While contemporary sociologists and journalists living in India and writing in English generally refer to the hijras as 'eunuchs' (e.g.

Sinha 1967, Sethi 1970, Mohan 1979, Bobb and Patel 1982, Patel 1983, 1988, Mitra 1983, 1984, Sharma 1984, Sayani 1986, Vyas and Shingala 1987, Mondal 1989, Shetty 1990, Raghuramaiah 1991, Allabadia and Shah 1992, Lakshmi and Kumar 1994), European and American researchers refer to them variously as 'transvestites' (e.g. Ross 1968, Freeman 1979, Preston 1987), 'an institutionalized third gender role' (Nanda 1985, 1990, Bullough and Bullough 1993), 'hermaphrodites' (Opler 1960, Ross 1968), 'passive homosexuals' (Carstairs 1956) and 'male prostitutes' (Carstairs 1956). The inconsistency of these translations underscores the inherent difficulty of translating the concept *hijṛā* into Western scholarship. Other English terms besides that of 'eunuch' occasionally employed by South Asian writers are 'abominable aberrations' (Raghuramaiah 1991), 'ambiguous sex' (Mohan 1979), 'hermaphrodites' (Singh 1956, Sethi 1970, Srinivas 1976, Mohan 1979, Pimpley and Sharma 1985), 'castrated human male' (Mohan 1979), 'hermaphrodite prostitutes' (Sanghvi 1984), 'labelled deviants' (Sharma 1989), 'male-homosexual transvestites' (Rao 1955), 'sex perverted male, castrated or uncastrated' (Sinha 1967), 'sexo-aesthetic inverts coupled with homosexual habits' (Sinha 1967), 'sexual inverts' or 'sexual perverts' (Rao 1955) and 'third sex' (Mondal 1989).

3. For discussions of eunuchs in Indian history, see Saletore (1974, 1978) and Sharma (1984); for discussions of transsexuality or 'dual' sexuality in Indian tradition and mythology, see O'Flaherty (1973, 1981), Nanda (1990), AIDS Bhedbhav Virodhi Andolan (1991) and Goldman (1993).

4. Lynton and Rajan frequently allude to the hijras' idiosyncratic language use in their short introduction to the hijras of Hyderabad; they explain, for example, that the hijras they interviewed speak Hindustani 'with many archaic expressions and constructions' and that their speech, while 'often ungrammatical', is 'full of imagery and sometimes has a rather poetic quality' (1974: 193). The authors provide very little linguistic detail in support of these compelling remarks, however, stating only that the hijras' 'manner of speech suggests a yearning for identity and identification with a social group', and moreover, that 'the confusion of their terminology is a constant reminder of the sexual confusion which brought them into the group' (p. 192).

5. Nanda refers specifically to Freeman's research in the 1970s, who noted that certain Oriya-speaking hijras (whom he calls 'transvestites') use 'women's expressions and feminine forms of address' (1979: 294). Freeman quotes the speech of a hijra named Kula in great detail, explaining that he 'delighted in using peculiar and distinctive expressions that called attention to himself' (295).

6. Indeed, an anonymous article in the political gossip paper *Bombay*

Blitz, entitled 'Wipe Out the Hijra Menace' (1981), refers to the hijra scathingly as 'it'. Because the hijras prefer to be referred to and addressed in the feminine, we have chosen to use the feminine pronouns 'her' and 'she' when referring to them.

7. The finality of the linguistic evidence in Sethi's narrative invites comparison with Lowe's (1983: 32) account of her first meeting with a hijra in Bombay named Lata:

> Lata was a surprise. If it hadn't been for Navalkar's keen eye, I would never have thought her a *hijra* at all. Her face was smooth and hairless and with eyebrows plucked to a fine arch, she was really quite pretty. Her sari hid any masculinity of build and her gestures were entirely feminine. She would use her arms and hands with the effectiveness of an actress. But Navalkar said the swaying walk was a dead giveaway. They all walked like cancan girls at rehearsals. **And once they spoke, their masculine tones left no doubt.** [emphasis ours].

A similar sentiment is expressed in Moses Manoharan's (1984: 27) brief introduction to the hijras in New Delhi: 'They dress in saris, have exotic hairstyles and wear heavy make-up, **but their voices give them away** – they're India's eunuchs. Now the eunuchs are raising their voices for a better deal after centuries as a despised and downtrodden community' [emphasis ours].

8. Throughout this chapter, we have used the transliteration system adopted by Snell and Weightman (1989: 7). The superscripted 'f' and 'm' represent feminine and masculine morphological marking, respectively.

9. While both men and women participate in *nautanki*, all of the actors performing in *sāng* are men. The women who do participate in *nautanki*, however, are frequently stereotyped as prostitutes, and women viewers are normally not welcomed in the audience. For more information on the Nautanki theatre in northern India, see Hansen (1992).

10. We have considerably simplified the complexity of gender marking in Hindi for the purposes of this chapter.

11. One of the hijras we spoke with, in order to indicate that three-fourths of all hijras have had operations, explained that 'rupayā mẽ bārah ānā' ['in one rupee 12 annas']. (In Indian currency, 16 annas make up one rupee.) This estimate suggests that only a minority of hijras are actually intersexed in the way Epstein (1990) and Kessler (1990) describe when they discuss the surgical reconstruction of new-born infants in America and Europe.

12. To preserve the hijras' anonymity, we have chosen pseudonyms for all of the hijras appearing in this chapter and have avoided giving the names of the four hijra communities we visited.

13. We have tried to transcribe each of the Hindi passages *as spoken*, maintaining any anomalies in gender agreement which occurred in the

tape-recorded conversations. In excerpt (4), for instance, there are a number of markings which are inconsistent with standard Hindi, such as when Sulekha treats the feminine noun *bāt* ['conversation'] as masculine, modifying it with the postposition $kā^m$ instead of $kī^f$. These agreement inconsistencies are related to the fact that the Hindi of most of the hijras referred to in this article was influenced by various regional dialects, particularly Bhojpuri. The transcription conventions we have used in the transliterated Hindi passages are adapted from Jefferson (see Atkinson and Heritage 1984: ix–xvi); they include the notable additions of a superscripted 'f' or 'm' to designate feminine and masculine morphological marking, and an asterisk to designate the flat-palmed clap used by the hijras for emphasis. (We have not used these same conventions in the English translations, since extralinguistic features like intonation and emphasis are not parallel.) Other transcription conventions include the following:

(0.4)   indicates length of pause within and between utterances, timed in tenths of a second

a - a   a hyphen with spaces before and after indicates a short pause, less than 0.2 seconds

but-   a hyphen immediately following a letter indicates an abrupt cutoff in speaking (interruption or self-interruption)

(( ))   double parentheses enclose non-verbal movements and extralinguistic commentary

( )   single parentheses enclose words which are not clearly audible (i.e. best guesses)

[ ]   brackets enclose words added to clarify the meaning of the text

what   bold face indicates syllabic stress

:   a colon indicates a lengthening of a sound (the more colons, the longer the sound)

.   a period indicates falling intonation

,   a comma indicates continuing intonation

?   a question mark indicates rising intonation at the end of a syllable or word

...   deletion of some portion of the original text

'a'   quotation marks enclose quoted or reported speech

< >   triangular brackets indicate beginning and end of conversational overlap

14. We should add that this insult is so offensive to middle-class Hindi speakers that the Banaras resident who typed our transcripts refused to include this word, typing an ellipsis in its place. The word is used differently from the American insult 'cunt'; it is primarily used in reference to men in order to indicate that they are somehow emasculated. The term *bhosṛī vālā* is itself masculine; its feminine counterpart *bhosṛī vālī* does not exist in contemporary usage. Ved Prakash Vatuk (personal communication) offers a succinct explanation as to why this curse is never used in reference to a woman: 'A

woman already has one, so why would it be a curse to tell her so?'
15. Rupa addresses our research assistant Vinita with the masculine term *beṭā* ['son'] instead of the feminine *beṭī* ['daughter'] throughout this passage. Hindi-speakers (especially parents) sometimes address younger women or children by *beṭā* in order to show affection, a reversal clearly derived from the value given to sons in Indian culture.
16. Sulekha later expands on this distinction:

> Everyone talks to their girlfriends and women companions. Everyone becomes girlfriends and talks with each other about what they feel inside. We need to have that kind of conversation, of course. But when you talk with your own man, it's a different thing altogether, and that's what I enjoy most. For example, I can easily sit around with other women and say, 'Eat *dīdī*, drink *dīdī*.' We'll sit together, we'll go for a walk together, we'll go to the cinema together, we'll see a movie together, we'll do everything together. But there's something more that goes on with a man. It's a lot more fun to talk to a man.

17. We owe this insight to Ved Prakash Vatuk (personal communication).
18. Sulekha uses the term *koṭha* ['room'] when referring to her hijra-family lineage, a term frequently used by Hindi speakers in reference to the room of a prostitute.

References

AIDS Bhedbhar Virodhi Andolan (eds) 1991 *Less than gay: a citizen's report on the status of homosexuality in India*. AIDS Bhedbhav Virodhi Andolan, New Delhi.

Allabadia Gautam N, Shah Nilesh 1992 India: begging eunuchs of Bombay. *Lancet* 339.8784: 48–9.

Atkinson J. Maxwell, Heritage John (eds) 1984 *Structures of social action: studies in conversation analysis*. Cambridge University Press, Cambridge.

Barrett Rusty 1994 'She is *not* white woman': the appropriation of white women's language by African American drag queens. In Bucholtz Mary, Liang A C, Sutton Laurel, Hines Caitlin (eds) *Cultural performances: proceedings of the third Berkeley women and language conference*. Berkeley Women and Language Group, Berkeley, CA pp 1–14.

Barrett Rusty 1996 The homo-genius speech community. In Livia Anna, Hall Kira (eds).

Bobb Dilip, Patel C J 1982 Eunuchs: fear is the key. *India Today*, 15 September pp 84–5.

Bourdieu Pierre 1977 The economics of linguistic exchanges. *Social Science Information* 16.6: 645–68.

Bullough Vern L, Bullough Bonnie 1993 *Cross-dressing, sex, and gender*. University of Pennsylvania Press, Philadelphia.

Carstairs George Morrison 1956 Hinjra and jiryan: two derivatives of

Hindu attitudes to sexuality. *British Journal of Medical Psychology* 29: 128–38.

Davidson D C 1884 Amputation of the penis. *The Lancet* 16 February: 293.

Ebden H 1856 A few notes, with reference to 'the eunuchs', to be found in the large households of the state of Rajpootana. *The Indian Annals of Medical Science* 6: 520–5.

Epstein Julia 1990 Either/or – neither/both: sexual ambiguity and the ideology of gender. *Genders* 7: 99–142.

Faridi Khan Bahadur Fazalullah Lutfullah 1899 Híjdás in *Gujarat Population, Musalmans. Gazetteer of the Bombay Presidency* Vol. 9, Part 2: 21–2 Government Central Press, Bombay.

Freeman James M 1979 *Untouchable: an Indian life history*. Stanford University Press, Stanford.

Gaudio, Rudolph P 1996 Not talking straight in Hausa. In Livia Anna, Hall Kira (eds).

Goldman Robert P 1993 Transsexualism, gender, and anxiety in traditional India. *Journal of the American Oriental Society* 113: 374–401.

Hall Kira 1994 A third-sex subversion of a two-gender system. In Gahl Susannah, Dolbey Andy, and Johnson Chris (eds) *Proceedings of the twentieth annual meeting of the Berkeley Linguistics Society*. Berkeley Linguistics Society, Berkeley pp 220–33.

Hall Kira 1995 *Hijra/Hijrin: language and gender identity*. Unpublished PhD dissertation. University of California at Berkeley.

Hall Kira 1996 Go suck your husband's sugarcane!: hijras and the use of sexual insult. In Livia Anna, Hall Kira (eds).

Hansen Kathryn 1992 *Grounds for play: the nautanki theatre of North India*. University of California Press, Berkeley.

Jacobs Sue-Ellen, Cromwell Jason 1992 Visions and revisions of reality: reflections of sex, sexuality, gender, and gender variance. *Journal of Homosexuality* 23.4: 43–69.

Jani Sushma, Rosenberg Leon A 1990 Systematic evaluation of sexual functioning in eunuch-transvestites: a study of 12 cases. *Journal of Sex and Marital Therapy* 16.2: 103–10.

Kessler Suzanne J 1990 The medical construction of gender: case management of intersexed infants. *Signs: Journal of Women in Culture and Society* 16.1: 3–26.

Lakshmi N, Kumar A Gururaj 1994 HIV seroprevalence among eunuchs. *Genitourinary Medicine* 70.1: 71–2.

Livia Anna 1995 Linguistic gender and liminal identity. *Pronoun envy: literary uses of linguistic gender*. Unpublished PhD dissertation. University of California at Berkeley.

Livia Anna 1996 Disloyal to masculinity. In Livia Anna, Hall Kira (eds).

Livia Anna, Hall Kira (eds) 1996 *Queerly phrased: language, gender, and sexuality*. Oxford University Press, New York.

Lowe Sunaina 1983 Portrait of a young hijra. *Imprint* June pp 29–38.

Lynton Harriet Ronken, Rajan Mohini 1974 The unworldly ones: the hijras. In *The days of the beloved*. University of California, Press, Berkeley pp 190–206.

Manoharan Moses 1984 Hijras raising voices for better conditions. *India West* 10 February p 27.

Mehta Sumant 1945 Eunuchs, Pavaiyās, and Hijaḍās. *Gujarat Sahitya Sabha* pp 3–75.

Mitra Nirmal 1983 The making of a 'hijra'. *Onlooker* 18 February pp 14–25.

Mitra Nirmal 1984 Bahuchara Mata and her rooster. *The India Magazine* April pp 44–53.

Mohan Chander 1979 The ambiguous sex on the war-path. *Hindustan Times, Weekly Sunday* August 26 p i.

Mondal Sekh Rahim 1989 The eunuchs: some observations. *Journal of Indian Anthropology and Sociology* 24: 244–50.

Mukherjee J 1980 Castration – a means of induction into the hijirah group of the eunuch community in India: a critical study of 20 cases. *American Journal of Forensic Medicine and Pathology* 1.1: 61–5.

Nanda Serena 1985 The hijras of India: cultural and individual dimensions of an institutionalized third gender role. *Journal of Homosexuality* 11.3/4: 35–54.

Nanda Serena 1990 *Neither man nor woman: the hijras of India*. Wadsworth Publishing Co, Belmont, CA.

Nanda Serena 1993 Hijras as neither man nor woman. In Abelove Henri, Barale Michèle Aina, Halperin David M (eds) *The lesbian and gay studies reader*. Routledge, New York pp 542–52.

Nanda Serena 1994 Hijras: an alternative sex and gender role in India. In Herdt Gilbert (ed) *Third sex, third gender: beyond sexual dimorphism in culture and history*. Zone Books, New York pp 373–417.

Naqvi Nauman, Mujtaba Hasan 1992 Neither man nor woman. *Newsline* December pp 80–9.

O'Flaherty Wendy Doniger 1973 *Siva, the erotic ascetic*. Oxford University Press, New York.

O'Flaherty Wendy Doniger 1981 *Women, androgyns, and other mythical beasts*. University of Chicago Press, Chicago.

Ogawa Naoko, Smith Janet S (Shibamoto) 1996 The gendering of the gay male sex class in Japan: a case study based on *Rasen no Sobyo*. In Livia Anna, Hall Kira (eds).

Opler Morris E 1960 The hijarā (hermaphrodites) of India and Indian national character: a rejoinder. *American Anthropologist* 62: 505–11.

Patel Haribhai G 1983 The hijada (eunuch) culture-complex: urgent research needs. *Bulletin of the International Committee on Urgent Anthropological and Ethnological Research* 25: 121–6.

Patel Haribhai G 1988 Human castration: a study of hijada (eunuch) community of Gujarat in India. *Man and Life* 14.1/2: 67–76.

Pimpley P N, Sharma S K 1985 Hijaras: A study of an atypical role. *The Avadh Journal of Social Sciences* 2: 41–50.

Preston Laurence W 1987 A right to exist: eunuchs and the state in nineteenth-century India. *Modern Asian Studies* 21.2: 371–87.

Raghuramaiah K Lakshmi 1991 *Night birds: Indian prostitutes from devadasis to call girls*. Chanakya Publications, Delhi.

Rao I Bhooshana 1955 Male homosexual transvestism: a social menace. *Antiseptic* 52: 519–24.

Ross Allen V 1968 *Vice in Bombay*. Tallis Press, London.

Saletore Rajaram Naroyan 1974 *Sex life under Indian rulers*. Hind Pocket Books, Delhi.

Saletore Rajaram Naroyan 1978 *Sex in Indian harem life*. Orient Paperbacks, New Delhi.

Sanghvi Malavika 1984 Walking the wild side. *The Illustrated Weekly of India* 11 March: 25–8.

Sayani Sanjay A 1986 Understanding the third sex [Interview with Siddharth Shah]. *The Sunday Observer* 9 November: 14.

Sethi Patanjali 1970 The hijras. *The Illustrated Weekly of India* 13 December: 40–5.

Sharma Satish Kumar 1984 Eunuchs: past and present. *The Eastern Anthropologist* 37.4: 381–9.

Sharma Satish Kumar 1989 *Hijras: the labelled deviants*. Gian Publishing House, New Delhi.

Shetty Kavitha 1990 Eunuchs: A bawdy festival. *India Today* 15 June: 50–5.

Singh Govind 1982 *hijṛō kā sansār*. Anupam Books, Delhi.

Singh Khushwant 1956 *Mano majra*. Grove Press, New York.

Singh Khushwant 1989 *Delhi*. Viking, Penguin Books, New Delhi.

Sinha A P 1967 Procreation among the eunuchs. *Eastern Anthropologist* 20.2: 168–76.

Snell Rupert, Weightman Simon 1989 *Hindi (Teach yourself books)*. Hodder & Stoughton, Kent.

Srinivas M N 1976 *The remembered village*. University of California Press, Berkeley.

Vyas M D, Shingala Yogesh 1987 *The life style of the eunuchs*. Anmol Publications, New Delhi.

'Wipe Out the Hijra Menace' 1981 *Bombay Blitz* 10 January: 3.

Yorke Michael (director), Prasad Aruna Har (screenwriter) 1990 *Eunuchs: India's third gender*. BBC Productions, London.

11 *Black feminist theory and African American women's linguistic practice*[1]

Mary Bucholtz

Introduction

Recent trends in feminist theory, and in social theory more generally, have made explicit the role of language in shaping, reproducing and challenging power relations. Judith Butler (1990, 1993), for example, has argued persuasively from a poststructuralist stance that the categories of sex and gender themselves are linguistically constructed through cultural discursive practices. Ironically, however, the new theoretical focus on language has not been accompanied by close, systematic attention to how the details of language are employed in particular situations for social purposes. Even feminist linguists working within different theoretical traditions, such as Julia Kristeva (1980), are more abstract than empirical in their approach to language and gender. Sociolinguists, trained in the study of how social categories and linguistic practices constitute each other, are well positioned to remedy this situation. Through the deployment of sociolinguistic methodologies that allow scrutiny of language in use, linguists can test and refine models of gender that emerge from other disciplinary perspectives. Likewise, as Deborah Cameron (this volume) argues, the interpretative resources of feminist scholars outside of linguistics may offer fruitful new explanations for language data.

This chapter draws together several strands of research on language use among African American women in order to demonstrate the benefits of strengthening the relationship between feminist scholarship in linguistics and in other social sciences. After discussing the present state of this relationship, I sketch the contours of a feminist theory, known as Black feminist thought, that has recently been articulated within sociology. This framework, centring as it does on the social practices of African American women, can usefully be brought into dialogue with new linguistic scholarship on gender and race. I outline this research and then describe the results of the present study, an investigation of how the identity-marking language of African American women on a radio panel discussion about race relations can be analysed within the framework of Black feminist thought. The implications of the study are two-fold: first, that close analysis of linguistic texts may be a promising method for exploring social theory, and, second, that Black feminist theory may shed light on the social meanings of the everyday speech practices of African American women.

Black feminist theory

A frequently voiced critique of feminist scholarship within all the social sciences, including linguistics, is that its focus has been limited, for the most part, to white, Western, middle-class, heterosexual adults. Many scholars have tended to make premature generalizations that define gender experience universally for all women, while other social categories, such as race, are either omitted or introduced in an additive fashion. So, for example, Black women are described as a peripheral group composed of the two marginal categories 'Black' and 'female' (Hull *et al.* 1982). A variety of theories of Black feminism, articulated by bell hooks (1984), Patricia Hill Collins (1990), and others, redress the inadequacies of these approaches. Black feminist thought, as it has developed within the USA, is not a unified philosophy, but in all its forms it makes women of African descent central to theory. It is rooted in an understanding of how such women may use historically grounded social practices to develop knowledge that is resistant to hegemonic discourse.

The form of Black feminist theory on which I will focus is that developed by sociologist Patricia Hill Collins. On the basis of interviews and close study of African American women's writings and artistic traditions, Collins locates potential commonalities in the experiences of African American women that in turn may give rise to a particular collection of shared perspectives towards those experiences. Such perspectives, which she terms 'subjugated knowledge', are produced and tested through a Black feminist epistemology, or theory of knowledge, that functions as an alternative to dominant ways of thinking. Collins points to four elements of an African American women's epistemology, each of which is validated by Black institutions: (1) the dialogic evaluation of knowledge claims, in which truth is arrived at through discussion with others; (2) an ethic of personal accountability, which holds all individuals responsible for moral behaviour; (3) an ethic of caring, often manifested as affective involvement in interaction; and (4) concrete experience as a criterion of knowledge, which is prized at least as highly as the authority of the scholar or the expert. As Collins herself notes, the characteristics of Black feminist thought share many affinities with principles articulated both by white feminists and by Afrocentric scholars. This similarity is unsurprising, for as Collins (1990: 219) argues, alternative epistemologies are crucial in offering resistance to dominant ideologies:

> Alternative knowledge claims in and of themselves are rarely threatening to conventional knowledge. Such claims are routinely ignored, discredited, or simply absorbed and marginalized in existing paradigms. Much more threatening is the challenge that alternative epistemologies offer to the basic process used by the powerful to legitimate their knowledge claims. If the epistemology used to validate knowledge comes into question, then all prior knowledge claims validated under the dominant model become suspect.[2]

Theories of knowledge such as Collins's that rest on an experiential foundation have an uneasy relationship to essentialism. To some critics, her theory suggests that only African American women may participate in the constitution of Black feminist epistemology, and that, conversely, *all* African American women engage in this process. The Afrocentric perspective that Collins takes has been challenged as a mechanism for levelling the heterogeneity of the African diaspora while serving as a litmus test for membership within this diffuse community (King 1992).[3] Collins has further been criticized as a so-called standpoint theorist, a term used for thinkers who argue that theoretical positions derive from individuals' experiences as members of social categories like gender, race, class and sexuality (cf. Harding 1986, Hartsock 1987, Smith 1987). Postmodernists have issued the most common criticism of this framework, charging that it relies on social categories that explode upon close analysis (Haraway 1985).

But deconstruction is not destruction, and to demonstrate that a category is incoherent is not to eliminate its strategic use as a resource for both dominant and subjugated interests. Moreover, because we live in a world that orients to categories, we cannot ignore their effects. Identities can be chosen, as poststructuralists point out, but the meaning of such choices does not rest with the individual alone, and the range of choices is itself limited by the constraints of physical appearance and other factors. In the same vein, Alice Freed (this volume) notes that, despite the incoherence of the category 'woman', individuals cannot escape being classified by observers according to gender. Yet postmodern feminists and feminists concerned with racial, sexual and other identities are not as far removed from one another as they may at first appear. Both are interested in undercutting normative social divisions, but whereas poststructuralists are concerned with revealing the socially constructed nature of category boundaries, as well as their transgressions and subversions, identity-based feminists are more interested in the political consequences of these deeply rooted distinctions for the daily lives of women.[4]

Collins (1990, 1992) positions her work in this debate as emerging from historically specific political considerations. Acknowledging the inadequacy of categories like 'woman' and 'African American', she argues that overstated accounts of African American women's unity may be nonetheless necessary at first in order to clear a space in which their diversity can be explored, much as the overgeneralized claims of white American feminists that introduced feminism into the academy later led to more nuanced studies. Collins additionally points out that the leadership of African American women in theory construction does not preclude the possibility of building coalitions with others who are sympathetic to the goals of the theory: Black feminist thought is not, then, a representation of all Black feminist understandings, but it offers one way of incorporating discussion of African American women's practices of resistance into the fabric of theoretical discourse.[5]

A tight theoretical space therefore exists between the political expediency of invoking social categories and the wholesale distortion that may be wrought by their use; I negotiate this space by focusing on a speech event in which racial categories are explicitly made salient, a discussion of race relations in the USA. Numerous linguistic practices of the African American women on the panel intersect with the criteria of Black feminist epistemology, but this observation does not imply that the women necessarily subscribe to a particular brand of Black feminist theory or even that they would identify themselves as feminists. My purpose in using Collins's work is instead to locate possible convergences between a socio-logical theory of knowledge and its reflexes in linguistic practice in the lives of African American women.

African American women's speech practices

Recent research on African American women's and girls' speech shows several points of intersection with Black feminist theory and exemplifies the important new research paradigms that have begun to surface in studies of the language use of African American women (e.g. Stanback 1985, Foster 1989, 1992, Nelson 1990, Etter-Lewis 1991, Morgan 1991, Rickford and McNair-Knox 1993). In keeping with the new scholarship on African American women throughout the social sciences, the innovations include increased attention to non-comparative analysis, which examines those aspects of Black women's speech that are not directly com-parable with Black men's or non-Black women's linguistic practices. Another point of divergence with earlier research is the frequent inclusion of middle-class African American women, and the consideration of a wide range of age groups, in contrast to most traditional analyses of African Americans' speech that have focused upon teenage boys of the lower social classes in order to get at a purportedly purer form of the vernacular (e.g. Labov 1972a). Mitchell-Kernan (1971) and Folb (1980), two early studies con-ducted by women, are rare exceptions to this trend. A final difference is that much recent research, rather than relying solely upon structured sociolinguistic interviews or ethnographic obser-vation, uses personal interviews that allow participants to provide their own understandings of the talk they produce. These inter-views may also draw upon a common racial and social background between researcher and informant to achieve a more intimate set-ting in which the vernacular is likely to be used and in which speakers are more willing to reveal their beliefs and attitudes. The new methods used by such scholars are not offered as a replace-ment for earlier research, but are an invaluable addition that expands the kinds of questions that linguists can ask.

I have selected two important studies (Foster 1989, Morgan 1991) for the insights they can bring to bear on Collins's descrip-tion of African American women's epistemologies.[6] The work of Michèle Foster (1989) offers a useful vantage point on Collins's framework. Foster studied the classroom interaction of an African American teacher in a predominantly Black community college and found that the instructor used performances to draw students into the lesson. These performances, in which teacher and student contributions became more symmetrical, were marked by a shift towards the structure and style of African American Vernacular English. Although Foster does not cast her data as exemplifying a specifically Black feminist perspective, the characteristics of this speech event connect closely with the elements of African American feminist epistemology described by Collins. The instructor encouraged students to draw upon their own experiences and to engage in dialogue in evaluating knowledge claims in the classroom, and she bolstered her own reliability as a producer of knowledge by creating in the classroom a community in which she was accountable both professionally, as an instructor, and personally, as an African American. The analytical harmony of Collins's theory and Foster's empirical data indicates that linguistic scholarship may be a productive means of illuminating and expanding the theoretical claims of social science.

Another study that is valuable for assessing the strengths of Black feminist theory is Marcyliena Morgan's (1991) research on indirectness in the discourse of African American women. Like Foster, Morgan does not identify her work as testing or exemplifying Black feminism; nevertheless, her commitment to using social theory to illuminate issues of praxis puts her in an intellectual alliance with Collins. Morgan reports that within the American slavery system Blacks developed what she terms an 'alternative reality', akin to Collins's 'subjugated knowledge', that continues today as a survival strategy of African Americans. Such an alternative reality, Morgan demonstrates, both shapes and is shaped by a characteristically African American communicative style that she calls a 'counterlanguage' (1991: 423), a concept developed from Michael Halliday's (1976) notion of 'anti-language'. One effect of counterlanguage is linked to speaker intentionality. Compared to European American women, the African American women whom Morgan studied were far more sensitive to the fact that a speaker may deny that she intended a particular meaning and thereby may attempt to avoid responsibility for her utterance. Because of this recognition, the African American women in Morgan's study were found to hold speakers within the speech community responsible for all possible interpretations of their words, an understanding of intentionality that diverges considerably from that of many non-African American speakers. The expanded vision of speaker accountability in Morgan's work has its counterpart within Collins's work in that knowledge producers are responsible for their knowledge claims. Additionally, Morgan's finding that the listener takes an active role in determining meaning corresponds to the dialogic construction of knowledge in Black feminist epistemology. Again, the concurrence of theory and data suggests that systematic study of the relationship between sociological and linguistic research could strengthen both enterprises.

In assessing Collins's framework against the findings of the two studies described above, it becomes clear that the direct and unproblematic assignment of the characteristics given by Collins to actual linguistic data may not be possible. In some sense microlinguistic forms both constitute and instantiate larger cultural phenomena, and yet there are dangers in making facile connections between these analytical levels. Penelope Eckert and Sally McConnell-Ginet (1992a, 1992b) suggest mediating between local and global analysis: it is practice, they argue, that constructs social realities from language, and practice that produces language in situated social realities. Within the communities that Foster and Morgan study, social practices – recurrent patterns of action and interaction – authorize certain linguistic forms to count as being imbued with and projecting the particular social meanings that Collins describes. Similarly, the linguistic practices under study in this chapter configure social alliances that can be interpreted within the frame of Black feminist thought.

Since the community that is produced through practice in this case is temporary, formed as it is around participation in a single radio programme, it serves as an especially vivid example of the instrumentality of fluid but patterned practices, rather than more static identities, as the source of alliance and resistance in social interaction. Thus the work of Eckert and McConnell-Ginet supports Collins's hypothesis that African American women's epistemology proceeds from historically rooted patterns of experience rather than essentialized social categories.

The panel-discussion study

A natural expansion of the body of work described above is the exploration of African American women's language in more formal, public and heterogeneous settings. Except for Foster (1989), little work has explored such situations although they are relevant to questions about the relationships among race, gender and practice. For this reason I take as the locus of my research the linguistic practices of African American women in media discourse. The study focuses upon a radio panel discussion convened in response to nationwide uprisings in the USA in 1992. These incidents of civil unrest followed the acquittal by a jury in Simi Valley, California, of four Los Angeles police officers charged with brutally beating an African American man, Rodney King. As shown in Table 11.1, two of the six panellists are African American women; both work as community advocates. The other panellists are all male; three are Black and the fourth is white. With the exception of one of the Black men, all the male panellists are university professors. The convenor of the discussion, an editor of a local newspaper, is a white man, and the moderator is a white South African man who is a journalist at the newspaper. These categories become relevant over the course of the discussion.

What makes the discussion striking is the systematic and creative way that some of the panellists restructure the discourse by using the features of the panel-discussion genre. In Bucholtz (1992) I offered a qualitative analysis that characterized this process. The present quantitative analysis of the data demonstrates that it is particularly the two African American women on the panel who adapt the norms of the discourse. The practices of these speakers are examined within the framework of Black feminist theory, and the theory is used to account for puzzling aspects of the data.[7]

In order to understand how the norms of the discourse are challenged in the interaction, it is necessary to describe those norms. I have previously argued (Bucholtz 1992) that the panel discussion is a mixed discourse genre with features both of news interviews and

Table 11.1   Participants in the panel discussion

	Sex	Racial/ethnic background	Occupation
CC	M	African American	professor
TD	M	African American	professor
GF	M	European American	professor
LF	M	White South African	journalist (moderator)
BG	M	European American	editor (convenor)
EH	F	African American	community organizer
JM	M	African American	youth project director
EP	F	African American	attorney

of conversation. These elements are often in conflict: conversation is an egalitarian type of talk in which topic, turntaking and participant roles are unplanned (Goffman 1981). Media interviews, in contrast, normatively have a fixed topic that is determined in advance, a turntaking system that allows some speakers but not others to select next speaker, and asymmetrical participant roles that limit question-asking to the interviewer and question-answering to the interviewee (Heritage and Greatbatch 1991). Additionally, interviews are mediated in nature, so that talk is performed not only for the benefit of copresent participants but also for an overhearing audience (Bell 1991). Interviewers are generally seen as facilitators rather than as bona fide interactants; they serve as surrogate interlocutors on behalf of the wider audience. The norms of the panel discussion are intermediate between those of the discourse types just described: speaker roles and turntaking rights are relaxed in comparison to the interview, but the interview system is still held to be normative; and participants usually orient to an overhearing audience.

Creative adaptation of the norms allows participants with less institutionalized power in the discourse – the panellists – to reduce the imbalance of power. By introducing norms of conversation into the interview genre, participants gain an interactional advantage in the discourse, not only because conversation permits a more egalitarian turntaking system, but also because alteration of the norms may be deployed as a strategy of dissent whereby speakers mark their resistance to the institutional discourse. As noted by Morgan (1993), speakers whose language goes on-record through, for example, electronic recording participate in power relations in multiple ways. On the one hand, their talk is subject to surveillance, in the Foucauldian sense, by those who hold institutional power (in her study, the academic researcher; in this work, the discussion moderator). On the other hand, those under scrutiny may take advantage of their position by bringing the powerful and relatively invisible monitor of their language into the foreground, by introducing this individual into their discourse either as an overt or covert topic or as a participant.

The discursive strategies of the African American women on the panel under analysis are of two kinds: those that subvert the role of the moderator in the discussion, and those that construct the panellists' social identities through political alliances. These strategies, both of which have particular linguistic forms associated with them, have the effect of bringing into relief social differences between the moderator and the panellists that have consequences for the larger social world. As will be shown in the discussion below, the strategies exemplify the four criteria of Black feminist epistemology as laid out by Collins: dialogic evaluation of knowledge; personal accountability; caring and involvement; and the valuation of concrete experience. I will first discuss those structures that are linked to challenges to the moderator's role and then turn to mechanisms that restructure the discourse around panellists' social identities and political agendas.

Challenges to the moderator

Acts of participant resistance to institutional structure can be located throughout the discourse. In particular, the female panellists use two linguistic resources – questions and deixis – to destabilize the discursive position of the moderator. As already mentioned, in a media interview the role of question-asking is normatively reserved for the interviewer. But as Table 11.2 shows, the women on the panel, EH and EP, take up this right for themselves during the interview. The results for these panellists are in boldface.

Table 11.2 Number of questions, by panellist*

CC	0%	(0)
TD	0%	(0)
GF	5%	(1)
EH	**50%**	**(11)**
JM	5%	(1)
EP	**40%**	**(9)**
Total	100%	(22)

* N's appear in parentheses. Findings are significant for $p < .001$.

Panelist questions that specify an addressee almost always select the moderator for that role. Moreover, the questions put to the moderator often challenge the moderator's control of the discourse in their content as well as their form, as in (1) and (2).[8]

(1)

```
1   EH:   Can I ask [a question?]
2   LF:              [Yeah. ] Mhm?
3   EH:   Do we have to be so dry in [here?]
4   LF:                              [Nuh. ] (.) Please.
```

```
5  EH:  Can we talk across the-
6  LF:                         =Jump in.
7  EH:  =I mean can we be real?
8  LF:                         =Yes. (h::)
9  EH:  =It's gettin' on my nerves. Okay. Th(h)ank y(h)ou.
```

In example (1), the first question, issued in line 1, conforms to the norms of the panel discussion in that the speaker acknowledges that she does not have a right to the floor without being selected by the moderator. Her next questions in lines 3, 5 and 7, on the other hand, challenge these norms by asking questions that force answers from the interviewer and require him to authorize a restructuring of the discussion, one in which every participant can select any other to speak. Such questions, then, do not function simply as questions but as a means of resisting the pre-existing institutional structure. EH's line of questioning, issued at the metapragmatic level (Silverstein 1993), can be viewed as empirical support for Collins's Black feminist epistemology, in that it sets up the preconditions for Black women's knowledge production to take place.

In example (2), the fissure that EH has created in the discourse structure provides an opportunity for the other African American female panellist, EP, to draw upon an alternative epistemology. The moderator has just asked another panellist to comment on white homeowners' flight from urban neighbourhoods. EP responds to the moderator's question with a query of her own, in line 3, concerning the perception among white Americans that Blackness is a stigma.

(2)
```
1  EP:  Now to me that's the more profound question L than (.)
2       why do neighbourhoods tilt,
3       why do you white people feel this way about how it is
        to be Black,
4       and what are you gonna do about that. (( ... ))
```

This sequence contains at least two components identified as important by a Black feminist theory of knowledge: the dialogic evaluation of knowledge claims and the personal accountability of the knowledge producer. The first is manifested in EP's unsolicited assessment in line 1 of the question issued by the moderator, LF. By offering an assessment as a preface to posing her own question, EP positions herself as someone with a right to make such evaluations of LF's contributions to the discourse. The evaluation may further be understood as participating in the ethic of caring as articulated by Collins, for affective involvement is characteristic of this epistemological criterion, besides being central to the act of assessment (Goodwin and Goodwin 1992). The questions themselves connect with another aspect of Collins's framework in their demand for accountability of the producer of knowledge claims. They do so by problematizing the moderator's omission of a more significant issue that is related to but absent from his original question, namely that 'white people feel this way about how it is to be Black'. EP's move to exact an account of this oversight from LF is effective because as a question it demands an answer; it demands that LF answer for his exclusion of crucial information in his shaping of the discourse. However, because EP introduces her question in a declarative form ('that's the more profound question') LF is able to avoid responding.

Personal accountability is also at issue in example (2) in the deictic form **you white people**. Although second-person pronouns in constructions of this kind do not occur frequently enough in the data to permit a meaningful quantitative analysis, it is revealing that they are produced only by the female panellists (three by EP and two by EH) and that they are always used to remove the moderator from his position of objectivity into a role constructed on the basis of race in which his personal responsibility for his implicit and explicit knowledge claims is highlighted.

The construction of social identities through political alliance

The strategies described above issue challenges to the moderator's institutionalized authority, and as such can be seen to support the alternative epistemological framework delineated by Collins. Collins's work can also shed light upon a second, complementary set of discursive practices employed by the two African American women on the panel. These practices allow the speakers to subvert their own imposed position in the interaction by constructing social identities and patterns of alignment for themselves that do not conform to the roles assigned to them by the institutional norms of the discourse.

The most direct way that this subversion is accomplished is through the symbolic embedding of features of the African American vernacular in speech that otherwise corresponds to the standard. This phenomenon counts as subversion because the standard is the normative code in public discourse.[9] At times, speakers on the panel draw on distinctive phonological features: consonant cluster simplification, monophthongization of /ay/, deletion of postvocalic /r/, and the use of alveolar stops for interdental fricatives.[10] Vernacular lexical items that the speakers use include such forms as **brother** for 'Black man', **cool out** for 'withdraw', and **rap** for 'account'. The patterns of vernacular use by speaker are given in Table 11.3.

Only TD, EH and EP symbolically employ African American Vernacular features in the discussion. Of the remaining panellists, CC and GF use Standard English and JM uses African American Vernacular English almost exclusively in the discussion. The figures given indicate the number of vernacular features each panellist uses as compared to the total use of the vernacular in the discourse. The table shows that EH and EP have the greatest tendency to engage in strategic switching between Standard English and African American Vernacular English. These findings contrast with accounts of the speech of women and middle-class African Americans that suggest that speakers do not use vernacular or non-prestige forms in formal settings (Labov 1972a, 1972b). The panellists' use of the vernacular as an emblem, rather than as the primary linguistic code, demonstrates that the social meaning of the language is retained, or even enhanced, within an institutional context. Likewise, in her study of the semiotics of code-switching in African American women's life narratives, Linda Williamson Nelson (1990) found that, for the women she interviewed, middle-class status did not diminish the cultural significance of vernacular forms and practices; in-group use of the vernacular marked

Table 11.3 Use of features of African American Vernacular English, by panellist*

	Phonological	Lexical	Syntactic	Total
TD	6 (17%)	1 (10%)	0	7 (15 %)
EH	21 (58%)	5 (50%)	0	26 (57%)
EP	9 (25%)	4 (40%)	0	13 (28%)
Total	36 (100%)	10 (100%)	0	46 (100%)

* Percentages given are of total number of features used by speakers of Standard English who employ African American Vernacular features. Findings are significant for $p < .01$.

solidarity. Hence, the meanings associated with African American Vernacular English allow the panellists to use it symbolically both to construct an identity and to manifest their opposition to the normative use of the standard in public discourse, a point that is also supported by Foster (1992).

It is striking that this use of the vernacular marks in-group membership precisely when the speakers are surrounded by out-group members: the participants who are imbued with the institutional power of the panel-discussion genre (the moderator and convenor) are white, as is the majority of the radio audience.[11] Within Black feminist theory, Collins terms the position of African American women in such contexts the 'outsider within'. This concept captures the fundamentally marginal location of Black women – and no doubt of all women of colour – within predominantly non-Black, non-female institutions such as the academy and the media. Collins perceptively comments that African American women may appropriate and exploit the position of the outsider within for strategic purposes, and this process is seen in the present data. The use of the vernacular constructs a racial identity for the women on the panel and marks them as simultaneously inside and outside the dominant discourse.

Another phenomenon that arises in the interaction, however, is more problematic, and its analysis benefits greatly from the resources found in Black feminist thought. Like the linguistic practices described above, the strategy at issue, the use of backchannelled or minimal responses such as **right** or **mhm**, permits the women on the panel to challenge their institutionally imposed discursive position. Backchannels are normatively withheld in radio interactions involving more than two participants, presumably because the audience is unable to identify the speaker. In the present data, however, the panellists EH, EP, and to a lesser extent, JM do issue backchannels, while the other panellists use very few or none. Table 11.4 shows the distribution of backchannels by panellist.

Accounting for these data raises a critical sociolinguistic issue: are these results due to shared racial identity, gender, the interaction of the two or some other factor? One possible explanation, following Frederick Erickson (1984) and others, is that the use of backchannels is an interactive device characteristic of African American speech style. But if this is so we would expect JM, who uses African American Vernacular English almost exclusively in the discussion, to have the highest number of backchannels, and as

Table 11.4   Use of backchannels, by panellist*

CC	0%	(0)
TD	0%	(0)
GF	4%	(5)
EH	**44%**	**(48)**
JM	15%	(16)
EP	**37%**	**(40)**
Total	100%	(109)

* N's appear in parentheses. Findings are significant for $p < .001$.

Table 11.4 shows, he does not. We might further expect that because TD uses a number of vernacular features, as shown in Table 11.3, he would also employ backchannels, but he does not. And we certainly would not expect GF, as the sole European American panellist, to produce any backchannels, and yet he does, a phenomenon I discuss further in Bucholtz (1992).

Nor can we simply attribute the results to gender, in keeping with numerous studies (e.g. Zimmerman and West 1975, Fishman 1983, Hirschman 1994) that find that women use more backchannels than men, for JM does produce significantly more backchannels than other men on the panel, although significantly fewer than either of the women. At this point some analysts might suggest an additive explanation: part of the effect is due to racial background and part is due to gender. But to accept such an explanation is to fail to account for crucial facts about the recipients of backchannels in the data. Backchannelled responses are not issued to all the participants equally, but neither are they issued exclusively to members of a particular gender, racial group or profession. For example, CC is an African American academic who receives no minimal responses, while GF is a European American academic and he does receive one. In a purely quantitative analysis, this difference is insignificant, but within the context of the interaction as a whole, it is in fact highly meaningful. If the two female panellists who issue the most backchannels are expressing their group affiliation by showing support for other group members, we cannot explain these apparent anomalies. Likewise, if they are using gendered communicative skills in order to sustain the conversation, we cannot explain why their minimal responses are not issued equally to all participants.

A less mechanistic explanation is in order, one in which speakers are actively making decisions about their linguistic practices. Collins's epistemological model provides just such an explanation, since according to Black feminist theory speakers test the merits of truth claims in interaction. It is appropriate to use this framework to understand the data, given that the puzzling backchannels are produced in response to statements that represent knowledge claims. Indeed, the dialogic evaluation of knowledge claims is one of Collins's criteria of a Black feminist theory of knowledge, and backchannels perform this function by encouraging speakers to build on claims that are considered to be valid. Similarly, the ethic of care that Collins associates with her epistemological structure is manifested in backchannel use, for minimal responses display interactional involvement, as in example (3).

```
(3)
  1  JM:   I mean really see I mean- see it's like— (.)
  2        I know folks that (1.9) how can I say it?
  3        I don't want to say it's that they've been out of the struggle,
  4        but out of touch.
  5  EH:   M[hm.
  6  JM:    [Let's put it like that. Like they were the first people (0.7)
           who called and say—
  7        I mean,
  8        you know what I'm sayin?
  9  EH:   I do I  [<get those calls> all the time.]
 10  JM:          [It's l(h)ike ]
 11  EP:                         [[Hhhhhh. ]]
 12  JM:                         [[Yeah they sayin— ]]
 13        cause some folks be sittin back in they easy
           chair [you know ]
 14  EP:        [Hhhhhh. ]
 15  EH:        [Mhm. Mhm.]
 16  JM:                        =driving three
 17        BMWs
 18  EH:   =Mhm.
 19  JM:   =the folks I can't get to help you know (.)
                                              [brothers]
 20  EH:                                      [Mhm. ]
 21  JM:   =and sisters on the street,
 22        right,
 23  EH:   That's right.
 24  JM:   And like,
 25        see I'm sayin,
 26        'See I told you'.
 27  EH:   Mhm.
 28  JM:   See?
```

Unquestionably, the backchannels in (3) are interactionally appropriate to the African American speech style that JM employs, but they are not provided merely to mark affiliation with that style, for not all of JM's turns at talk elicit backchannels. Conversely, when a speaker with a very different interactional style, such as the European American professor GF, makes a claim that EH considers valid, she offers a supportive minimal response, as example (4) shows. This response differs in form from previous backchannels, but it functions similarly.

(4)
1 GF: What would it **mean** for (.) for white people to do
          something uh constructive here?
2   Well one thing **every**body would have to do:,
3   there's no question **about** this,
4   is pay higher taxes.
5 EH: Thank you.

Identity will of course shape to some extent what claims an individual considers to be valid, but it is clear that the relationship between identity and interaction is not unmediated. Linguistic practices take on meaning only in the context of a particular local site and only with reference to other linguistic practices such as genre and community norms. Although the absence of European American women in the interaction makes it impossible to vitiate rival accounts of African American women's backchannels in these data, an analysis based on Black feminist thought accounts fully for the data and may offer an alternative to theories rooted in rigid understandings of identity or social roles.

Conclusion

This chapter shows how linguistic methods can be used to assess feminist theories that are produced in other disciplines and, conversely, how such theories can provide insights into linguistic data. The analysis demonstrates how the linguistic practices of two African American women subvert the institutionalized relationship between themselves and the moderator of a radio programme in which they participate. Collins's model of Black feminist epistemology is supported by the particular form that the reconstructed discourse genre takes in the data, and Collins's theory can illuminate interactional phenomena that are otherwise difficult to explain. Finally, by using subversive moves – questions and assessments, deixis, vernacular features and backchannelling – the speakers effectively restructure the speech situation, offering an alternative to the dominant institutional conventions. These discursive moves provide potential strategies for speakers in other settings.

The phenomena that create this process of reversal are articulated in the epistemological concerns traced in Collins's work: dialogic evaluation; personal accountability; affective involvement; and concrete experience, as well as the stance of the outsider within.[12] The success of the two African American women in unsettling the discourse corroborates the observation by Collins reproduced at the beginning of this chapter: namely, alternative epistemologies are deeply threatening to the dominant ideological system. The Black feminist theory that Collins proposes is certainly not the only theory that may be used to illuminate these or other data on the speech of African American women – in fact, Collins's approach lays the groundwork for further theory construction. Yet this particular theory provides a single explanation for a variety of otherwise disparate sociolinguistic processes. The restructuring of the panel discussion through these features serves to highlight the institutional context of the discourse and the personal accountability of all participants, including the moderator of the discussion. The result of such strategies is to challenge the power differences that inhere in institutional and social subject positions – that is, as found by Gwendolyn Etter-Lewis (1991), Marcyliena Morgan (1991) and Linda Williamson Nelson (1990), and as suggested by Collins's model, the strategies are designed as a challenge to hegemonic discourse.[13]

While there is no inevitable isomorphism between Black women's lives and Black feminist epistemology, the interface between Black feminist theory and African American women's speech practices in specific local sites provides insights into how theory is reproduced outside the confines of the academy. Finally, although this chapter is necessarily more suggestive than conclusive, I hope to have shown that feminist linguists and other feminist social scientists have much to offer one another.

Notes

1. I would like to thank Vicky Bergvall, Janet Bing, Colleen Cotter, Sue Ervin-Tripp, Alice Freed, Leanne Hinton, Robin Lakoff, Bonnie

McElhinny and John Rickford for providing many insightful comments on earlier versions of this chapter. Any weaknesses that remain are my own responsibility.

2. As Robin Tolmach Lakoff (1990) points out, acts of resistance of this magnitude lead to strategies of containment by the dominant social group, usually by labelling such acts 'illogical'. In the data that follow, this reaction is not observable in the discourse itself, but it is interesting to speculate about where, if anywhere, this consignment process took place.

3. Kathryn Shields-Brodber (personal communication) rightly points out that the very name 'Black' feminist thought implies an equally essentialized unitary position of all Black women world wide, while presenting only the perspective of North American women who are descendants of slaves. Despite the availability of this essentialist reading, I will not presume to rename the theory but will ask readers to bear in mind that the discussion should be understood to be limited by the geographical and historical boundaries given above.

4. The compatibility of the two perspectives is also noted by Bonnie McElhinny (1993), and they are successfully mediated within the innovative and influential work of Gloria Anzaldúa (1990) and Donna Haraway (1991). Although some theorists, often called cultural feminists, may lose sight of the constructed and limited nature of the perspectives they study (Belenky et al. 1986, Ruddick 1989), most scholars who use social categories as a resource in their work make clear that they do so as a political and historically specific intervention rather than as a move to reify these structures as universal (Spivak 1988).

5. Of course, researchers who are not members of the community they study will inevitably miss certain insights; as a European American I myself face this limitation. At the same time, however, it is imperative that white feminist linguists do not restrict the use of feminist theory to the contributions of other white researchers. To do so would be to reproduce patterns of exclusion and misrepresentation that weaken the quality of linguistic research. Moreover, the data under analysis here seem appropriate for analysis by a white researcher because the discussion was directed to a white audience, as discussed in note 11 below. Finally, Janet Bing has pointed out to me that strategies of subversion used by the African American women on the panel are also of utility to white feminists and other political progressives who oppose hegemonic public discourse.

6. The scholars who conducted these studies do not make reference to Collins or other African American feminist theorists, and they might not agree with the connections I see between such theories and their own work. The associations that I trace, then, are not to be construed as the definitive reading of this complex and nuanced research, but

rather as a way of understanding social theory through the testimony of linguistic data.

7. This study necessarily incorporates a number of methodologies, ranging from conversation analysis to variationist approaches, that do not often co-occur in a single research report. Although such integrative analysis is not entirely without precedent (cf. Macaulay 1991), it has been undertaken primarily in the service of describing dialect rather than of making sense of discourse. The collaboration among methodological resources is essential to capture the complexity of the unfolding interaction. Sociolinguistic techniques locate linguistic forms in social space, while discourse-analytic principles of interaction-based analysis expand the linguistic context of social relations. Hence both components are necessary for a full understanding of how social categories are produced, replicated and resisted in discourse.

8. The following transcription conventions have been observed. Each intonational unit of longer utterances appears on a separate line.

.	falling intonation
,	fall–rise intonation
?	rising intonation
—	self-interruption; break in the intonational unit
-	self-interruption; break in the word, sound abruptly cut off
:	length
bold	emphatic stress
(.)	pause of 0.5 seconds or less
(n.n)	pause of greater than 0.5 seconds, measured by a stopwatch
h	exhalation (e.g. laughter, sigh); each token marks one pulse
(( ))	transcriber comment; non-vocal noise
< >	uncertain transcription
[ ]	overlap beginning and end
[[ ]]	second overlap in proximity to first
=	latching (no pause or overlap)

9. This symbolic use of socially meaningful linguistic markers is distinct from code-switching, in which entire grammatical structures of two different linguistic systems are juxtaposed, and which is normally oriented towards an in-group and is not utilized with non-bilingual or non-bidialectal outsiders (Gumperz 1982). Significantly, only those phonological forms and lexical items that are culturally associated with African American Vernacular English are embedded in the speech of the African American women participating in the panel discussion.

10. This collection of phonological variables has long been known to be characteristic of African American Vernacular English (Wolfram 1969, Labov 1972a, Baugh 1983).

11. Although the local radio station was unable to provide a racial breakdown of its listenership, the national broadcasting company of which the station is a part reports its listenership as 89 per cent white, 11 per cent all other races.

12. The small number of personal anecdotes prevents me from conducting a quantitative analysis of the role of concrete experience as a means of assessing truth claims. However, the majority of personal anecdotes in the panel discussion are offered by the two African American women.

13. It is important to recognize that the speakers' achievement was local and temporary in its effects; neither the radio station nor the sponsoring newspaper implemented the changes in journalistic focus and institutional structure that the women proposed as ways of overcoming racism. And although researchers may be tempted to celebrate the panellists' intervention in public discourse, subsequent media treatment of Black community issues – from African Americans' response to the O.J. Simpson verdict, to coverage of the Million Man March on Washington – indicates that any such celebration would be premature.

References

Anzaldúa, Gloria 1990 En rapport, in opposition: cobrando cuentas a las nuestras. In Anzaldúa Gloria (ed) *Making face, making soul/Haciendo caras*. Aunt Lute Foundation, San Francisco pp 142–48.

Baugh, John 1983 *Black street speech: its history, structure, and survival*. University of Texas Press, Austin.

Belenky Mary Field, Clinchy Blythe McVicker, Goldberger Nancy Rule, Tarule Jill Mattuck 1986. *Women's ways of knowing: the development of self, voice, and mind*. Basic Books, New York.

Bell Allan 1991 *The language of news media*. Basil Blackwell, Oxford.

Bucholtz Mary 1992 The mixed discourse genre as a social resource for participants. In *Proceedings of the nineteenth annual meeting of the Berkeley Linguistics Society*. Berkeley Linguistics Society, Berkeley, CA pp 40–51.

Butler Judith 1990 *Gender trouble: feminism and the subversion of identity*. Routledge, New York.

Butler Judith 1993 *Bodies that matter: on the discursive limits of 'sex'*. Routledge, New York.

Cameron Deborah this volume: The language-gender interface: challenging co-optation.

Collins Patricia Hill 1990 *Black feminist thought*. Unwin Hyman, Boston.

Collins Patricia Hill 1992 Reply to review symposium on *Black feminist thought*. *Gender & Society* 6.3: 517–19.

Eckert Penelope, McConnell-Ginet Sally 1992a Think practically and look locally: language and gender as community-based practice. *Annual Review of Anthropology* 21: 461–90.

Eckert Penelope, McConnell-Ginet Sally 1992b Communities of practice: where language, gender, and power all live. In Hall Kira, Bucholtz Mary, Moonwomon Birch (eds) pp 89–99.

Erickson Frederick 1984 Rhetoric, anecdote, and rhapsody: coherence strategies in a conversation among black American adolescents. In Tannen Deborah (ed) *Coherence in spoken and written discourse*. Ablex, Norwood, NJ pp 81–154.

Etter-Lewis Gwendolyn 1991 Standing up and speaking out: African American women's narrative legacy. *Discourse & Society* 2.4: 425–38.

Fishman Pamela 1983 Interaction: the work women do. In Thorne Barrie, Kramarae Cheris, Henley Nancy (eds) *Language, gender, and society*. Newbury House, Rowley, MA pp 89–101.

Folb Edith A 1980 *Runnin' down some lines: the language and culture of black teenagers*. Harvard University Press, Cambridge, MA.

Foster Michèle 1989 'It's cookin' now': a performance analysis of the speech events of a Black teacher in an urban community college. *Language in Society* 18.1: 1–29.

Foster Michèle 1992 'Are you with me?': power, solidarity, and community in the discourse of African American women. In Hall Kira, Bucholtz Mary, Moonwomon Birch (eds) 132–43.

Freed Alice F this volume: Language and gender research in an experimental setting.

Goffman Erving 1981 *Forms of talk*. University of Pennsylvania Press, Philadelphia.

Goodwin Charles, Goodwin Marjorie Harness 1992 Assessments and the construction of context. In Duranti Alessandro, Goodwin Charles (eds) *Rethinking context: language as an interactive phenomenon*. Cambridge University Press pp 147–89.

Gumperz John 1982 *Discourse strategies*. Cambridge University Press, Cambridge.

Hall Kira, Bucholtz Mary, Moonwomon Birch (eds) 1992 *Locating power: proceedings of the second Berkeley women and language conference*. Berkeley Women and Language Group, Berkeley, CA.

Halliday Michael A K 1976 Anti-languages. *American Anthropologist* 78: 570–84.

Haraway Donna J 1985 A manifesto for cyborgs: science, technology, and socialist feminism in the 1980s. *Socialist Review* 15.80: 65–107.

Haraway Donna J 1991 *Simians, cyborgs, and women: the reinvention of nature*. Routledge, New York.

Harding Sandra 1986 *The science question in feminism*. Cornell University Press, Ithaca, NY.

Hartsock Nancy C M 1987 The feminist standpoint: developing the ground for a specifically feminist historical materialism. In Harding Sandra (ed) *Feminism and methodology*. University of Indiana Press, Bloomington pp 157–80.

Heritage John, Greatbatch David 1991 On the institutional character of institutional talk: the case of news interviews. In Boden Deirdre, Zimmerman Don H (eds) *Talk and social structure*. University of California Press, Berkeley pp 93–137.

Hirschman, Lynette 1994 Female-male differences in conversational interaction. *Language in Society* 23.3: 427–42.

hooks bell 1984 *Feminist theory: from margin to center*. South End Press, Boston.

Hull Gloria T, Scott Patricia Bell, Smith Barbara (eds) 1982 *But some of us are brave*. The Feminist Press, New York.

King Deborah 1992 Review of Patricia Hill Collins' *Black feminist thought*. *Gender & Society* 6.3: 512–15.

Kristeva Julia 1980 *Desire in language*. Columbia University Press, New York.

Labov William 1972a *Language in the inner city: studies in the Black English Vernacular*. University of Pennsylvania Press, Philadelphia.

Labov William 1972b *Sociolinguistic patterns*. University of Pennsylvania Press, Philadelphia.

Lakoff Robin Tolmach 1990 *Talking power*. Basic Books, New York.

Macaulay Ronald K S 1991 *Locating dialect in discourse: the language of honest men and bonnie lassies in Ayr*. Oxford University Press, New York.

McElhinny, Bonnie 1993 *We all wear the blue: language, gender, and police work*. Stanford University PhD dissertation.

Mitchell-Kernan Claudia 1971 *Language behavior in a black urban community*. Language-Behavior Research Laboratory, Berkeley, CA.

Morgan Marcyliena 1991 Indirectness and interpretation in African American women's discourse. *Pragmatics* 1.4: 421–51.

Morgan Marcyliena 1993 The role of narrative shift and audience in stylistic variation. Paper presented at the 67th annual meeting of the Linguistic Society of America, Los Angeles, CA.

Nelson Linda Williamson 1990 Code-switching in the oral life narratives of African-American women: challenges to linguistic hegemony. *Journal of Education* 172.3: 142–55.

Rickford John R, McNair-Knox Faye 1993 Addressee- and topic-influenced style shift: a quantitative sociolinguistic study. In Biber Douglas, Finegan Edward (eds) *Sociolinguistic perspectives on register*. Oxford University Press, New York pp 235–75.

Ruddick Sara 1989 *Maternal thinking*. Ballantine, New York.

Silverstein Michael 1993 Metapragmatic discourse and metapragmatic function. In Lucy John A (ed) *Reflexive language: reported speech and metapragmatics*. Cambridge University Press, Cambridge pp 33–58.

Smith, Dorothy E 1987 *The everyday world as problematic: a feminist sociology*. Northeastern University Press, Boston.

Spivak Gayatri Chakravorti 1988 *In other worlds: essays in cultural politics*. Routledge, New York.

Stanback Marsha Houston 1985 Language and black woman's place: evidence from the black middle class. In Treichler Paula A, Kramarae Cheris, Stafford Beth (eds) *For alma mater: theory and practice in feminist scholarship*. University of Illinois Press, Urbana pp 177–93.

Wolfram, Walt 1969 *A sociolinguistic description of Detroit Negro speech*. Center for Applied Linguistics, Washington, DC.

Zimmerman Don, West Candace 1975 Sex roles, interruptions, and silences in conversation. In Thorne Barrie, Henley Nancy (eds) *Language and sex: difference and dominance*. Newbury House, Rowley, MA pp 105–29.

Index

Bold entries under author indicates chapter in this book.